Djurgården
See pages 86–101

LILLA VÄRTAN

DJURGÅRDEN

Saltsjön

**Malmarna &
Further Afield**
See pages 102–135

**Excursions
from Stockholm**
See pages 142–153

| 0 metres | | 500 |
| 0 yards | | 500 |

EYEWITNESS TRAVEL

new by date shown

STOCKHOLM

EYEWITNESS TRAVEL

STOCKHOLM

Main Contributor: **Kaj Sandell**

DK

DK | Penguin Random House

Produced by Streiffert Förlag AB, Stockholm
Chief Editor Bo Streiffert
Project Editor Guy Engström
Editors Guy Engström, Monica Nilsson
Designer Bo Streiffert
Picture Research Guy Engström

Dorling Kindersley Ltd
Managing Editor Anna Streiffert
Art Director Gillian Allan

Main Contributor Kaj Sandell

Contributors
Lisa Carlsson, Jan & Christine Samuelson,
Christina Sollenberg Britton, Stockholm Visitors Board

Maps Stig Söderlind

Photographers
Erik Svensson, Jeppe Wikström

Illustrations
Urban Frank, assisted by Jan Rojmar

English Translation Philip Ray

Reproduced by PDC Tangen, Norway
Printed and bound in Malaysia by Vivar Printing Sdn. Bhd

First published in Great Britain in 2000 by Dorling Kindersley Ltd
80 Strand, London WC2R 0RL

16 17 18 19 10 9 8 7 6 5 4 3 2 1

Reprinted with revisions 2001, 2004, 2007, 2010, 2012, 2014, 2016

Copyright 2000, 2016 © Dorling Kindersley Ltd, London
A Penguin Random House company

A CIP Catalogue record is available from the British Library.

ISBN 978 0 24120 871 7

Floors are referred to throughout in accordance with European usage;
ie the "first floor" is the floor above ground level.

Front cover main image: Aerial view of Gamla Stan

MIX
Paper from
responsible sources
FSC FSC™ C018179
www.fsc.org

The information in this Dorling Kindersley Travel Guide is checked regularly.
Every effort has been made to ensure that this book is as up to date as possible at
the time of going to press. Some details, however, such as telephone numbers,
opening hours, prices, gallery hanging arrangements and travel information, are
liable to change. The publishers cannot accept responsibility for any consequences
arising from the use of this book, nor for any material on third-party websites, and
cannot guarantee that any website address in this book will be a suitable source of
travel information. We value the views and suggestions of our readers very highly.
Please write to: Publisher, DK Eyewitness Travel Guides, Dorling Kindersley, 80 Strand,
London WC2R 0RL, Great Britain, or email: travelguides@dk.com.

◀ Colourful houses in Gamla Stan, Stockholm

Contents

Wooden sculpture on the 17th-century warship *Vasa*

Introducing Stockholm

Kaknästornet, Stockholm's tallest building at 155 m (508 ft)

Late winter walk along the shores of Kungsholmen

A packet of traditional round Swedish crispbread

The renovated Royal Chapel at the Royal Palace

The Royal Palace in Gamla Stan

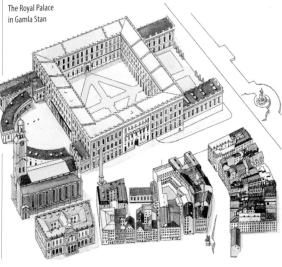

INTRODUCING STOCKHOLM

GREAT DAYS IN STOCKHOLM

In Stockholm you are never far from water, and the city's 14 islands offer a beguiling mix of culture and nature. Although beautiful when seen from the water, this city is also a pleasure to explore on foot, particularly around Gamla Stan's medieval lanes and the leafy island of Djurgården. To help you make the most of your visit, here are ideas for four themed days out, followed by itineraries based on length of stay on pages 10–11. All the sights are accessible using public transport. Prices include travel, food and admission charges. Family prices are for two adults and two children.

Looking over the Nordiska museet towards the city centre

Museums Meander

Two Adults allow at least 800 kr

- **A sunken ship and Swedish history on Djurgården**
- **Lunch near Kungsträdgården park**
- **Skeppsholmen – "museum island"**

Morning
Start the day on the island of Djurgården at the **Vasamuseet** *(see pp94–6)*. The impressive 17th-century warship *Vasa* is worth a visit of at least 90 minutes, and try not to miss the informative video. Next door, the **Nordiska museet** *(see pp92–3)* gives a glimpse into Swedish life over the centuries. Allow 2 hours. Leaving the island over **Djurgårdsbron** *(see p90)*, turn left, and a 15-minute waterside walk down Strandvägen brings you to **Kungsträdgården** *(see p66)*. Around this park are plenty of places for a lunch break.

Afternoon
Refreshed, head for Skeppsholmen, passing the stately **Grand Hotel** *(see p81)* and the **Nationalmuseum** *(see pp84–5)*. Once there, you can choose between the **Moderna museet** *(see pp82–3)* and the **ArkDes** *(see p80)*. Finish with a late "*fika*" (coffee break) in the museum café, or try the restaurant with its view over the water.

Palaces and Waterways

Two Adults allow at least 830 kr

- **Kungliga Slottet (the Royal Palace)**
- **The city from the water**
- **Drottningholm Palace**

Morning
Start the day with a touch of royalty at **Kungliga Slottet** *(see pp50–53)*, the Royal Palace, in Gamla Stan. Choose any combination of tours – the Royal Apartments, the Tre Kronor Museet or Gustav III's Museum of Antiquities – which will take up most of the morning. Then, just before noon, step outside for the Changing of the Guard, complete with full horse parade over Norrmalm Bridge. Afterwards, take a gentle walk through the cobblestone streets of Gamla Stan to **Stortorget** *(see p56)* for lunch at any one of the cafés lining the square. The charming Chokladkoppen is an excellent choice, popular with tourists and locals alike. During the winter holidays, one of the oldest *Julmarknad* (Christmas Markets) is held here.

Drottningholm Palace by boat

◀ *View of Stockholm from the Fersen Terrace with the Palace Makalos, by Elias Martin*

Afternoon

After lunch, enjoy Stockholm from the water. An hour canal cruise to **Drottningholm Palace** *(see pp146–9)*, the residence of the Swedish royal family, provides a waterfront tour of the city on the way to the palace just outside of town. Be sure to visit the Chinese Pavilion and the beautiful summer gardens in the palace grounds. "Under the Bridges of Stockholm" is another popular canal tour, which takes two hours and passes all of the city's major landmarks. Coffee and cakes are available on board. For both tours, it is worth booking in advance during peak times *(see p204)*.

The busy Stortorget square in the heart of Gamla Stan

A Walk from Nature to Culture

Two Adults allow at least 300 kr

- The mountain park of Vita Bergen
- Shopping and eating in trendy SoFo
- Old Södermalm and Mosebacke

Morning

Begin on the island of Söder-malm at **Vita Bergen** *(see p132)*, a beautiful mountain park. Here you will find allotment-gardens, worker's houses from the early 18th century and the monumental **Sofia Kyrka** *(see p132)*. Then head downhill and into trendy "SoFo" (the area south of Folkungagatan). A

variety of boutiques and cafés are located here, with Folkunga-gatan itself leading towards **Medborgarplatsen** *(see p133)*. Traditional Swedish lunch can be had at an outdoor restaurant on the square.

Afternoon

From Medborgarplatsen it is not far to **Katarina Kyrka** *(see p130)* and the characteristic 18th-century cottages of old Södermalm. For a more contemporary view of Söder, the stretch of Götgatan between Medborgarplatsen and Slussen has an eclectic mix of shops, many selling Swedish design. The area east of here is **Mosebacke** *(see p130)*. Here you will find the **Södra Teatern** *(see p176)* and a public terrace, offering amazing views of the city. A more glamorous viewing point is the restaurant at the top of **Katarina-hissen** *(see p129)*, accessible from **Slussen** *(see p128)*.

A Full Family Day

Family of 4 allow at least 1,800 kr

- A trip to the Skansen zoo and open-air park
- Amusements at Gröna Lund
- The world of Pippi Longstocking and a theatre visit at Junibacken

Morning

Start the day at the world's oldest open-air museum and zoo of Scandinavian wildlife, **Skansen** *(see pp100–101)*,

Having fun at Skansen, an open-air museum on the island of Djurgården

located on the island of Djurgården. Here you can visit period houses preserved and transported from all over Sweden, watch traditional glass blowing, and walk through a typical Swedish town, complete with market and post office. After such a busy morning, take a well-deserved break in one of the many cafés in the grounds of the park.

Afternoon

After lunch, make your way to **Gröna Lund** *(see p97)*, an amusement park where you can ride one of the roller coasters, float through the Tunnel of Love or relax on the Ferris wheel. Alternatively, enter the world of celebrated children's author Astrid Lingren at **Junibacken** *(see p90)* to explore her well-loved collection of books; little ones can play in Pippi Longstocking's house, Villekulla Cottage. It also has one of Sweden's leading children's theatres.

People enjoying picnics at Nytorget in "rustic chic" SoFo

Night view of the Royal Palace

3 Days in Stockholm

- Shop for souvenirs and handicrafts in Västerlånggatan
- View Moderna museet's interesting modern art collection
- Amble the quaint streets of Södermalm, with its old workers' cottages

2 Days in Stockholm

- Explore Gamla Stan's historic buildings and medieval cobbled streets
- Pay a visit to Sweden's oldest museum, Livrustkammaren
- Chill out in Kungsträdgården, the former royal kitchen gardens

Day 1

Morning See the sights in picturesque **Gamla Stan** (pp46–61), starting with the 16th-century **Tyska Kyrkan** (pp56–7), with its spectacular ebony and alabaster pulpit. A short walk up Slottsbacken leads to **Stortorget** (p56), scene of the Stockholm Bloodbath in 1520. Admire the Gothic and Baroque interior of nearby **Storkyrkan** (p55), before heading to **Livrustkammaren** (p54), Sweden's oldest museum.

Bernt Notke's statue of *St George and the Dragon* in Storkyrkan, Gamla Stan

At noon, catch the Changing of the Guard at the **Royal Palace** (pp50–53), before visiting some of its 608 grand rooms. Head west to tiny Riddarholmen, home to **Riddarholmskyrkan** (p58), final resting place of the Swedish sovereigns.

Afternoon Visit **Stadshuset** (pp116–17), scene of the annual Nobel Prize festivities, built in National Romantic style. Further east, in **City** (pp62–75), go to the cultural hub of **Kulturhuset** (p69) and enjoy one of its free art exhibitions. Take a break in **Kungsträdgården** (p66), the former royal kitchen gardens, then admire the Renaissance façade of **Kungliga Operan** (pp66–7) and the opulent **Grand Hôtel** (p81) on the waterfront, before settling in at **Berns** (p83), a Stockholm dining and drinking institution.

Day 2

Morning Take a ferry to **Djurgården** (pp86–101) and spend a couple of hours at **Vasamuseet** (pp94–6). Housing the world's only preserved 17th-century warship, this is one of the city's must-see museums. Weather permitting, take a picnic and have lunch alfresco in one of the peninsula's parks.

Afternoon Visit **Skansen** (pp100–101), the world's first open-air museum, home to 150 historic buildings from across Sweden. Here you can watch craftsmen demonstrate traditional skills. Round off the day with family favourite **Gröna Lund** (p97), Sweden's oldest amusement park.

Day 1

Morning Spend a few hours at the **Royal Palace** (pp50–53) and **Livrustkammaren** (p54) in **Gamla Stan** (pp46–61), leaving time for the Changing of the Guard at noon. Head west to **Riddarholmskyrkan** (p58) to view the ornate vaults of former Swedish monarchs. Wander back east to **Stortorget** (p56), admiring the Baroque façades of **Storkyrkan** (p55) and the Hanseatic **Tyska Kyrkan** (pp56–7), then browse the handicraft shops in **Västerlånggatan** (p57).

Afternoon Head across the waters to **City** (pp62–75). Pay a visit to **Kulturhuset** (p69) for an art exhibition and relax in the park of **Kungsträdgården** (p66), then stop for afternoon tea at the **Grand Hôtel** (p81), enjoying views of Gamla Stan, **Kungliga Operan** (pp66–7) and **Stadshuset** (pp116–17). Later, experience the thrilling rides at **Gröna Lund**'s (p97) amusement park.

Day 2

Morning Start the day at **Moderna museet** (pp82–3). Next, take a stroll around the former naval base of **Skeppsholmen** (pp78–9) for a look at the restored buildings and traditional wooden boats, including **af Chapman** (p81), now a trendy youth hostel.

Afternoon Take a short ferry ride across to Djurgården to visit the open-air museum of **Skansen** (pp100–101). Return by ferry to Nybroplan for a drink at **Berns** (p83) before taking in a show at **Dramaten** (pp74–5) or **Kungliga Operan** (pp66–7).

Day 3

Morning Explore **Södermalm** (*pp128–35*), Stockholm's charming south. Leave from **Slussen** (*p128*) and enjoy great views from the top of the 38-m (125-ft) high **Katarinahissen** (*p129*). Next, go up to quaint **Mosebacke** (*p130*); visit the 17th-century **Katarina Kyrka** (*p130*), then continue to **Fjällgatan** (*p131*) and the old-fashioned **Söder Cottages** (*p131*). Climb up to **Vita Bergen** (*p132*) for more pleasant views and 18th-century homesteads. Take a ferry from **Fåfängan** (*p132*) in the east.

Afternoon Disembark at **Djurgården** (*pp86–101*) and spend the rest of the day visiting the unique **Vasamuseet** (*pp94–6*), followed by **Nordiska museet** (*pp92–3*). Housed in a Renaissance-style building, this museum has a vast collection of objects dating from the 16th century to the present day.

5 Days in Stockholm

- **Explore the museums of Djurgården**
- **Spend a day sailing around the Stockholm Archipelago**
- **Visit Drottningholm, a UNESCO World Heritage Site on the island of Lovön**

Day 1

Morning Start the day with a visit to the art galleries in **Kulturhuset** (*p69*). Pass by **Kungliga Operan**'s (*pp66–7*) ornate façade, then relax in **Kungsträdgården** (*p66*) and take a look at the Art Deco **Dramaten** (*pp74–5*) theatre.

Afternoon Walk to Blasieholmen, past the **Grand Hôtel** (*p81*), and stop off to explore the modern art collection at **Moderna museet** (*pp82–3*), before visiting **Skeppsholmen** (*pp78–9*), a former naval base with traditional wooden boats. Amble back for evening drinks at **Berns** (*p83*), one of the city's best nightspots.

Södermalm's Katarina Kyrka, dating from the late 1600s

Day 2

Morning Admire the impressive **Stadshuset** (*pp116–17*) before walking across to Riddarholmen, in **Gamla Stan** (*pp46–61*). Visit **Riddarholmskyrkan** (*p58*), with its ancient royal sarcophagi, and stop at **Livrustkammaren** (*p54*) for 500 years of royal history. Catch the Changing of the Guard at the **Royal Palace** (*pp50–53*) at noon, then go on to **Storkyrkan** (*p55*). Wander down shopping street **Västerlånggatan** (*p57*) to view Baroque and Renaissance-style **Tyska Kyrkan** (*p56–7*), reaching the southern end of Gamla Stan at **Slussen** (*p128*).

Afternoon Explore quaint and trendy **Södermalm** (*pp128–35*), starting with **Katarinahissen** (*p129*) for pleasant views over the city. Follow the picturesque streets to **Fåfängan** (*p132*), returning via mountainous **Vita Bergen** (*p132*) and **Fjällgatan** (*p131*), with its traditional buildings, and Stigbergsgatan, home of the **Söder Cottages** (*p131*). Be sure to stop at **Katarina Kyrka** (*p130*), now restored to its

former glory after a fire. Return to Gamla Stan for an evening drink in one of its cosy bars.

Day 3

Morning Take a ferry to **Djurgården** (*pp86–101*), visiting **Vasamuseet** (*pp94–6*) and the adjacent **Nordiska museet** (*pp92–3*) for interesting insights into Swedish history and culture.

Afternoon Enjoy the historic buildings and laid-back atmosphere at **Skansen** (*pp100–101*), a charming open-air museum. End the day at **Gröna Lund**'s (*p97*) amusement park.

Day 4

Full Day Spend a day on the Stockholm Archipelago. There are some 30,000 islands here, but one must-see stop is **Sandhamn** (*p153*). Take a tour boat along the Strömma Canal and soak up the idyllic seaside atmosphere in historic Sandhamn, returning to Stockholm in the evening.

Day 5

Morning Visit the royal palace of **Drottningholm** (*pp146–9*), a UNESCO World Heritage Site on Lovön, in Lake Mälaren. Admire the beautiful rooms, stroll in the Baroque Garden and pay a visit to the Chinese Pavilion.

Afternoon Explore **Hagaparken** (*pp124–5*), the mid-18th-century royal park north of Stockholm. Take a look at Gustav III's castle ruin and the 18th-century Chinese Pagoda, and set time aside for Fjärils- & Fågelhuset, with their exotic birds and butterflies.

Beautiful autumn colours, Hagaparken

Putting Stockholm on the Map

Sweden is Europe's fourth largest country, covering 486,661 sq km (187,900 sq miles). Its southern-most point is on the same latitude as Edinburgh; its northern extremity is 280 km (174 miles) north of the Arctic Circle. Sweden borders Norway in the west and Finland in the east. Since 2000 it has been connected to Denmark in the south via a bridge over the Öresund strait. The capital, Stockholm, is in the south-east. It has around one million inhabitants. The city is built on islands, which separate the Baltic Sea from Lake Mälaren *(see pp42–3)*.

Gulf

84

76

Gävle

Grisslehamn

NORWAY

Torsby

62

SWEDEN

70

E4

Kapells

See inset map below

Oslo

E45

60

E18

Drammen

E18

Karlstad

Örebro

E20

STOCKHOLM

Moss

Sandefjord

E18

Fredrikstad

E18

E18

73

Larvik

Strömstad

Vänern

51

Nynäsham

E6

Mellerud

Mariestad

45

E4

Örebro

Skagerrak

E20

Vättern

Norrköping

Trollhättan

E4

Linköping

Kristiansand,
Newcastle

Borås

E22

Gothenburg

40

Jönköping

Västervik

33

Gotla

Hirtshals

E6

E4

Oskarshamn

E39

Frederikshavn

26

E22

Aalborg

Varberg

23

Växjö

Öland

25

Ljungby

25

Halmstad

30

Kalmar

E45

Grenå

E4

23

Karlskrona

Aarhus

E6

Helsingborg

E22

Baltic

DENMARK

Helsingör

E22

Copenhagen

Simrishamn

Odense

E20

E20

Malmö

Ystad

Trelleborg

Bornholm

E47

Rönne

Rödby

Gedser

Sassnitz

Gdyni

Kiel

Puttgarden

Stralsund

Slupsk

Gda

Travemünde

Rostock

Greifswald

Koszalin

Hamburg

A20

GERMANY

Swinoujscie

POLAND

Nowogard

A19

A20

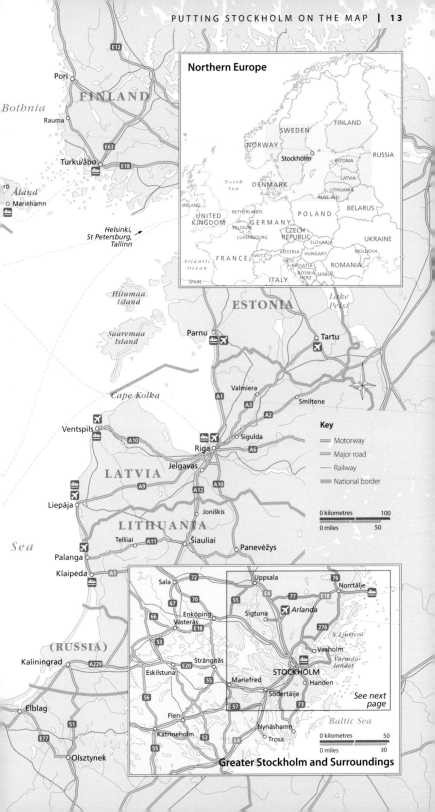

Northern Europe

NORWAY
SWEDEN
FINLAND
Stockholm
ESTONIA
RUSSIA
North Sea
DENMARK
LATVIA
LITHUANIA
RUSS. FED.
BELARUS
IRELAND
UNITED KINGDOM
NETHERLANDS
GERMANY
POLAND
UKRAINE
BELGIUM
LUXEMBOURG
CZECH REPUBLIC
SLOVAKIA
Atlantic Ocean
FRANCE
SWITZ.
AUSTRIA
HUNGARY
MOLDOVA
SLOV.
CROATIA
ROMANIA
SPAIN
ITALY
BOSNIA HERZ.
SERBIA

Bothnia

Pori
FINLAND
Rauma
Turku/Åbo
rö
Åland
Mariehamn

Helsinki,
St Petersburg,
Tallinn

Hiiumaa Island
ESTONIA
Lake Peisi
Parnu
Tartu
Saaremaa Island

Cape Kolka
Valmiera
Smiltene

Ventspils
Sigulda
Riga
Jelgavas

Key
— Motorway
— Major road
— Railway
— National border

Sea

LATVIA
Liepāja

LITHUANIA
Joniškis
Telšiai
Šiauliai
Panevėžys
Palanga
Klaipėda

| 0 kilometres | 100 |
| 0 miles | 50 |

(RUSSIA)
Kaliningrad

Sala
Uppsala
Norrtälje
Enköping
Sigtuna
Arlanda
Västerås
Vaxholm
S. Ljusterö
Värmdö-landet
Strängnäs
STOCKHOLM
Eskilstuna
Mariefred
Handen
Södertälje
See next page
Flen
Elblag
Nynäshamn
Baltic Sea
Katrineholm
Trosa
Olsztynek

| 0 kilometres | 50 |
| 0 miles | 30 |

Greater Stockholm and Surroundings

Stockholm and Surroundings

Stockholm's first buildings were erected on a small island in the narrow Strömmen channel between the Baltic and Lake Mälaren. When the town started to expand, buildings sprang up on the "Malms", the areas on either side of Strömmen. Today Stockholm stretches over 14 islands, with high-rise suburbs sprawling almost all the way out to the royal country palaces. The network of underground and suburban trains, buses and ferry services offers easy transport to sights beyond the city centre *(see pp142–53)*.

For keys to symbols *see back flap*

Stockholm

Solna
Hersby
Sundbyberg
Solna
Norra
Djurgården
Bromma
Huvudsta
Karlberg
Ladugårds-
gärdet
Riksby
Stockholm C
STOCKHOLM
Hornstull
Stockholm
Södra
Nacka
Midsommar-
kransen
Årstaberg
Johanneshov
Segeltorp
Långbro
Älvsjö
Enskede
Bandhagen
Skarpnäcks

0 kilometres 5
0 miles 3

Ranas
Skedviken
Rimbo
Karsta
Karby
276
Österåker
Åkersberga
Svinninge
Resaro
N. Ljusterö
S. Ljusterö
Möja
Grinda
Möja
Vaxholm
Bogesunds-
landet
Ormingelandet
Värmdö
Vindö
274
Gustavsberg
Värmdö-
landet
Djurö
Baltic Sea
222
Stavsnäs
Sandhamn
228
Brunn
222
Runmarö
Sandön
Saltsjöbaden
Ingarö
229
Tyresö
Brevik
Nämndö
260
åninge
Dalarö
227
Gålö
Myšingen
Ornö

Key

═══ Motorway
═══ Major road
─── Minor road
─── Railway
☐ Greater Stockholm

0 kilometres 10
0 miles 10

THE HISTORY OF STOCKHOLM

Legends and theories about Stockholm's origins have been many and varied, and sometimes even contradictory. But they have a common factor – control over the waterways. The generally accepted founder of Stockholm is the 13th-century regent Birger Jarl, who, according to the medieval Erik's Chronicle, wanted to build a fortress to protect Lake Mälaren from marauding pirates.

A thousand years ago the waters around the island now known as Gamla Stan were busy with warships, trading vessels and pirate ships using the narrow channel between the Baltic and Lake Mälaren. In those days boat was the quickest and safest method of travel.

In the first literary mention of what was to become Stockholm, the Icelandic poet and saga writer Snorre Sturlasson (1179–1241) described a barrier of piles across a waterway, which he named Stock-sundet, the present Norrström. The island formed by this piling became known as Stockholm. Excavations in the late 1970s revealed the remains of a large number of piles in the water dating from the 11th century. Snorre also mentioned a 12th-century castle tower, which would have predated Birger Jarl's fortress, the predecessor of the present Royal Palace.

Documents show that Stockholm was already a city in 1252, four years after Birger Jarl became regent. Many towns in Sweden started to expand in the early 13th century. Stockholm was a late starter but soon caught up. A document from 1289 describes Stockholm as the biggest place in the kingdom. But it was not the capital city, because the king was always on the move. Birger Jarl's son, King Magnus Ladulås, did not regard Stockholm as his capital either. For a long time the city's importance lay in its role as a trading centre. It became an important port for the German-dominated Hanseatic League, which controlled Swedish overseas trade from the 13th century until the late 17th century.

The frontiers of the Nordic countries remained undefined for some time, but with a background of similar languages and cultures, Sweden, Norway and Denmark signed the Kalmar Union in 1397. Finland at that time was still part of Sweden. The era of union became one of conflict and violence. At the battle of Brunkeberg in Stockholm in 1471 the Danish king tried to take control of Sweden, but was defeated by the regent Sten Sture. A new Danish campaign in 1520 culminated in the notorious Stockholm Bloodbath at Stortorget *(see p56)*, when more than 80 Swedish noblemen were executed.

1008 Olof Skötkonung converts to Christianity and is baptized in Västergötland

Birger Jarl, Stockholm's founder

c.1250 Birger Jarl founds Stockholm

1350 Code of Magnus Eriksson replaces provincial laws

1364 Albrecht of Mecklenburg chosen as Sweden's King

1397 Kalmar Union links the Nordic countries

1520 Swedish noblemen executed in Stockholm Bloodbath

1000	**1100**	**1200**	**1300**	**1400**	**1500**

800–975 Vikings settle and trade at Birka *(see p150)*

1275 Magnus Ladulås chosen as Sweden's king at Mora

1101 Three Kings' Meeting fixes Scandinavian frontiers

1280 Ordinances of Alsnö give nobility freedom from taxation

1349–50 Plague ravages Sweden

1471 Sten Sture the Elder defeats the Danish King Kristian at Brunkeberg

◀ *The Parhelion Painting* in Storkyrkan (Stockholm's cathedral), depicting a remarkable light phenomenon seen in 1535

The newly chosen king, Gustav Vasa, making his ceremonial entry into Stockholm, Midsummer Day 1523

The Vasa Era

One of those who managed to avoid execution in the Stockholm Bloodbath was the young nobleman Gustav Eriksson. At the end of 1520 Gustav organized an army to oust the Danish King Kristian from Sweden. Gustav was successful and on 6 June 1523 – later to become Sweden's National Day – he was named king with the title Gustav Vasa.

When Gustav Vasa took the throne he discovered a nation in financial crisis. He called on Parliament to pass a controversial law transferring the property of the Church to the State, which then became the country's most important source of economic power. Another important result of this policy was the gradual separation from Catholicism and the adoption of the Lutheran State Church.

During his reign Gustav Vasa implemented tough economic policies in order to concentrate central power in Stockholm. This effective dictatorship also resulted in the Swedish Parliament's decision in 1544 to make the monarchy hereditary.

Descendants of Gustav Vasa oversaw the rise of Sweden into one of Europe's great powers. During the reign of Gustav's son Erik XIV, there were wars against Denmark, Lübeck and Poland. His brothers dethroned him, and he died in prison, probably of a pea soup poisoned by his brother Johan III. During the reign of Karl IX, the third son, Sweden waged war against Denmark and Russia.

Gustav II Adolf and Kristina

Portrait of Erik XIV (1561)

When the next king, Gustav II Adolf, came to power in 1611, Sweden was involved in wars against Russia, Poland and Denmark. Under his rule Sweden steadily increased its influence over the Baltic region. Stockholm started to develop into the country's political and administrative centre. In 1630 Gustav II Adolf, together with his influential chancellor Axel Oxenstierna, decided to intervene in the Thirty Years' War on the side of the Protestants, using religious motives as a pretext. Sweden had some notable military successes during the war, but paid a heavy

1523 Gustav Vasa chosen as king in Strängnäs and marches into Stockholm	**1542** Nils Dacke and supporters stage a peasant revolt in Småland	*Vasa dynasty's coat of arms*	**1560** Gustav Vasa dies	**1568** Erik XIV imprisoned by his brothers at Gripsholms Slott **1577** Erik XIV dies, probably poisoned	**1611** Gustav II Adolf comes to power

1525		**1550**		**1575**		**1600**

1527 Reformation: Parliament confiscates Church property	**1544** Hereditary monarchy established for Gustav Vasa's male descendants	**1561** Eric XIV is crowned king, and his brothers' powers are curbed **1569** Johan III crowned in Stockholm	**1570** Nordic Seven Years' War ends **1587** Johan III's son Sigismund chosen as king of Poland	**1612** Axel Oxenstierna named State Chancellor

price for winning the bloody battle at Lützen in 1632, as the king was killed in action.

Gustav II Adolf's only child, Kristina, came to the throne at the age of six. During her reign (1633–54), life at the court was influenced by the world of science and philosophy. Kristina corresponded with leading academics and invited the French philosopher René Descartes, who died in Stockholm in 1650 only a few months after he had arrived. The Tre Kronor castle became the permanent royal residence. Kristina's reluctance to marry resulted in her cousin, Karl Gustav, becoming Crown Prince. Kristina abdicated and left for Rome, where she converted to Catholicism.

Karl XII with the widowed queen on his arm leaving the burning Tre Kronor fortress

Queen Kristina, fascinated by science and corresponding with leading scientists

The Carolian Era

Karl X Gustav (1654–60) was the first of three Karls to reign. At the height of Sweden's era as a great power, and in one of the most audacious episodes in the history of war, he conquered Denmark by leading his army across the frozen waters of the Great Belt *(see p21)*. Karl XI (1660–97) secured the southern Swedish provinces,

and divided the land more evenly between the crown, nobility and peasants.

While the body of Karl XI lay in state at Tre Kronor in 1697 a fire broke out, destroying most of the building. The new monarch was the teenage Karl XII (1697–1718). He faced mammoth problems when Denmark, Poland and Russia formed an alliance in 1700 with the aim of crushing the power of Sweden. Karl XII set off to battle.

Denmark and Poland were soon forced to plead for peace, but Russia resisted. A bold push towards Moscow was unsuccessful, and the Swedish army suffered a devastating defeat at Poltava in 1709. This marked the beginning of the end for Sweden as a great power.

Karl XII, the most controversial Swedish monarch, returned to Sweden in 1715 after an absence of 15 years. His plans to regain Sweden's position of dominance never came to pass, and he was killed in Norway in 1718.

By now, Sweden was in crisis. Crop failures and epidemics had annihilated one-third of Stockholm's population, and the state's finances were drained.

Sweden's Era as a Great Power

For more than a century (1611–1721) Sweden was the dominant power in northern Europe, and the Baltic was effectively a Swedish inland sea. The country was at its most powerful after the Peace of Roskilde in 1658, when Sweden acquired seven new provinces from Denmark and Norway. Outside today's frontiers the Swedish Empire covered the whole of Finland, large parts of the Baltic, and important areas of northern Germany. Over 111 years as a great power Sweden spent 72 of them at war, with many treasures brought back to the new palaces. It was also an era of cultural development and efficient government.

Swedish Empire

☐ Sweden's empire after the Peace of Roskilde, 1658

The Tre Kronor Castle
Built as a defensive tower in the 1180s, the Tre Kronor castle was the seat of Swedish monarchs from the 1520s and became the administrative centre of the Swedish Empire. It was named after the three crowns on the spire, which burned down in 1697.

The columns of troops ride out over the shifting ice towards Danish Lolland.

The Thirty Years' War

A major European war raged between 1618–48, largely on German soil. Sweden entered the war in 1631 in an alliance with France. Gustav II Adolf was a fine military leader and had modernized the Swedish army, which immediately had major successes at the battles of Breitenfeld (1631) and Lützen (1632), where the king, however, was killed. Later, the Swedes pressed into southern Germany and also captured and plundered Prague (1648). Some rich cultural treasures were brought back to Sweden from the war. In 1648 the Peace of Westphalia gave Sweden several important possessions in northern Germany.

The death of Gustav II Adolf at the Battle of Lützen in 1632

Stockholm in 1640
The city's transformation from a small medieval town into a capital city can be seen in the network of straight streets, similar to the present layout.

Karl XI's Triumphs
The roof painting in Karl XI's gallery at the Royal Palace (1693) by the French artist Jacques Foucquet shows in allegoric form the king's victories at Halmstad, Lund and Landskrona.

Powerful Nobility
The nobility were very influential in the Empire era, and many successful soldiers were ennobled. The Banér family coat of arms from 1651 is adorned by three helmets and barons' crowns.

Count Carl Gustaf Wrangel *(see p58).*

King Karl X Gustav
himself leads the Swedish army of 17,000 men.

Bondeska Palatset
One of the leading buildings of the era (1662–73), this palace was designed by Tessin the Elder and Jean de la Vallée for the State Treasurer Gustav Bonde *(see p60).*

Crossing the Great Belt

When Denmark declared war on Sweden in autumn 1657, the Swedish army was in Poland. Marching west, Karl X Gustav captured the Danish mainland, but without the navy, he could not continue to Copenhagen. However, unusually severe weather froze the sea, making it possible for the soldiers to cross the ice of the Great Belt, and the Danes had to surrender.

Karl XII's Pocket Watch
The warrior king's watchcase dates from 1700. It shows the state coat of arms, as well as those of the 49 provinces that belonged to Sweden at that time.

Karl XII's Last Journey
After being hit by a fatal bullet at Fredrikshald in Norway (1718), the king's body was taken first to Swedish territory then on to Uddevalla for embalming. Painting by Gustav Cederström (1878).

Gustav III (r. 1771–92) with the white armband he wore when mounting his *coup d'état* in 1772

The Age of Liberty and the Gustavian Era

A new constitution came into force in 1719, transferring power from the monarch to parliament. As a result, Sweden developed a system of parliamentary democracy similar to that of Britain in the early 18th century.

The "Age of Liberty" coincided with the Enlightenment, with dramatic advances in culture, science and industry. The botanist Carl von Linné became one of the most famous Swedes of his time. Another was the scientist, philosopher and author Emanuel Swedenborg. The production of textiles expanded in Stockholm, and Sweden's first hospital was constructed on Kungsholmen.

Changes in the balance of power around 1770 gave the new king, Gustav III, an opportunity to strike in an attempt to regain his monarchical powers. On 19 August 1772 Gustav accompanied the guards' parade to the Royal Palace, where, in front of his life-

guards, he declared his intention to mount a bloodless *coup d'état*. The guards and other military units in Stockholm swore allegiance to the king, who tied a white handkerchief round his arm as a badge and rode out into the city to be acclaimed by his people. Absolute power had been restored.

Gustav III was influenced by the Age of Enlightenment and by French culture, which had a great effect on Swedish cultural life *(see pp24–5)*. But over the years opposition grew to the king's absolute powers, largely because of his costly war against Russia. In 1792 he was murdered by a nobleman, Captain Anckarström, during a masked ball at the Opera House *(see p25)*.

Gustav III was succeeded by his son, Gustav IV Adolf. During his reign Sweden was dragged into the Napoleonic wars. After a war against Russia in 1808–9, Sweden lost its sovereignty over Finland, which at the time accounted for one-third of Swedish territory. The king abdicated and left Stockholm to flee the country.

The Era of Karl Johan and Bourgeois Liberalism

By the early 19th century the absolute powers of the monarch had been removed

Napoleon's former marshal, Jean-Baptiste Bernadotte, as King Karl XIV Johan surrounded by his family

1719 New constitution transfers power from the king to Parliament

1738 Parliamentary power is established in the Age of Liberty as the "Hat" party wins elections

1754 The Royal family moves into Royal Palace

1790 Swedish defeat over Russia at Battle of Svensksund

1780s Immigrants are given wide religious freedom

1809 Sweden lose Finland, and Gusta IV Adolf abdicate

1792 Gustav III murdered

1720 **1740** **1760** **1780** **180**

1721 Swedish defeat in the Great Northern War results in territorial losses and the end of the country's golden age

1741 Carl von Linné appointed professor at Uppsala

Carl von Linné (1707–78)

1772 Gustav III crowned and mounts *coup d'état,* giving the king absolute power

1786 Swedish Academy founded

1778 National costume decreed. Death penalty removed for some crimes

Newspaper readers outside the *Aftonbladet* office in 1841

for all time, and the privileges of the aristocracy were undermined even more in 1809 with a new constitution that divided power between the king, the government and parliament.

With a new class structure and the effect of the French Revolution, a new middle class emerged with aspirations of being more influential. One of the best-known newspapers founded around this time was the liberal mouthpiece, *Aftonbladet*.

Difficulties in finding a suitable new monarch led eventually to the choice of one of Napoleon's marshals, Jean-Baptiste Bernadotte, who took on the more authentic Swedish name of Karl Johan. Founder of the present royal dynasty, Karl XIV Johan continued to speak French and never fully learned the Swedish language. His French wife, Queen Desideria, found Stockholm a cultural backwater compared with Paris.

In 1813 a Swedish army with Karl Johan at its head became involved in a campaign against Napoleon. The Battle of Leipzig ended in defeat for France, but, more

significantly, Denmark had to hand over Norway to Sweden. The Norwegians were reluctant to unite with Sweden, but a union between the two countries was agreed – this lasted from 1814 to 1905. A long era of peace began, and with it came a dramatic increase in the country's population, which grew by 1 million to 3.5 million by 1850.

Many Swedes were driven into poverty, because there was not enough work to go round. Mass emigration followed. From the 1850s to the 1930s about 1.5 million people left Sweden. Most of the emigrants travelled to North America in search of a better life.

Folk Movements and Industrialization

As Sweden was transformed from an agricultural society into an industrialized country, the problems posed by the population surplus were gradually tackled.

Stockholm's Eldkvarn mill, destroyed by fire in 1878

An industrial revolution started around 1850, gathering momentum in the late 19th century, and the textile, timber and iron industries provided the main sources of employment. In 1806 the nation's first steam-driven mill, Eldkvarn, was built on the site of the present-day City Hall in Stockholm. It continued production until destroyed by fire in 1878.

Folk movements sprang up in the 19th century, and these still play an important role in Swedish life. A temperance movement emerged against a background of alcohol abuse – in the 1820s annual consumption of spirits was 46 litres (80 pints) per person.

1810 Parliament chooses ean-Baptiste Bernadotte s Crown Prince

1869 Emigration to North America increases due to crop failures

1876 L M Ericsson starts manufacture of telephones

August Strindberg

1908 Royal Dramatic Theatre opens

1842 Primary schools established by decree in every parish

1820	1840	1860	1880	1900

1818 Karl XIV Johan is crowned King of Sweden and Norway

1859 Sweden's first railway opens

1879 August Strindberg's novel *The Red Room* is published

1814 Sweden gains Norway in peace treaty with Denmark

1850 Sweden has 3.5 million population, 93,000 living in Stockholm

1905 Parliament dissolves union with Norway

The Era of Gustav III

Gustav III (1771–92) is one of the most colourful figures in Swedish history. The king's great interest in art, literature and the theatre made the late 18th century a golden age for Swedish culture, and several prestigious academies were founded at this time. After a bloodless revolution in 1772 Gustav III ruled with absolute power and initiated a wide-ranging programme of reform. But his attacks on the privileges of the nobility and his adventurous and costly foreign policy made him powerful enemies. In 1792 he was murdered during a masked ball at Stockholm's Opera House.

The Swedish Academy
The academy was founded by Gustav III in 1786 to preserve the Swedish language. Members received a token depicting the king's head at every meeting.

A courtier entertains by reading aloud.

Gustav III studies architectural designs.

Gustav III's Coronation, 1772
The coronation of the all-powerful monarch in Stockholm's cathedral was a magnificent ceremony, portrayed here by C G Pilo (1782). Every detail was overseen by Gustav himself, who used his flair for the dramatic in politics as well.

Court Life at Drottningholm
Hilleström's painting (1779) gives an insight into court life at Drottningholm, where the king resided between June and November. In the present-day Blue Salon, Gustav III and Queen Sofia Magdalena socialized with their inner circle. Behaviour was modelled on the French court, and etiquette was even stricter at Drottningholm than at Versailles.

The Battle of Svenskund
Gustav III was not known as a successful warrior king, but in 1790 he led the Swedish fleet to its greatest victory ever, when it defeated Russia in a major maritime battle in the Gulf of Finland.

Life in the Inns
The city abounded with inns, frequently visited by the 70,000 inhabitants. J T Sergel's sketch shows a convivial dinner party.

Murder at the Masked Ball
In 1792 Gustav III fell victim to a conspiracy at the Opera House. He was surrounded by masked men and shot by Captain Anckarström on the crowded stage. He died of his wounds 14 days later.

Gustav III's Mask and Cocked Hat
Despite his mask, Gustav III was easy to recognize at the Opera House since he was wearing the badges of two orders of chivalry. The drama intrigued the whole of Europe and inspired Verdi's opera *Un Ballo in Maschera*.

Flogging of the King's Murderer
Among the conspirators, only Anckarström was condemned to death. Before he was taken to his execution in Södermalm, he was flogged on three successive days on the square in front of Riddarhuset.

Queen Sofia Magdalena does her needlework.

Bust of Catherine the Great of Russia, the king's cousin

Gustavian Style

The mid-18th century saw the emergence of Neo-Classicism, with the focus on antiquities and Greek and Roman ideals. Gustav III embraced this trend with great enthusiasm and supported the country's talented artists and authors. He established his own Museum of Antiquities *(see pp52–3)* with marble sculptures that he brought home from Italy. In handicrafts, the sweeping lines of Rococo elegance were replaced by the stricter forms of what has become known as Gustavian Style. Rooms at the Royal Palace were renovated with decoration and furnishings adapted to suit this style.

Chair designed in the Gustavian Style

Swedish Court Costume
In 1778 Gustav III introduced a costume based on French lines to restrain fashion excesses. This is the male court costume for daily wear.

Universal Suffrage

Sweden's population reached 5 million around 1900 despite mass emigration to America. Many people moved to the towns to work in industry, and by the early 20th century Stockholm's population was about 300,000, a fourfold increase since the year 1800.

Increasing social awareness and the rise of the Social Democrat and Liberal parties in the early 20th century gave impetus to the demands for universal suffrage. Radical authors such as August Strindberg became involved. There ensued a political battle, which was not resolved until 1921, when universal suffrage was introduced for both sexes.

Branting and Gustav V in conversation, 1909

Another question which was hotly debated in the 19th century was the role of the king and the extent of his powers. In his "courtyard speech" at the Royal Palace in 1914 King Gustav V called for military rearmament. This led to a constitutional crisis and the resignation of the Liberal government. After the 1917 election the king was forced to accept a government that contained republican-friendly Social Democrats, including the future prime minister, Hjalmar Branting (1860–1925). By then it was parliament, not the king, that decided what sort of government Sweden should have.

The Growth of the Welfare State

In 1936 the Social Democrats and Farmers' Party formed a coalition that developed what was to become known as the welfare state. The Social Democrat prime minister, Per Albin Hansson (1885–1946), defined the welfare state as a socially conscious society with financial security for all.

Reforms introduced under this policy included unemployment benefit, paid holidays and childcare. As a result, poverty in Sweden virtually disappeared during the 1930s and 1940s.

The right of everyone to good housing was also part of welfare state policy. Under the principle of "work-home-centre", a new Stockholm suburb, Vällingby, was planned and built in the early 1950s. The idea was to transform the dormitory suburbs into thriving communities where people would both live and work. The concept was unsuccessful. It soon became apparent that the people who lived there still worked somewhere else, and vice versa. The great shortage of housing in the 1960s led to the "million" programme, which involved the building of a million homes in an extremely short time. These areas soon became known as the "new slums" despite high standards of construction.

Calls for democratic reforms in June 1917 led to riots like this one outside the parliament building in Stockholm

1914 Gustav V gives his "courtyard speech".	**1932** Suicide of industrial magnate Ivar Kreuger is followed by stockmarket crash	**1940** Sweden–German agreement on transit of German military personnel	**1955** Obligatory national health insurance		**1958** Women can be ordained as priests
1921 Universal suffrage for men and women					**1967** Right-hand driving introduced
1920		**1940**			**1960**
Selma Lagerlöf, winner of the Nobel Prize for Literature	**1930** Rise of Functionalist style in architecture, stimulated by the Stockholm Exhibition	**1939** Sweden has coalition government and declares neutrality in World War II	**1950** First public TV broadcast in Sweden	**1964** Art exhibition Moderna Museet shows works by Andy Warhol, Roy Lichtenstein and Claes Oldenburg	**1973** Gustav VI Adolf dies and is succeeded by grandson, Carl XVI Gustaf

The War Years

Sweden declared its neutrality during both World War I and II. Its policy of continuing to trade with nations involved in the conflict during World War I provoked a number of countries into imposing a trade blockade on Sweden. The situation became so serious that hunger riots broke out in some towns.

Neutrality stamp issued in 1942

World War II produced an even more difficult balancing exercise for Swedish neutrality, largely because its Nordic neighbours were at war. With a combination of luck and skill, Sweden remained outside the conflict, but the concessions it had to make were strongly criticized both nationally and internationally.

The Post-War Era

Although the Social Democrats dominated government from the 1930s to the 1970s the socialist and non-socialist power blocs in Swedish politics have remained fairly evenly matched since World War II.

The policy of non-alignment has not proved an obstacle to Swedish involvement on the international scene, including the United Nations. The country has offered asylum to hundreds of thousands of refugees from wars and political oppression.

The centre of Vällingby, which attracted attention among city planners worldwide in the 1950s

Prime minister Olof Palme (1927–86), probably the best-known Swedish politician abroad, was deeply involved in questions of democracy and disarmament, as well as the problems of the Third World. He was renowned for condemning undemocratic acts by dictators. Palme's assassination on the streets of Stockholm in 1986 sent a shock wave across the world, but strangely the murder has still not been solved.

Important changes took place during the closing decades of the 20th century. These included a new constitution in 1974, which removed the monarch's political powers. In 1995 Sweden joined the European Union, after a referendum approved entry by only the narrowest of majorities.

Sveavägen, the site of Palme's murder, 1986

The start of the new millennium marked a change in the role of the church in Sweden, which severed its connections with the state after more than 400 years.

The last decade has seen a significant number of jobs created in high technology companies, and the almost total absence of heavy industry has made Stockholm one of the world's cleanest cities. In 2010, it was granted the European Green Capital Award by the EU Commission, making Stockholm Europe's first green capital.

1974 The monarch loses all political powers	**1980** New constitution gives women the right of succession to the throne	**2000** Öresund bridge opens between Denmark and Sweden		**2010** Crown Princess Victoria marries Daniel Westling	
				2012 Princess Estelle born to Crown Princess Victoria and Prince Daniel	

Crown Princess Victoria

1980	2000	2020

1986 Prime minister Olof Palme murdered in Stockholm

1995 Sweden joins European Union

2007 Legendary film maker Ingmar Bergman dies

1974 ABBA pop group wins Eurovision Song Contest

2000 Swedish Church separated from the State

2003 Foreign minister Anna Lindh murdered in Stockholm

STOCKHOLM THROUGH THE YEAR

Stockholm's heart never misses a beat despite the vagaries of the climate. Although summer is a glorious time to visit the capital, the city shimmering in ice and snow is also an amazing experience, and numerous popular events take place throughout the year. Stockholm's countless sporting fixtures attract top-class international stars. Its many concerts, both pop and classical, indoor and outdoor, feature performers from around the world. Sweden's national festivals are celebrated in the traditional way in Stockholm and are always popular attractions for both locals and visitors alike. The capital's proximity to the surrounding countryside and water provides an extensive range of opportunities for all kinds of outdoor activities throughout the year.

Spring

As in all the Nordic countries, people long for spring after the dark days of winter, and it has a big impact on life in the capital. Sun-lovers sit on the steps of Konserthuset (Concert Hall) and Kungliga Dramatiska Teatern (Royal Dramatic Theatre); people work on their boats; football competes with ice hockey for attention; spring flowers come into bud in Kungsträdgården; and the traditional *semla* cream buns go on sale to break the Lenten fast.

March
Stockholm International Boat Show *(early Mar)*. The spring's major boat exhibition at Stockholm International Fairs in Älvsjö.
Outdoors Fair *(Mar)*. Held at Stockholm International Fairs in Älvsjö, this exhibition focuses on camping, tourism and outdoor equipment.

Enjoying the first sunny weather of the spring at Djurgårdsbrunnsviken

Garden Fair *(Mar)*. Everything for the gardener is on show at Stockholm International Fairs in Älvsjö.

April
Stockholm Art Week *(early Apr)*. A week of art events, exhibitions and fairs. Many of the city's art galleries, museums and exhibition venues arrange special events and programmes.
Swedish Football Championship *(last weekend in Apr)*. Series starts at Råsunda and Söder stadiums.
Gröna Lund *(end of Apr)*. Djurgården's amusement park, the oldest in the country, opens for its 130-day season. Exciting rides and attractions include roller coasters and a free-fall tower. There are also stages hosting music and other shows, and there's a wide range of places to eat. Gröna Lund's beautiful gardens include 30,000 pansies and 25,000 summer flowers.
Stockholm Culture Night *(end of Apr)*. Stockholm's main cultural institutions come together to organize a series of free events throughout the city, including concerts, parties and guided tours. Many museums, galleries and libraries stay open until midnight.
Walpurgis Night at Skansen *(30 Apr)*. Traditional celebrations to welcome the arrival of spring with massed standard bearers, folk dancing, torchlight procession, student choirs, bonfire and fireworks.
King's Birthday *(30 Apr)*. The king is greeted at Kungliga

Walpurgis Night bonfire at Evert Taubes Terrass, Riddarholmen

Slottet (Royal Palace) with a military parade, and children present flowers and gifts.

May
Round Lidingö Race *(2nd Sat in May)*. This long-distance sailing race attracts hundreds of boats of all shapes and sizes.
Archipelago Fair *(late May)*. This is the fair for all those looking to sell, purchase or exchange their leisure boats.
Elite Race *(last weekend in May)*. Trotting competition at Solvalla with top horses from all over the world.
Kungsträdgården *(late May)*. The programme of summer entertainment in the park starts on the main stage.
Gärdet Race *(late May)*. Over 500 vintage cars take part in this race around the city. As part of the festivities, there are food stands, music shows and a classic boat show.

Average Daily Hours of Sunshine

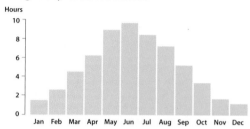

Sunshine Chart
Stockholm's climate can vary markedly from hot, sunny days followed by a cooler rainy spell during the summer to winters with freezing temperatures and snow. From mid-June to mid-July it never really gets dark. Winter days are very short, although there can still be a strong sun at times.

Summer

Stockholm is at its best at this time of year. Although May can be warm, summer does not really start until early June, when the schools break up. In late June the sun shines almost round the clock, and with it comes a vibrant outdoor life with picnics and street festivals. The capital gets a little emptier at peak holiday-time in July. When the schools go back in late August, Swedes celebrate the arrival of two annual culinary delights: crayfish and fermented Baltic herring.

Traditional Midsummer celebrations at Skansen, the open-air museum

June

Summerburst *(early Jun)*. Festival of electronic music in Gärdet.
Stockholm Outdoor *(early Jun)*. Scandinavia's largest festival for outdoor activities.
Stockholm Early Music Festival *(early Jun)*. Renowned musicians from Sweden and Europe perform music from the Medieval, Renaissance and Baroque periods.
A Taste of Stockholm *(early Jun)*. Kungsträdgården becomes the world's largest outdoor restaurant.
Archipelago Boat Day *(early Jun)*. Classic steamboats assemble at Strömkajen near the Grand Hôtel for a round trip to Vaxholm.
ASICS Stockholm Marathon *(first Sat in Jun)*. One of the world's 10 biggest marathons with around 13,000 runners.
National Day *(6 Jun)*. Celebrations at Skansen take place in the presence of the royal family.
Nationaldagsgaloppen *(6 Jun)*. Horse racing at Gärdet.
Midsummer Eve *(last Sat but one in Jun)*. A major Swedish

festival celebrated at Skansen over three days. It starts at 2pm on Midsummer Eve with the traditional raising of the maypole and ring dancing.
ÅF Offshore Race *(end Jun)*. A major international sailing event, which starts in Stockholm and finishes at Sandhamn.
Drottningholms Slottsteater *(Jun–Aug)*. A season of concerts, opera and dance is performed in the 18th-century court theatre.

July

Stockholm Street Festival *(early Jul)*. Buskers, magicians and other performers entertain at Kungsträdgården.
Stockholm BAUHAUS Athletics *(end Jul)*. A major international athletics competition at Stockholm Stadion.

August

Crayfish Season *(Aug)*. Parties throughout the capital feast on crayfish and sing traditional drinking songs.

Crayfish

Stockholm Pride *(Aug)*. Week-long gay and lesbian festival with a parade, events and music.
Stockholm Music & Arts *(early Aug)*. Festival held in Skeppsholmen.
Midnight Race *(mid-Aug)*. Night-time running that takes place over a distance of 10 km (6 miles) in Söder. The event attracts around 16,000 people.
Stockholm Culture Festival *(mid-Aug)*. For six days, the streets and squares of the city centre become the stage for 600 cultural events.
Philharmonikerna i det Gröna *(2nd Sun in Aug)*. The Royal Philharmonic Orchestra performs for free to picnicking music-lovers on the lawn by Sjöhistoriska museet.
Baltic Sea Festival *(late Aug)*. Various Swedish orchestras perform classical pieces at the Berwaldhallen concert hall.
Popaganda *(late Aug)*. Artists display their works at the public baths of Eriksdalsbadet.

Average Monthly Rainfall

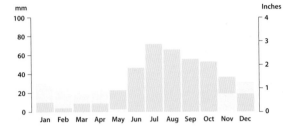

Rainfall Chart
Some years Stockholm can have very rainy summers, but in others the weather can be dry for several weeks at a time. Heavy snowfall in winter may lie until March, but some winters have been known to be virtually free of snow.

Autumn

Early autumn mornings can be crisp and clear. Summer often stages a successful and lengthy last-ditch stand, before the trees explode in a cascade of colours.

Globen, Tele2 and other indoor arenas draw increasingly large attendances, and cultural activities in theatres and art galleries get under way again, although many outdoor events continue well into the autumn, weather permitting.

Chanterelles

September

Now is the time to pick apples, pears and plums in the garden. Summer cottages are shut, and boats are laid up for the winter, but there is still a lot going on in the capital.

Tjejmilen *(early Sep)*. Djurgården is the setting for the world's biggest race for female athletes.
Stockholm Oktoberfest *(early Sep)*. A popular Bavarian-style beer festival with music.
Music at the Palace *(Sep)*. The summer concert season starts in the Hall of State and the Royal Chapel at Kungliga Slott.
Stockholm Beer and Whisky Festival *(last weekend in Sep & first in Oct)*. Lively festival with lots of beer, whisky and cider.
Stockholm Half-Marathon *(mid-Sep)*. This easy course starts and finishes outside the Royal Palace, taking runners through many inner-city areas.
Traditional Fair at Skansen *(last weekend in Sep)*. Among the items on sale are textiles, woodcrafts and toys.
Lidingö Race *(end of Sep)*. The world's largest cross-country race with competitors of all ages.
Svensk Travkriterium *(end of Sep)*. Harness racing at Solvalla.

October

This is a busy time for theatres, cinemas, restaurants and clubs. There are fewer outdoor events, with people heading instead for the parks and forests for autumn strolls.
Bake & Chocolate Festival *(mid-Oct)*. The world's best bakers and chocolatiers gather at Stockholmsmässan.

Annual Stockholm International Horse Show at Globen

If Stockholm Open *(mid-Oct)*. This ATP World Tour tennis tournament takes place at Kungliga Lawn Tennishallen.

November

As darkness falls over the city, there is a wide selection of events to choose from.
Granturismo *(early Nov)*. An exhibition of some of the world's finest and fastest cars.
Scandinavian Sail and Motor Boat Show *(mid-Nov)*. Exhibition at Stockholm International Fairs with everything for large motor boats or yachts.
Skating Premiere *(mid-Nov)*. Skating with music starts on a rink in Kungsträdgården.
Stockholm International Film Festival *(mid-Nov)*. Ten-day event with public screenings and the presentation of awards.
Stockholm International Horse Show *(late Nov)*. World Cup competition in dressage and jumping plus entertainment at Globen.
Christmas displays *(late Nov)*. Shop windows and streets are seasonally decorated.

Profusion of autumn colours in Hagaparken

Average monthly temperature

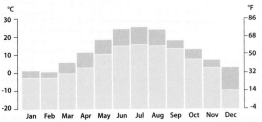

Temperature Chart
Stockholm has a maritime climate and is much milder than one might expect. The summers are usually fairly cool, but sometimes there is hot sunshine for several weeks running. Winter temperatures often fall below freezing, but it is rarely severely cold. The average maximum and minimum temperatures are shown.

Winter

Winter can vary from temperatures a few degrees above freezing with slush on the streets to sparkling sunny days with the city under a dazzling white blanket of snow, ice-covered water and temperatures well below zero. Stockholmers get out their skis, skates, or toboggans, or go for long walks. There are also several cultural and sporting events.

December

Sometimes the eagerly awaited Christmas season seems a long way off, but there is no shortage of activities in early December, when some of the year's most important events are staged.
Christmas Walking Tours *(Dec)*. A great way to enjoy the city's Christmas decorations and lights.
Christmas at Skansen *(Dec)*. This open-air museum *(see pp100–1)* beautifully demonstrates how Christmas was celebrated in pre-industrial society.
Nobel Day *(10 Dec)*. A ceremony at Konserthuset (Concert Hall) honours the year's Nobel Prize

Lucia, the "Queen of Light", with her attendants at Skansen

laureates. In the evening the royal family attends a banquet at Stadshuset (City Hall).
Lucia Celebrations *(13 Dec)*. Sweden's white-clad Lucia, the "Queen of Light", with her girl attendants and "star boys", serves the Nobel laureates early morning coffee with saffron buns and performs traditional songs. In the evening a Lucia procession winds through the city to celebrations and fireworks at Skansen. Many Swedish homes, schools and workplaces have their own Lucia.
Christmas Markets *(from early Dec)*. An array of Christmas goods on sale at traditional markets at Skansen, Rosendals Slott, Kungsträdgården, Stortorget in Gamla Stan and Drottningholms Slott.
Christmas *(24–26 Dec)*. Filled with traditions, Christmas is the most important Swedish holiday. The main event is Christmas Eve, when an abundant *smörgåsbord* is followed by gifts, often delivered by a family member disguised as Father Christmas.
Christmas Sales *(first weekday after Christmas)*. Shops start their sales.
New Year *(31 Dec–1 Jan)*. A major festival, when many Stockholmers go out on the town. Traditional celebrations at Skansen include a reading of Tennyson's poem "Ring Out, Wild Bells" on the stroke of midnight. Churches across the

Fireworks display over Stockholm on New Year's Eve

city ring their bells, and there is a spectacular fireworks display.

January
Stockholm Fashion Week *(end of Jan)*. As well as fashion, events focus on interior design.

February
Antiques Fair *(mid-Feb)*. Stockholm International Fairs, Älvsjö, hosts antiques lovers.
Globen Gala *(mid-Feb)*. International athletics stars converge on the Globen arena for one of the world's best indoor competitions.

Public Holidays

New Year (1 Jan)
Epiphany (6 Jan)
Good Friday
Easter Monday
Ascension Day (6th Thu after Easter)
Labour Day (1 May)
Whit Monday (May/Jun)
Midsummer Eve (end Jun)
Christmas Day (25 Dec)
Boxing Day (26 Dec)

STOCKHOLM AT A GLANCE

The old conception of Stockholm as a small, rustic capital of a cold country far away to the north is no longer valid – the city has a rich cultural heritage and has become a dynamic Continental-style capital.

Stockholm is an unbelievably beautiful city, surrounded by clear water and unspoilt countryside that stretches right into the heart of the urban area. Stockholm's 750-year history has produced many beautiful buildings, as

well as plenty of impressive cultural treasures that can be discovered in its fine museums.

To make your visit as rewarding as possible the following ten pages give a quick guide to the best museums and palaces, the most distinguished architecture and outstanding modern design. Activities along the city's quaysides and waterways are also described. Below is a selection of sights that should not be missed.

Stockholm's Top Ten Sights

Stadshuset
See pp116–17

Nordiska museet
See pp92–3

Skansen
See pp100–101

Drottningholm
See pp146–9

Historiska museet
See pp106–7

Moderna museet
See pp82–3

Stockholm's Archipelago
See pp152–3

Nationalmuseum
See pp84–5

Royal Palace and its Guard
See pp50–53

Vasamuseet
See pp94–6

◄ The magnificent Western Staircase in the Royal Palace

Stockholm's Best: Museums

Stockholm has around 100 museums, with remarkable collections covering every conceivable subject and interest. The "Top Ten" shown here are of particular note. Kungliga Slottet (the Royal Palace), for instance, is effectively four museums in one, while the most spectacular is the museum housing the *Vasa* warship, salvaged from the depths of Stockholm's harbour after 333 years and now an international attraction.

Hallwylska museet
Thanks to a methodical countess and her impeccable taste, this lavishly decorated palace from the late 19th century has become a magnificent museum with a wide-ranging collection of objects displayed in an original setting.

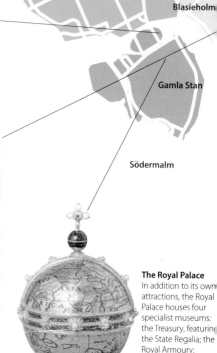

Vasastaden

City

Blasieholm

Gamla Stan

Södermalm

Medeltidsmuseum
Parts of the city wall from the 1530s can be seen in this underground Medieval museum, which focuses on the capital's origins. The wall's reconstruction shows medieval building techniques.

0 metres	500
0 yards	500

Nationalmuseum
The Nationalmuseum of Fine Arts, Sweden's largest art museum, has fine collections of 17th- and 18th-century Swedish paintings and handicrafts, 17th-century Dutch and 18th-century French art. Rubens's *Bacchanalia on Andros* dates from the 1630s.

The Royal Palace
In addition to its own attractions, the Royal Palace houses four specialist museums: the Treasury, featuring the State Regalia; the Royal Armoury; Gustav III's Museum of Antiquities; and the Tre Kronor Museum.

Moderna museet
The Fantastic Paradise (1966) by Niki de Saint Phalle and Jean Tinguely marks the way up to the Moderna museet, with its collection of modern international and Swedish art.

Historiska museet
Behind the sculpted bronze gateways of the Swedish History Museum is a wealth of material, including a section on Viking life. The Gold Room shows priceless prehistoric finds, such as the Timboholm Treasure (400–450 BC).

Östermalm

Sjöhistoriska museet
The stern of the royal flagship *Amphion*, dating from the late 18th century, is one of the many treasures on display in the National Maritime Museum, designed by architect Ragnar Östberg.

Djurgården

ppsholmen

Nordiska museet
This colossal building from 1907 houses many different artifacts illustrating everyday Swedish life and customs, dating from the 1520s.

Vasamuseet
A fatal capsizing in 1628 and a successful salvage operation 333 years later gave Stockholm its most popular museum. Over 98 per cent of the renovated warship *Vasa* is original.

Skansen
The world's first open-air museum, founded in 1891, shows the Sweden of bygone days with farms and manor houses, urban scenes and craftspeople at work. Nordic fauna and flora are also on display.

Exploring Stockholm's Museums

Stockholm's wide range of museums gives the visitor a chance to experience exhibitions covering a multitude of different interests. Many are housed in magnificent historic palaces or institutions with notable collections and the resources to bring each subject to life. In addition, there are numerous specialist museums, including the homes of highly regarded artists. Various important private collections are open to the public. This guide lists more than 50 of the best museums Stockholm has to offer.

Karl XII's uniform, 1718, on show at Livrustkammaren

Palace Museums

The period when Sweden was a great power (1611–1721) resulted in a number of beautiful buildings, many of which are now museums. Foremost among these are the royal palaces in and around the city. **Kungliga Slottet** (Royal Palace, pp50–53) is a museum in itself. It also houses **Skattkammaren** (the Treasury) with Sweden's royal regalia, crowns and a large silver font for the baptism of royal children.

Also in the Royal Palace are **Gustav III's Antikmuseum**, containing the antique marble sculptures that Gustav III brought home from his Italian travels, and **Livrustkammaren** (Royal Armoury, p54) where visitors can see a variety of items used at the court through the centuries. **Museum Tre Kronor** reflects the history of the earlier castle.

Other royal museums include **Rosendals Slott** (p98), a pre-fabricated building from the

1820s in Karl Johan (Empire) style, on Djurgården. **Gustav III's Paviljong** (pp124–5) in Hagaparken has furnishings and decorations that are fine examples of the late 18th-century Gustavian style. **Ulriksdals Slott** (p127) has some interesting interiors, including a living room for King Gustav VI Adolf and Queen Louise.

In a class of its own is **Drottningholms Slott** (pp146–9), a UNESCO World Heritage site, which includes a notable theatre museum.

Historical Museums

Several of Stockholm's museums focus on various historic aspects. **Historiska museet** (Swedish History Museum, pp106–7) has treasures from prehistoric times in its magnificent Gold Room, as well as a wonderful section on the Vikings.

Nordiska museet (pp92–3) and the open-air **Skansen** (pp100–101) show Swedish customs and traditions alongside traditional wooden homes. **Stockholms Stadsmuseum** (City Museum, p129) tells the story of Stockholm and its citizens. It is also home to a reference library.

The city's earliest history is highlighted at **Medeltidsmuseum** (Medieval Museum, p61).

Etnografiska museet (National Museum of Ethnography, p110) features anthropological artifacts from all around the world.

The culture and history of Stockholm's Jewish population is the theme of **Judiska museet** (p120).

Medelhavsmuseet (Museum of Mediterranean and Near Eastern Antiquities, p67), with its marvellous 1905 stairwell, focuses on architecture and sculptures from the countries around the Mediterranean. **Östasiatiska museet** (Museum of Far Eastern Antiquities, p80) contains large collections of arts and crafts from China, Japan, Korea and India.

Art Museums

The wide range of collections at the **Nationalmuseum** (National Museum of Fine Arts, pp84–5) cover European and Swedish paintings up to the early 20th century, as well as Swedish handicrafts and design. **Moderna museet** (pp82–3) on Skeppsholmen has an outstanding collection of contemporary Swedish and international art. **ArkDes** (p80), highlights Swedish building techniques over the last 1,000 years and provides an overview of the wider international picture.

Three magnificent art galleries are located in beautiful buildings on Djurgården. **Liljevalchs Konsthall** (p97) focuses on 20th-century Swedish and international art, while **Waldemarsudde** (p99) and **Thielska Galleriet** (p99) both specialize in Swedish and Nordic art from the late 19th to the early 20th century.

The **Schefflerska Palatset** (Haunted Palace, p118) shows Stockholm University's collection of classic Swedish

Decorative Viking brooch, Historiska museet

paintings, from the 16th to the 19th century, as well as artistic Swedish glass.

Millesgården *(p152)* on Lidingö is where the sculptor Carl Milles lived and worked, and where he is now buried. Some of his best works are on show in a beautiful outdoor setting with a panoramic view of Stockholm.

Marine Museums

A city located on water offers plenty of interest for anyone interested in ships and the sea.

One of the city's biggest attractions, **Vasamuseet** *(pp94–6)* shows the magnificent and almost intact warship *Vasa*, which sank in Stockholm harbour after a maiden voyage of only 1,300 m (1,400 yd). In addition to the painstakingly restored hull, there are other exhibits that give an insight into life on board a 17th-century warship.

Close to *Vasa* are **Museifartygen** (Museum Ships, *p91*), including one of the last Swedish lightships, *Finngrundet* (1903), and the powerful ice-breaker *St Erik* (1915), featuring Europe's largest marine steam engine.

Sjöhistoriska museet (National Maritime Museum, *pp108–9*) houses a fine collection of model ships as well as an interesting display of figure heads.

A short boat trip takes visitors to the **Fjäderholmarna** islands, where there are two boat museums devoted to traditional and recreational boating. There is also an angling museum and the Baltic aquarium, dramatically set into the side of a rock face *(p152)*.

Museums in Private Homes

One of the pearls among Stockholm's museums, **Hallwylska museet** *(p75)* is an opulent private residence from the late 19th century, complete with original furnishings. The home of the dramatist and

Drawing room in the lavishly decorated Hallwylska museet

author August Strindberg, the **Strindbergsmuseet Blå Tornet** (Strindberg's Blue Tower Museum, *p71*) gives an insight into his life. A statue of Strindberg by Carl Eldh stands near **Carl Eldhs Ateljémuseum** (Studio Museum, *pp122–3*), the sculptor's former residence.

Museums for Special Interests

Stockholm has many museums catering for special interests. **Kungliga Myntkabinettet** (Royal Coin Cabinet, *p54*) explains the history of money and shows coins and other methods of payment dating back 1,000 years.

Junibacken *(p90)* is a charming museum, bringing

Stage costume from *Les Ballets Suédois* (1920s), Dansmuseet

to life the classic children's books by Astrid Lindgren.

Leksaksmuseet (Toy Museum, *p133*) is an attraction for all ages, though it is children who will be utterly mesmerized by its mechanical toys, models, dolls and dolls' houses.

A traditional wine shop and distillery can be seen at **Spritmuseum** (Museum of Spirits, *p91*). Another human weakness, tobacco, is documented at Skansen's Tobaksmuseet (Museum of Matches and Tobacco).

Postmuseum (Postal Museum, *p57*) contains more than 4 million stamps from around the world.

Spårvägsmuseet (Transport Museum, *p132*) has some 40 original trams and a large collection of models. In the same area is the **Almgrens Sidenväveri & Museum** (Almgren's Silk-Weaving Mill & Museum, *p129*).

The life of the popular 18th-century troubadour Carl Michael Bellman *(p98)* is portrayed at the **Bellmanmuseet** *(p134)* on Långholmen.

Dansmuseet (Dance Museum, *p67*) reflects all aspects of dance with a superb and varied international collection.

Swedish Museum of Performing Arts *(p74)* has some 6,000 instruments and the country's biggest musical archive, which includes records covering 20,000 traditional ballads.

Stockholm's Best: Architecture

Sweden was spared the ravages of World War II, so
Stockholm has preserved a rich variety of architectural
treasures. Gamla Stan was the city's first built-up area.
The surrounding districts known as Malmarna *(see p103)*
remained mainly rural until an intensive period of
building begun in the second half of the 19th century.
From 1930 the city started to expand further and this
period is reflected in a band of Functionalist-style
buildings. Suburbs including Farsta and Vällingby were
built after 1945. In the 1990s, new buildings began
appearing in the inner city on former industrial sites.

Kungliga Dramatiska Teatern
(Fredrik Lilljekvist, 1901–8). The Royal
Dramatic Theatre is one of Stockholm's
few monumental Jugendstil buildings.
The façades are of white marble and,
inside, the staircase and foyer are
embellished with lavish gold decorative
work. *(See pp74–5.)*

Vasastaden

The Royal Palace
(Nicodemus Tessin the Younger, 1690–1704;
completed under Carl Hårleman). Work on
the Royal Palace, based on plans by Tessin
the Younger, started after the fire in 1697. The
façade exhibits influences of Roman palaces;
the magnificent interiors are of French and
Swedish design. *(See pp50–53.)*

City

Kungsholmen

Nybroviken

Gamla stan

Wrangelska Palatset
(Originally built 1629; extensively rebuilt under Jean de la Vallée and
Nicodemus Tessin the Elder, 1652–70). This is one of several majestic palaces
built on Riddarholmen in the imposing style popular during the 17th century.
Original details include the gateway and the courtyard arcade. *(See p58.)*

The Tessin Trio

Nicodemus Tessin the Younger (1654–1728), who designed the Royal Palace *(see
pp50–53)*, can be regarded as Sweden's leading architect because he influenced
not only building design but also city
planning, landscape gardening and
handicrafts. His father, Nicodemus Tessin
the Elder (1615–81), designed several
country mansions, with Drottningholm
Palace being his master work *(see pp146–9)*.
The third-generation Tessin, Carl Gustaf
(1695–1770), along with Carl Hårleman,
introduced the Rococo style to Sweden.

**Etching of the Royal Palace, to which
all three Tessins contributed**

| 0 metres | | 500 |
| 0 yards | | 500 |

Stockholm's Surrounding Areas

Tessinparken
(Arvid Stille; 1930 city plan by Sture Frölén). Functionalist style on a large scale was tested on the three-storey buildings on pillars at Tessinparken. *(See p112.)*

Stadsbiblioteket
(Erik Gunnar Asplund, 1920–28). The City Library is Stockholm's most admired example of the 1920s Neo-Classical style. The book hall has a fascinating cylindrical shape and many fine interior details. *(See p119.)*

Söder Cottages
Wooden cottages for port workers were built from the early 18th century. Quite a few remain in the Söder area, for example at Åsöberget and on Fjällgatan. *(See p131.)*

Globen Arena was designed in a spectacular spheric shape. *(See p135.)*

Drottningholm, a World Heritage site, features exquisite buildings and parks dating from 1600 to 1880. *(See pp146–9.)*

Skogskyrkogården Cemetery, a World Heritage site, combines landscape design and architecture. *(See p135.)*

0 kilometres 5

0 miles 3

Nordiska museet
(Isak Gustaf Clason, 1889–1907). This museum was conceived as a national monument to Nordic culture. The impressive building in a Scandinavian version of Renaissance style is only one-fourth of its original planned size. *(See pp92–3.)*

Östermalm

Djurgården

ops-
men

Södermalm

Moderna museet
(Rafael Moneo, 1995–8). The spacious Modern Museum was designed to be novel yet not to disturb the historically sensitive surroundings of the island of Skeppsholmen. *(See pp82–3.)*

Swedish Style

Swedish design first attracted international attention at the 1925 World Exhibition in Paris, when glassware in particular took the world by storm, and the concept of "Swedish Grace" was launched. The nation's design tradition is characterized by its simplicity and functionality with an emphasis on natural materials. Swedish designers and architects are renowned for creating simple, attractive "human" objects for everyday use. The 1990s marked the beginning of a new golden age in which contemporary Swedish design once more won worldwide acclaim.

Stoneware, Hans Hedberg
Swedish stoneware from the 1940s, 1950s and 1960s attracts worldwide attention, and collectors tend to snap up anything they can find.

Armchair (1969), Bruno Mathsson
Bruno Mathsson, one of Sweden's most celebrated 20th-century furniture designers, is one of the creators of what came to be known as the "Swedish Modern" style. He designed the first version of the Pernilla armchair in 1942.

Simplicity is the concept most closely associated with Swedish style. **Pale wood** is characteristic of its design.

Rag mats are produced using an old Swedish weaving tradition taken up by Karin Larsson, whose skill as a textile designer is now widely recognized.

Bureau (1952), Josef Frank
Frank was born in Austria but worked in Sweden and was another disciple of the "Swedish Modern" style. He is best known for his printed textiles for Svenskt Tenn *(see p186)*, but also designed furniture.

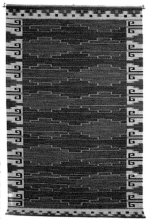

Carpet (1931), Märta Måås-Fjetterström
From 1919 Måås-Fjetterström wove her highly regarded carpets at her studio in southern Sweden. Her work was inspired by folklore and nature, and she created a design concept that was new but still deeply rooted in tradition.

Silver coffee pot (1953), Sigurd Persson

Persson had an almost unrivalled ability to handle metal. He made a big impact on the history of design with both his every-day industrial work and his exclusive artistic creations.

Flowers and plants along a windowsill and no curtains typify the Larssons' ideas on interior decoration.

Chair (1981), Jonas Bohlin

The Concrete chair became the most remarkable piece of Swedish furniture design in the 1980s. A graduation project, it represented a completely new approach to furniture design.

Bookshelf (1989), John Kandell

Books are placed flat on the *Pilaster* bookshelf instead of being stacked in the usual way. The lines are simple and typically Scandinavian. The maker, Källemo, is one of Sweden's most unconventional furniture manufacturers.

Gustavian late 18th-century style elements have remained a strong feature in Swedish design through the centuries, and made a particular comeback in the 1990s.

Carl Larsson's Sundborn

The home created by the artist Carl Larsson (1853–1919) and his wife Karin became an inspiration to the world when it featured in his watercolour series A Home. *The mixture of old and new, pure colours, plants and windows without curtains was an expression of the "Beauty for All" movement.*

Vase (1998), Ann Wåhlström

Wåhlström is one of the new young glass designers at Kosta Boda. Her vase, *Cyklon*, is a good example of contemporary Swedish glass.

Where to See Swedish Design

Asplund
Sibyllegatan 31. **Map** 3 E3. Contemporary Swedish and international design. W asplund.org

Design House Stockholm
Hamngatan 18–20. **Map** 3 D4. Exclusive and functional design with a Scandinavian touch.
W designhousestockholm.com

Jacksons
Sibyllegatan 53. **Map** 3 E3. W jacksons.se

Orrefors Kosta Boda
Birger Jarlsgatan 15. **Map** 3 D3. W orrefors.com or
W kostaboda.com

R.O.O.M.
PUB, Plan 03, Hötorget. **Map** 2 C4. W room.se

Svenskt Tenn
Strandvägen 5. **Map** 3 E4.
Josef Frank, etc. W svenskttenn.se

Stockholm, the City on the Water

Stockholm is sometimes referred to as "The Venice of the North", built as it is on 14 islands surrounded by the clear waters of Lake Mälaren and Saltsjön, an inlet from the Baltic Sea. For most visitors, seeing "the green city on the water" is a remarkable experience. Stockholm's quaysides and waterways offer a range of activities not normally associated with a capital city, which are made possible only because of the pollution-free environment. The waterside location is Stockholm's most beautiful feature.

Canoe Slalom on Strömmen
Spectacular canoe slalom competitions are held every year in the rushing water of the Strömmen channel below Gustav Adolfs Torg.

Sailing Race on Riddarfjärden
The waters of Stockholm are always busy with sailing boats. A ride along Riddarfjärden is particularly spectacular at night.

City

Kungsholmen

Riddarfjärden

Gamla Stan

Strömmen

Ske
Ho

Långholmen

Södermalm

Swimming in the Heart of the City
During the summer months, swimmers bathe in the clean, warm water (about 20°C/68°F) in the city centre. Långholmen (*see p134*) has sandy beaches and smooth rocks offering an ideal setting for a refreshing dip.

For map symbols *see back flap*

Fishing for a Living
For 400 years fishermen have cast their nets from boats near Kungliga Slottet (Royal Palace). Today only four boats remain. Of the 30 species found here, smelt is the most commonly caught fish.

Vintage Mahogany Boat
Lovingly renovated vintage motor boats with shining mahogany and brass fittings are often seen on the waterways of Stockholm, as well as the more exclusive Riva racing boats.

Exploring on Your Own
Kayaks, pedalos, rowing boats, motor boats and sometimes sailing dinghies can be hired near the Djurgården Bridge by visitors who want to explore the waters of Stockholm on their own.

```
0 metres        500
0 yards         500
```

Key

 ••• Paved walking path

Östermalm

Djurgårdsbrunnsviken

Djurgården

Saltsjön

Fishing for Perch
The clean waters of the inner city are rich in edible fish. Anglers spin for sea trout, and here, on Djurgårdsbrunn Canal, bait-fishing for perch is popular, as is fly-fishing in autumn.

Cruise Ship Manoeuvres in Stockholm's Harbour
Cruise ships are an impressive sight, when seen from the heights of Södermalm, as they make their way through the narrow channel to their centrally located quay.

Aerial view of the city, around the royal palace ▶

STOCKHOLM AREA BY AREA

GAMLA STAN

Relics of Stockholm's early history as a town in the 13th century can still be found on Stadsholmen, the largest island in Gamla Stan (Old Town). The whole island is one huge area of historical heritage, with the many sights just a few metres apart.

The Royal Palace is the symbol of Sweden's era as a great power in the 17th and early 18th centuries (see pp20–21), and its magnificent state rooms, apartments and artifacts are well matched to the Roman Baroque-style exterior. The historic buildings

standing majestically around Slottsbacken underline Stockholm's role as a capital city.

This area has a special atmosphere with much to offer: from the bustling streets of souvenir shops, bookstores and antiques shops to elegant palaces, churches and museums. Many medieval cellars are now restaurants and cafés, while the narrow streets recall a bygone era.

Bridges lead to Riddarholmen, with its 17th-century palaces and royal crypt, and to Helgeandsholmen for the newer splendours of Riksdagshuset (the Parliament building).

Sights at a Glance

Palaces and Museums

1 Kungliga Slottet (Royal Palace) pp50–53
2 Livrustkammaren
3 Kungliga Myntkabinettet
4 Tessinska Palatset
10 Postmuseum
12 Wrangelska Palatset
15 Stenbockska Palatset
17 Bondeska Palatset
19 Medeltidsmuseum

Historic Buildings

14 Birger Jarls Torn
16 Riddarhuset
18 Riksdagshuset

Streets and Squares

6 Stortorget
8 Mårten Trotzigs Gränd
9 Västerlånggatan
13 Evert Taubes Terrass

Churches

5 Storkyrkan
7 Tyska Kyrkan
11 Riddarholms-kyrkan

▢ Restaurants pp166–71

1 Bistro & Grill Ruby
2 Bistro Pastis
3 Den Gyldene Freden
4 Djuret
5 Frantzen
6 Magnus Ladulas
7 Mr French
8 Pubologi
9 Le Rouge
10 Vapiano Gamla Stan

See also Street Finder pp206–18

0 metres 250
0 yards 250

◄ **Detail from a striking stained-glass window in Storkyrkan**

For map symbols see back flap

Street-by-Street: Slottsbacken

Slottsbacken is much more than just a steep hill
linking Skeppsbron and the highest part of Gamla Stan
(Old Town). It also provides the background for ceremonial
processions and the daily changing of the guard, and is the
route for visiting heads of state and foreign ambassadors,
when they have an audience with the king at the Royal Palace
(Kungliga Slottet). Alongside Slottsbacken the palace displays
its most attractive façade, with the entrance to the Treasury
(Skattkammaren), State Room (Rikssalen) and Palace Church
(Slottskyrkan). Nicodemus Tessin the Younger's ambition to
make Stockholm a leading European city in monumental
terms was realized in 1799 with the addition of the Obelisk.

The Olaus Petri statue by
Storkyrkan stands in front of
a tablet telling the history
of the cathedral
since 1264.

Outer Courtyard

Axel Oxenstiernas Palats (1653) is, for
Stockholm, an unusual example of the
style known as Roman Mannerism. For
30 years, Axel Oxenstierna (1583–1654)
was a dominant figure in Swedish
power politics.

The Obelisk by Louis
Jean Desprez was
erected in 1799 to thank
the citizens for their
support of Gustav III's
Russian war in 1788–90.

Stock Exchange *(see p56)*

TRÅNGSUND

STOR-
TORGET

❺ ★ **Storkyrkan**
An impressive cathedral with a
late Gothic interior, it is full of
treasures from many different eras.

❻ **Stortorget**
This square is the heart of the "city
between the bridges", with a well
dating from 1778. It was the scene of
the Stockholm Bloodbath in 1520.

Key

— Suggested route

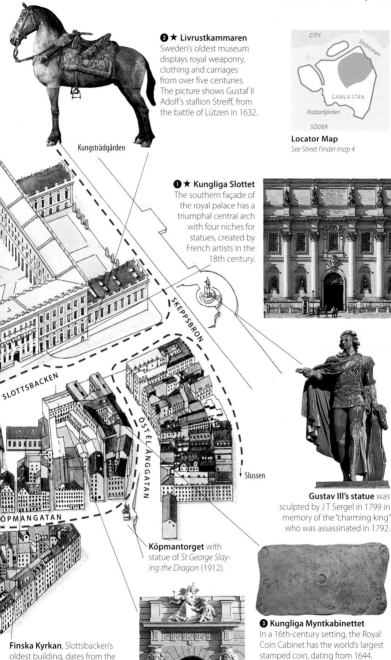

❷ ★ Livrustkammaren
Sweden's oldest museum displays royal weaponry, clothing and carriages from over five centuries. The picture shows Gustaf II Adolf's stallion Streiff, from the battle of Lützen in 1632.

Kungsträdgården

Locator Map
See Street Finder map 4

CITY
Strömmen
GAMLA STAN
Riddarfjärden
SÖDER

❶ ★ Kungliga Slottet
The southern façade of the royal palace has a triumphal central arch with four niches for statues, created by French artists in the 18th century.

SKEPPSBRON

SLOTTSBACKEN

ÖSTERLÅNGGATAN

KÖPMANGATAN

Slussen

Gustav III's statue was sculpted by J T Sergel in 1799 in memory of the "charming king" who was assassinated in 1792.

Köpmantorget with statue of *St George Slaying the Dragon* (1912).

❸ Kungliga Myntkabinettet
In a 16th-century setting, the Royal Coin Cabinet has the world's largest stamped coin, dating from 1644.

Finska Kyrkan, Slottsbacken's oldest building, dates from the 1640s. It was originally a court for ball games for the palace, but since 1725 it has been the religious centre for the Finnish community.

❹ Tessinska Palatset
Built by and for Nicodemus Tessin the Younger, architect of the Royal Palace, in 1694–7, this palace has been the residence of the Governor of Stockholm County since 1968.

0 metres	100
0 yards	100

❶ Kungliga Slottet (Royal Palace)

Defensive installations or castles have stood on the island of Stadsholmen ever since the 11th century. The Tre Kronor (Three Crowns) fortress was completed in the mid-13th century, but during the following century it became a royal residence. The Vasa kings turned the fortress into a Renaissance palace, but this burned to the ground in 1697. In its place the architect Nicodemus Tessin the Younger created a new palace in Roman style with an Italianate exterior and a French interior toned down by Swedish influences. The palace's 608 rooms were decorated by Europe's foremost artists and craftsmen. King Adolf Fredrik was the first king to move into the palace, in 1754. It is no longer the king's private residence, but remains one of the city's leading sights.

★ **Changing of the Guard**
Stockholm's most popular tourist event is the daily changing of the guard, which takes place at midday in the Outer Courtyard.

Entrance to the State Apartments

The Western Staircase
Tessin was especially proud of the two staircases, made from Swedish marble and porphyry. On the western staircase stands a bust of the gifted architect.

★ **The Hall of State**
This opulent hall has an atmosphere of ceremonial splendour and forms an ideal setting for Queen Kristina's silver throne, probably the palace's most famous treasure.

Entrance to the Treasury and Royal Chapel

KEY

① **The Guest Apartments**

② **The Bernadotte Apartments** are situated on the floor below Karl XI's Gallery.

③ **Tre Kronor Museum** entrance from Lejonbacken.

④ **Carl Hårleman** played an important role in the design of the palace. His bust adorns this niche.

⑤ **Logården** is the terrace between the palace's east wings.

⑥ **Livrustkammaren** (see p54).

The Royal Chapel
This delightful little church has a rich interior decorated by many different artists. The pulpit is the work of J P Bouchardon.

Gustav III's State Bedchamber
Sergel's bust of Gustav III (1779) stands in the room where the king died after being shot at the Opera House. The decor by J E Rehn dates from the 1770s.

★ Karl XI's Gallery
One of the most magnificent rooms in the palace, this fine example of Swedish Late Baroque is used for banquets hosted by the king and queen. In the cabinet is this priceless salt-cellar dating from 1627–8.

VISITORS' CHECKLIST

Practical Information
Gamla Stan.
Map 4 B2.
Tel 08-402 61 30.
[w] kungahuset.se
The Royal Apartments, The Treasury, Gustav III's Museum of Antiquities, Tre Kronor Museum:
Open mid-May–mid-Sep: 10am–5pm daily; mid-Sep–mid-May: 10am–4pm Tue–Sun. **Closed** during official functions of the Court. tours in English at 1 & 2pm.
The Royal Chapel: **Open** Jun–Aug: noon–4pm Wed & Fri. Mass 11am Sun (year round).

Travel information
Gamla Stan, Kungsträdgården.
2, 43, 55, 71, 76.

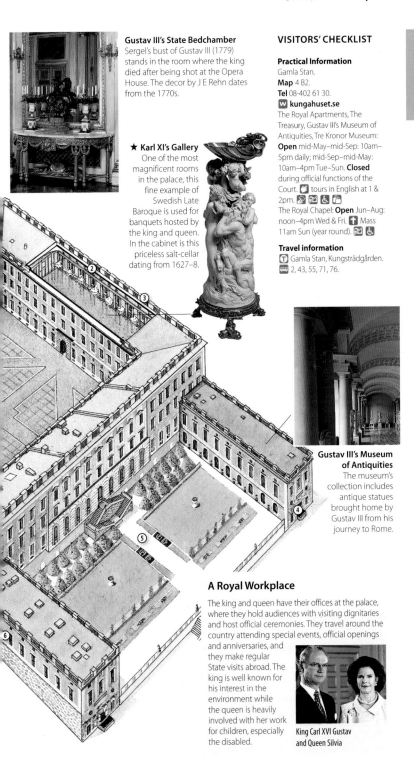

Gustav III's Museum of Antiquities
The museum's collection includes antique statues brought home by Gustav III from his journey to Rome.

A Royal Workplace

The king and queen have their offices at the palace, where they hold audiences with visiting dignitaries and host official ceremonies. They travel around the country attending special events, official openings and anniversaries, and they make regular State visits abroad. The king is well known for his interest in the environment while the queen is heavily involved with her work for children, especially the disabled.

King Carl XVI Gustav and Queen Silvia

Exploring the Royal Palace

The public areas of the Royal Palace allow you to walk through grand rooms of sumptuous furnishings and priceless works of art and craftsmanship. The Hall of State and the Royal Chapel are both characterized by their magnificent lavish decor and Gustav III's Museum of Antiquities contains ancient marble sculptures from the king's journey to Italy. The palace also houses the Treasury with the State regalia; the Tre Kronor Museum, which depicts the palace before the 1697 fire; and the Livrustkammaren *(see p54)*.

The Pillar Hall in the Bernadotte Apartments with original decor

Karl XI's Gallery, the finest example of the Late Baroque period in Sweden

The State Apartments

The royal family has lived at Drottningholm Palace *(see pp146–49)* since 1982, but official functions, including banquets hosted by the king during visits by foreign heads of state, still take place in the royal palace's State Apartments. Other official dinners are staged here, as well as the festivities held every year to honour the Nobel laureates.

Banquets are served in Karl XI's Gallery, the finest example of Swedish Late Baroque, modelled on the Hall of Mirrors at Versailles. Each window is matched with a niche on the inner wall, where some of the palace's priceless works of arts and crafts are exhibited. Most remarkable is the salt-cellar made from ivory and gilded silver designed by the Flemish painter Rubens (1577–1640). The room known as "The White Sea" serves as a

drawing room. Gustav III's State Bedchamber, where the king died after being shot at the Opera House in 1792 *(see pp24–5)*, is the height of Gustavian elegance. Along with Queen Sofia Magdalena's State Bedchamber, it was designed by the architect Jean Eric Rehn. The lintels on the doors to the Don Quixote Room, named after the theme of its tapestries, feature paintings by François Boucher and are among the palace's most treasured pieces.

The Guest Apartments

An imposing part of the palace, these apartments are where visiting heads of state stay. The beautiful rooms include the Meleager Salon, where official gifts and decorations are exchanged, and a large bedroom with a sculpted and gilded bed. Other impressive rooms are the Inner Salon, with decor inspired by the excavations in Pompeii, and the Margareta Room, named after the present king's grandmother and displaying some pictures painted by her.

The apartments contain remarkable works of craftsmanship by such 18th-century masters as the cabinet-maker Georg Haupt *(see p84)*, chair-maker Ephraim Ståhle and the sculptor Jean Baptiste Masreliez.

King Karl XIV Johan's egg cup

The Bernadotte Apartments

This magnificent suite has earned its name from the gallery displaying portraits of the Bernadotte dynasty. The apartments have some notable ceiling paintings and mid-18th-century chandeliers, and are used for many a ceremonial occasion. The elegant Pillar Hall is the venue for investitures, and the East Octagonal Cabinet, with probably the palace's best Rococo decor, is where the king receives foreign ambassadors. Along with the western cabinet, its interior has remained just as it was planned by Carl Hårleman more than 250 years ago.

Oscar II's very masculine Writing Room, dating from the 1870s, also still looks much as it did in his day. However, it is clear the palace was kept up to date with technical advances. Electricity was installed in 1883, and the telephone only one year later.

The Hall of State

Rococo and Classicism were brought together in perfect harmony by the architects Nicodemus Tessin the Younger and Carl Hårleman, when they designed the two-storey Hall of State. It provides a worthy framework for Queen Kristina's silver throne, a gift for the coronation in 1650 and one of the most valuable treasures in the palace. The throne was given to the Queen by Magnus Gabriel de la Gardie and was made in Augsburg, Germany, by the goldsmith Abraham Drentwett. The canopy was added 100 years later for the coronation of King Adolf Fredrik and was designed by Jean Eric Rehn.

The decor of the Hall of State is lavish. Colossal sculptures of Karl XIV Johan and Gustav II Adolf flank the throne, while those on the cornice symbolize Peace, Strength, Religion and Justice.

Until 1975 the Hall of State was the scene of the ceremonial opening of the Swedish Parliament (Riksdagen), which included a march past of the royal bodyguard in full regalia. It is now used more for other official occasions and, like the Royal Chapel, is a venue for summer concerts *(see pp176–7)*.

The Hall of State, the most important ceremonial room in the palace

The Royal Chapel

It took 50 years to build the Royal Palace, and a lot of effort went into the French Rococo interior decoration of the Royal Chapel. The work was carried out largely by Carl Hårleman under the supervision of Nicodemus Tessin the Younger. As with the Hall of State, the co-operation between the two produced a magnificent result, enhanced by the contributions of several foreign artists. The chapel was completed when the palace reopened in 1754.

A number of remarkable artifacts have been added over the centuries. The most recent was a group of six 17th-century-style bronze crowns, as well as two crystal crowns.

It also has some rare relics of the original Tre Kronor fortress: new benches that had been ordered by Tessin. They had been rescued during the palace fire in 1697 and preserved but not put in the chapel until the 19th century. The benches were made by Georg Haupt, grandfather of the cabinet-maker of the same name who was to create some of the palace's most prized furnishings.

Gustav III's Museum of Antiquities

Opened in 1794 in memory of the murdered king, the Museum of Antiquities initially housed more than 200 exhibits, mainly acquired during Gustav's Italian journey in 1783–4 and then supplemented with more purchases later.

In 1866 the museum's collection was moved to the city's National Museum *(see pp84–5)*. During the 1950s the main gallery was renovated, followed by the smaller galleries 30 years later, which enabled the collection to be returned to its original setting.

The most prized exhibits are in the main gallery, the best known being the sculpture of Endymion, the eternally sleeping young shepherd and lover of the Moon Goddess Selene. The 18th-century sculptor Johan Tobias Sergel is represented by *The Priestess*, ranked as the collection's second most important piece. She is flanked by two large candelabras.

The Treasury

Situated at the bottom of 56 well-worn steps, below the Hall of State on the south side of the palace, is the entrance to the Treasury (Skattkammaren), where the State regalia, the most potent symbols of the monarchy, are kept.

On the rare occasions that King Erik XIV's crown, sceptre, orb and the keys of the kingdom are taken out of their showcase, they are placed beside the

Erik XIV's crown, made by Cornelis ver Weiden in Stockholm in 1561

uncrowned King Carl XVI Gustaf. The 1-m (3-ft) high silver baptismal font, which took the French silversmith Jean François Cousinet 11 years to make, is 200 years old and is still used for royal baptisms. Hanging in the Treasury is the only undamaged tapestry among six dating from the 1560s, salvaged from the 1697 fire.

Tre Kronor Museum

In the oldest parts of the ruined Tre Kronor fortress, preserved under the north side of the royal palace, is the Tre Kronor (Three Crowns) Museum. About half of a massive 12th-century defensive wall and brick vaults from the 16th and 17th centuries provide a unique setting for the museum, which illustrates the palace's history of almost 1,000 years.

Two models of the Tre Kronor fortress show changes made to the fortress during the second half of the 17th century and how it looked by the time of the fire. Among items rescued from the ashes are a schnapps glass, amber pots and bowls made from mountain crystal.

A glass bowl saved from the 1697 fire, displayed in the Tre Kronor Museum

❷ Livrustkammaren

Slottsbacken 3. **Map** 4 C2. **Tel** 08-402 30 30. Ⓣ Gamla Stan. 🚌 2, 43, 55, 76. **Open** Jan–Apr, Sep–Dec: 11am–5pm Tue–Sun (to 8pm Thu); May–Jun: 11am–5pm daily; Jul–Aug: 10am–5pm daily. 🎧 Eng: Jul–Aug. 🎫📷✉📶🛗 ⓦ livrustkammaren.se

Situated in the Royal Palace, Livrustkammaren (The Royal Armoury) is the oldest museum in Sweden. In 1628, Gustav II Adolf had a few costumes that had been stained with his blood during war preserved, so that they could be seen and reflected upon here in the Royal Armoury. They were displayed along with his magnificent weapons and suits of armour, including those worn by his predecessors. Formerly a monument to the Vasa kings, the Royal Armoury grew to hold a collection com- memorating five royal dynasties. Ceremonial costumes and coaches from the royal stables are also on display.

The museum now exhibits artifacts from different cultural themes such as knights, royal ceremonies and the history of dress, along with exhibits related to politics and drama in the lives of the Swedish regents and across European history more generally. In 1978, the collection was returned to the Royal Palace after many transfers over centuries between different buildings in the capital.

❸ Kungliga Myntkabinettet

Slottsbacken 6. **Map** 4 C3. **Tel** 08-519 553 00. Ⓣ Gamla Stan. 🚌 2, 43, 55, 76. **Open** 10am–5pm daily. **Closed** public hols. 🎧 by arrangement. 🎫 free on Mon. 🛗 📷📶📶 ⓦ myntkabinettet.se

The Royal Coin Cabinet is a museum holding a priceless collection of currency and highlighting the history of money from the 10th century to the present day – from the little cowrie shell via the drachma and denarius to the cash card of the 21st century. The museum also gives an insight into the art of medal design over the past 600 years and shows both traditional portrait medals and more modern examples like those that have been awarded to Nobel laureates.

Sweden's first coin, struck in about AD 995

Visitors can also see the first Swedish coin, struck in the late 10th century by King Olof Skötkonung. Other rarities include Queen Kristina's coin from 1644, weighing 19.7 kg (42 lb) and reckoned to be the world's heaviest coin. From the island of Yap, in Micronesia, the museum has acquired what is thought to be the world's largest means of payment, a so-called "rai-stone", which greets visitors in the foyer.

The kids' playroom is great fun. Among its highlights are a pirate ship with a treasure chest of gold coins and a kitsch collection of piggy banks.

The elegant Baroque garden in Tessinska Palatset's courtyard

❹ Tessinska Palatset

Slottsbacken 4. **Map** 2 C3. Ⓣ Gamla Stan. 🚌 2, 43, 55, 59, 76. **Closed** to the public.

The Tessin Palace at Slotts- backen is considered by many to be the most beautiful private residence north of Paris. It is the best-preserved palace from Sweden's era as a great power in the 17th century and was designed by and for Tessin the Younger (1654– 1728), the nation's most renowned architect.

Completed in 1697, the building is located on a narrow site, which widens out towards a courtyard with a delightful Baroque garden. The relatively discreet façade with its beautiful porch was inspired by the exterior design of Roman palaces. The decor and garden were influenced by Tessin's time in Paris and Versailles.

Tessin, who became a count and State Councillor, spent large sums on the building's ornamentation. Sculptures and paintings were provided by the same French masters whose work had graced the Royal Palace. Later, however, his son, Carl Gustaf, had to sell the palace for financial reasons.

The building was acquired by the City of Stockholm as a residence for its Governor in 1773. In 1968 it became the residence of the Governor of the County of Stockholm.

The coronation carriage of King Adolf Fredrik and Queen Lovisa Ulrika in Livrustkammaren

❺ Storkyrkan

Trångsund 1. **Map** 4 B3. **Tel** 08-723 30
16. Ⓣ Gamla Stan. 🚌 2, 43, 55, 59, 76.
Open Sep–May: 9am–4pm; Jun: 9am–
5pm; Jul–Aug: 9am–6pm. 🛐 11am Sat
& Sun. 🎧 Eng: Jul–15 Aug: 10am–1pm
Mon–Fri; to 2pm Sat & Sun (tour of the
tower: Jul–15 Aug: 2pm & 5pm). ♿ ✉
(during services). 📷 🆆 **stockholms
domkyrkoforsamling.se**

Stockholm's 700-year-old cathedral is of great national religious
importance. It was from here that
the Swedish reformer Olaus Petri
(1493–1552) spread his Lutheran
message around the kingdom. It
is also used for royal ceremonies,
weddings and funerals.

A small village church was
built on this site in the 13th
century, probably by the city's
founder Birger Jarl. It was
replaced in 1306 by a much
larger basilica, St Nicholas, and
has been enlarged and altered
over the centuries.

The Gothic character of the
interior, acquired in the 15th century, was revealed in 1908, when,
during restoration work, plaster
was removed from the pillars,
exposing the characteristic red
tiling. The late Baroque period
provided the so-called "royal
chairs" and the pulpit, while the
façade was adapted to bring it
into keeping with the rest of the
area around the Royal Palace. The
66-m (216-ft) high tower, added
in 1743, has 4 bells, the largest
of which weighs about 6 tonnes.

Storkyrkan's façade in the Italian Baroque style, seen from Slottsbacken

The cathedral houses some
priceless artistic treasures,
including *St George and the
Dragon*, regarded as one of
the finest late Gothic works
of art in Northern Europe.
The sculpture, situated to
the left of the altar, was carved
from oak and moose horn
by Lübeck sculptor Berndt
Notke. Unveiled in 1489, it
commemorates Sten Sture
the Elder's victory over the
Danes in 1471 *(see p17)*.

The Last Judgment (1696) is a
massive Baroque painting by
David Klöcker Ehrenstrahl. The
3.7-m (12-ft) high bronze candelabra before the altar, likely to
be German, has adorned the
cathedral for some 600 years.
One of the cathedral's most
prized treasures is the silver
altar, which gave the interior a
completely new appearance in
the 1650s. It was a gift from the
diplomat Johan Adler Salvius.

The pews nearest to the
chancel, the "royal chairs", were
designed by Nicodemus Tessin
the Younger in 1684 to be used
by royalty on special occasions.
In 1705, the pulpit was installed
above the grave of Olaus Petri.

On 20 April 1535, a light
phenomenon was observed
over Stockholm – six rings
with sparkling solar halos. *The
Parhelion Painting (see p16)*,
recalling the event, hangs in
Storkyrkan and is thought to
be the oldest portrayal of the
capital. It shows the modest
skyline dominated by the
cathedral, at that time still
the basilica of St Nicholas.

The sculpture *St George and the Dragon* by Bernt Notke (1489) in Storkyrkan

The imposing Stock Exchange on the north side of Stortorget

❻ Stortorget

Map 4 B3. Ⓣ Gamla Stan. 🚌 2, 3, 43, 53, 55, 76. Nobelmuseet **Tel** 08-534 818 00. **Open** Sep–May: 11am–8pm Tue, 11am–5pm Wed–Sun; Jun–Aug: 10am–8pm daily. **Closed** 1 Jan, Midsummer eve (in Jun), 24, 25 & 31 Dec. 🎧 in English daily. ♿ 📷 ⌀ 🅿 📖 🌐 nobelmuseum.se

It was not until 1778, when the Stock Exchange (Börsen) was completed, that Stortorget, the square in the heart of the Old Town, acquired a more uniform appearance. Its northern side had previously been taken up by several buildings that served as a town hall. Since the early Middle Ages the square had been a natural meeting point, with a well and market place, lined with wooden stalls on market days.

A pillory belonging to the jail, which was once sited on nearby Kåkbrinken, used to stand on the square. It is now in the Town Hall on Kungsholmen (see p114).

The medieval layout is clear on Stortorget's west side, where the red Schantzska Huset (No. 20) and the narrow Seyfridtska Huset were built in around 1650. The Schantzska Huset remains unchanged and has a lovely limestone porch adorned with figures of recumbent Roman warriors. The artist Johan Wendelstam was responsible for most of the notable porches in the Old Town. The 17th-century gable on the Grilska Huset (No. 3) is also worth closer study.

The decision to construct the Stock Exchange was taken in 1667, but many wars delayed the start of the building by 100 years. The architect was the talented Erik Palmstedt (1741–1803), who also created the decorative cover for the old well. However, 200 years of trading on the floor of the Stock Exchange came to an end in 1990. Opened in 2001 to mark the centenary of the Nobel Prize (see p70), the **Nobelmuseet** explores the work and ideas of 880 creative minds by means of short films, exhibitions and original artifacts. On the upper floor, the Swedish Academy (closed to the public) holds its ceremonial gatherings, a tradition maintained since Gustav III gave his inauguration speech in 1786.

❼ Tyska Kyrkan

Svartmangatan 16. **Map** 4 B3. **Tel** 08-411 11 88. Ⓣ Gamla Stan. 🚌 2, 3, 43, 53, 55, 76. **Open** 1 May– 15 Sep: 11am–3pm daily; 16 Sep– 30 Apr: 11am–3pm Wed, Fri & Sat. **Closed** during services. 🔔 11am Sun, German. 🎧 by appt in Swedish & German. ♿ 🌐 svenskakyrkan.se

The German church is an impressive reminder of the almost total influence that Germany had over Stockholm during the 18th century. The Hanseatic League trading organization was in control of the Baltic and its ports, which explains why the basic layout of Gamla Stan resembled that of Lübeck. Germany's political influence was only broken after the Stockholm Bloodbath and Gustav Vasa's accession to the throne in 1523 (see p18), but its cultural and mercantile influence remained strong, as German merchants and craftsmen settled in the city.

The church's parish assembly, which today has some 2,000 members, was founded in 1571. The present twin-nave church was built in 1638–42, as an extension of a smaller church that the parish had used since 1576.

In German Late Renaissance and Baroque style, the interior has a royal gallery, added in 1672 for German members of

The Stockholm Bloodbath

Stortorget is intimately linked with the Stockholm Bloodbath of November 1520. The Danish King Kristian II besieged the Swedish Regent, Sten Sture the Younger, until he capitulated, and the Swedes chose Kristian as their king. He promised an amnesty and ordered a three-day feast at Tre Kronor fortress. Near the end of the festivities, the revellers were suddenly shut in and arrested for heresy. The next day more than 80 noblemen and Stockholm citizens were beheaded in the square.

Detail of a painting of the Bloodbath (1524)

The royal gallery in the 17th-century Tyska Kyrkan

the royal household. The pulpit (1660) in ebony and alabaster is unique in Sweden, and the altar, from the 1640s, is covered with beautiful paintings surrounded by sculptures of the apostles and evangelists.

The sculptures on the south porch by Jobst Hennen date from 1643 and show Jesus, Moses and three figures portraying Faith, Hope and Love.

Mårten Trotzigs Gränd, the narrowest street in the city

❽ Mårten Trotzigs Gränd

Map 4 C4. Ⓣ Gamla Stan. 🚌 2, 3, 43, 53, 55, 76.

At only 90 cm (35 inches) wide, Mårten Trotzigs Gränd is the city's narrowest street, and climbing up the 36 steps gives a good idea of how different parts of the Old Town vary so much in height and how tightly packed together the houses are.

Mårten Trotzigs Gränd is named after a German merchant called Traubzich, who owned two houses here at the end of the 16th century. After being fenced off at both ends for 100 years, the street was reopened in 1945.

❾ Västerlånggatan

Map 4 B3. Ⓣ Gamla Stan. 🚌 2, 3, 43, 53, 55, 59, 76.

Once a main road outside the city proper, built along parts of the original town wall, Västerlånggatan now runs through the heart of the Old

Town, and is usually thronging with people – tourists and locals – shopping or strolling. Starting at Mynttorget in the north, where the Chancery Office (Kansli-huset) and Lejonbacken are, the lively and atmospheric street finishes at Järntorget in the south, where the export of iron was once controlled. Alongside is Bancohuset, which served as the headquarters of the State Bank from 1680 to 1906.

The building at No. 7 has been used by the Swedish Parliament since the mid-1990s. Its late 19th-century façade has a distinctive southern European influence.

No. 27 was built by and for Erik Palmstedt, who also designed the Stock Exchange and the well at Stortorget. No. 29 is a very venerable building, dating from the early 15th century. The original pointed Gothic arches were revealed during restoration in the 1940s.

No. 33 is a good example of how new materials and techniques in the late 19th century made it possible to fit large shop windows into old houses. The cast-iron columns, which can be seen in many other places, also date from this period.

No. 68, Von der Lindeska House, has a majestic 17th-century façade and a beautiful porch with sculptures of Neptune and Mercury.

❿ Postmuseum

Lilla Nygatan 6. **Map** 4 B3. **Tel** 010-436 44 39. Ⓣ Gamla Stan. 🚌 3, 53. **Open** 11am–4pm Tue–Sun, Sep–Apr, also Wed 4–7pm. 🎫 by arrangement. ♿ 🚻 📷 🎥 🖥 🅦 postmuseum.se

An attraction in itself, the Postmuseum building takes up a whole area bought by the Swedish Post Office in 1720.

Västerlånggatan, Gamla Stan's most popular shopping street

About 100 years later the majestic-looking Post Office was built, incorporating parts of the 17th-century buildings already there. Stockholm's only Post Office until 1869, it was turned into the Postal Museum in 1906.

Letters have been sent in Sweden since 1636, and the museum's permanent exhibits include a portrayal of early "peasant postmen" fighting the angry Åland Sea in their boat *Simpan*. Also on display is the first post bus, which ran in northern Sweden in the early 1920s.

Mauritian stamp in the Postmuseum

The collection includes no fewer than four million stamps, among which are the first Swedish stamps, produced in 1855. Also on display is the "Penny Black", the world's first stamp (dating from 1840), and some stamps issued by Mauritius in 1847.

The museum library holds a large collection of literature on philately and postal history. Among the many interactive displays and exhibits, there is also a charming workshop, *The Little Post Office*, where children can discover what it was like to work in a 1920s post office.

⓫ Riddarholms- kyrkan

Birger Jarls Torg. **Map** 4 A3. **Tel** 08-402 61 30. 🚇 Gamla Stan. 🚌 3, 53. **Open** 15 May–13 Sep: 10am–5pm daily; 14 Sep–29 Nov: 10am–4pm Sat & Sun. 🎧 Eng: noon. **Closed** 30 Nov– 14 May. 🎫 📷 ♿ 🎒

This church on the island of Riddarholmen is best known as a place for royal burials. Its interior is full of ornate sarcophagi and worn gravestones, and in front of the altar are the tombs of the medieval kings Karl Knutsson and Magnus Ladulås.

Built on the site of the late 13th-century Greyfriars abbey, founded by Ladulås, the majestic brick church was gradually enlarged over the centuries. After a serious fire in 1835, the church acquired its present lattice-work, cast-iron tower.

The church is surrounded by ornate burial vaults, which date back as far as the 17th century. The coffins rest on a lower level with space for a memorial above. The most recent was built in 1858–60 for the Bernadotte dynasty.

The vaults contain the remains of all the Swedish sovereigns from Gustav II Adolf in the 17th century to the present day with two exceptions: Queen Kristina was buried at St Peter's in Rome in 1689 and Gustav VI Adolf, who died in 1973, was interred at Haga (see pp124–5). The most magnificent sarcophagus is that of the 19th-century king, Karl XIV Johan, which had to be towed here by

Wrangelska Palatset, a royal residence after the Tre Kronor fire of 1697

sledge from his porphyry work-shops in the Älvdalen region in northern Sweden.

Particularly moving are the graves of royal children who met an early death, including the many small tin coffins that surround the last resting place of Gustav II Adolf and his queen, Maria Eleonora.

⓬ Wrangelska Palatset

Birger Jarls Torg 16. **Map** 4 A3. 🚇 Gamla Stan. 🚌 3, 53. **Closed** to the public.

Only two parts of the fortification work that Gustav Vasa undertook around 1530 still remain – Birger Jarl's Tower and the southernmost tower of what became the Wrangel Palace. Built as a residence for the nobleman Lars Sparre in 1629, it was extensively rebuilt only a few decades later. The owner by then was Carl Gustaf Wrangel, a field marshal during the Thirty Years'War, who chose Jean de la Vallée as his architect. The result was Stockholm's largest palace in private hands.

In 1693 Wrangel lost many valuable possessions in a major fire, and four years later his palace became a royal residence when the Royal Family moved to Riddarholmen after the Tre Kronor fortress was ravaged by another fire. The palace then became known as

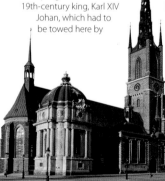
Riddarholmskyrkan with the external burial vault by Tessin and Hårleman

the King's House, and it was here in 1697 that the 15-year-old Karl XII took the oath of office after the death of his father. Three years later the young king left his palace to go to war; he would never return to Stockholm. Gustav III was born here, ten years before the Royal Family moved back to the new Royal Palace in 1754.

The Court of Appeal now uses the whole building, where in 1792 the assassin of Gustav III was manacled in the dungeons during his trial.

The court also rents the Rosenhane Palace (Birger Jarls Torg 10) and the Hessenstein House (Birger Jarls Torg 2), which was built in 1630 by Bengt Bengtsson Oxenstierna. It was named after Fredrik Wilhelm von Hessenstein, the son of Fredrik I and his lover Hedvig Taube. Later it was occupied by Carl Gustav Tessin, son of the Royal Palace architect and a leading cultural figure in his day.

The city founder Birger Jarl's statue on the square that bears his name

⑬ Evert Taubes Terrass

Norra Riddarholmshamnen. **Map** 4 A3. Ⓣ Gamla Stan. 🚌 3, 53.

A statue of Evert Taube (1890–1976), the much-loved troubadour and ballad writer, stands on the terrace below Wrangelska Palatset looking out over the waters of Riddarfjärden. In an ideal position, given the poet's close links to the sea, the bronze sculpture was created by Willy Gordon in 1990. Close by, Christer Berg's *Solbåten* (the Sun Boat), an elegant sculpture in granite, was unveiled in 1966. Inspired by the shape of a shell, from some angles it looks like a sail.

Bronze statue of Evert Taube

⑭ Birger Jarls Torn

Norra Riddarholmshamnen. **Map** 4 A3 Ⓣ Gamla Stan. 🚌 3, 53. **Closed** to the public.

When the St Klara convent on Norrmalm was pulled down in 1527 following the Reformation, Gustav Vasa used some of its stonework to build a defensive installation on Riddarholmen. The northernmost of the two towers came to be known as Birger Jarls Torn in the 19th century, when some thought it had been erected 600 years earlier. The tower has been linked with one of the legends that surround the founding of

Stockholm by Birger Jarl. The story goes that the inhabitants of the town of Sigtuna floated a log on Lake Mälaren after a fire in 1187. It drifted on to the shore where the tower now stands, and it was this log – or "stock" in Swedish – that gave the capital its name. A famous painting in Storkyrkan (*see p16*), dating from 1535, shows the waves breaking over the rocks beneath the tower.

The 16th-century Birger Jarls Torn

⑮ Stenbockska Palatset

Birger Jarls Torg 4. **Map** 4 A3. Ⓣ Gamla Stan. 🚌 3, 53. **Closed** to the public.

Both externally and internally the Stenbock Palace is the best-preserved building on Riddarholmen. It was built in the 1640s by the State Councillor

Stenbockska Palatset, the best-preserved nobleman's residence on Riddarholmen

Fredrik Stenbock and his wife Katarina de la Gardie, and the family's coat of arms can be seen above the porch. The palace underwent major extension work in 1863 when it was taken over by the State Archives. Then in 1969–71 it was restored as the headquarters of the Supreme Administrative Court.

Many leading Swedish and foreign architects and artists have all played their part in enhancing the palace's outstanding appearance. The roof beams and flooring are from the Stenbock period, and the staircase was designed by Nicodemus Tessin the Elder.

Several beautiful ceilings are the work of the masters of stucco, Carlo Carove (c.1672) and Giuseppe Marchi (1704), and there is a cabinet created by Rococo architect Carl Hårleman.

1200	1300	1400	1500	1600	1700	1800	1900

1250s The island, then called Kidskär, is a cattle-grazing area outside the settlement

1270–85 The Greyfriars' abbey is founded. Kidskär is renamed Gråmunkeholmen. The abbey church is used for royal burials

1527 Following the Reformation, the monks are evicted from the island

1625–35 Land is donated to noblemen and distinguished officers. The name is changed to Riddarholmen

Late 17th century The prosperity of the nobility starts to diminish

1697–1754 The royal family takes over Wrangelska Palatset after Tre Kronor fortress is destroyed by fire

1830s Hornska House used for Parliament by priests and burghers

1866–67 The Parliament building and Hebbe House are rebuilt for new two-chamber Parliament

1905 Parliament moves to new building on Helgeandsholmen

Wrangelska Palatset

Riddarhuset, built in the 17th century in lavish Dutch Baroque style

⓰ Riddarhuset

Riddarhustorget 10. **Map** 4 A3.
Tel 08-723 39 90. Ⓣ Gamla Stan.
🚌 3, 53. **Open** 11am–noon
Mon–Fri. 🅿 🔲 by arrangement.
🖥 **riddarhuset.se**

Often regarded as one of
Stockholm's most beautiful
buildings, Riddarhuset
(House of Nobility) stands
on Riddarhustorget, which as
late as the mid-19th century
was still the city's centre.

Built in 1641–7 on the initiative
of the State Chancellor, it was
designed by the architects Simon
and Jean de la Vallée, Heinrich
Wilhelm and Justus Vingboons.
The nobility, whose privileges
were granted in 1280, then
had a base for meetings
and events. The building
is still used as a focal
point for the nobility,
hosting the triennial
Assembly of Nobles.

The building is a
supreme example of
Dutch Baroque design
and colouring. Over the entrance
on the northern façade is the
nobility's *Arte et Marte* (Art
and War) with Minerva, Goddess
of Art and Science, and Mars,
God of War, on either side.

The sculptures on the
vaulted roof symbolize the
knightly virtues. On the south
side is *Nobilitas* (Nobility) holding
a small Minerva and spear. She is
flanked by *Studium* (Diligence)
and *Valor* (Bravery). Facing the
north is the male equivalent,
Honor, flanked by *Prudentia* (Prud-
ence) and *Fortitudo* (Strength).

The interior is equally
impressive. The lower hall is
dominated by a magnificent

The motto at
Riddarhuset

double staircase, which leads up
to the Knights' Room. This has a
masterly ceiling painting by David
Klöcker Ehrenstrahl (1628–98) and
Riddarhuset's foremost treasure, a
sculpted ebony chair that dates
from 1623. The walls are covered
by some 2,320 coats of arms.

⓱ Bondeska Palatset

Riddarhustorget 8. **Map** 4 B3.
Ⓣ Gamla Stan. 🚌 3, 53. **Closed** to
the public.

The seat of the Supreme Court
since 1949, the Bonde Palace
was created in 1662–73 by
architects Jean de la Vallée and
Nicodemus Tessin the
Elder in the style of a
French town house. The
year previously, the
State Treasurer Gustav
Bonde had bought
the site opposite
Riddarhuset to build a
palace with the idea of
renting out most of it.
Since then the Bonde Palace
has had several owners and was
damaged by fires in 1710 and

Bondeska Palatset, now the seat of the
Supreme Court

1753. In 1730 the building
became the property of the city
and served as the City Hall until
1915. After that, there was little
interest taken in the palace until
renovation planned by the
architect Ivar Tengbom was
begun in the late 1940s. It had
even been suggested that the
building should be demolished,
but public opinion ensured
that it remained intact.

⓲ Riksdagshuset

Riksgatan 3A. **Map** 4 B2. **Tel** 08-786 40
00. Ⓣ Gamla Stan. 🚌 3, 53.
Open tours & meetings in the
Chamber. 🔲 ring for details on tours
of the building & art works. 🅰 📷
🖥 **riksdagen.se**

The Parliament Building
(Riksdagshuset) and State
Bank (Riksbank) on Helgeandsholmen were inaugurated in
1905 and 1906 respectively.
Since 1983, when Parliament
returned here after 12 years at
Sergels Torg, the two buildings
have been combined and
enlarged. Parliament also
occupies five premises in Gamla
Stan. All the buildings are
connected by underground
passages and together amount
to 130,000 sq m (1,400,000 sq
ft), with a staff force of about
600, plus 300 in the political
parties' offices.

Parliamentary debates can
be watched from the public
gallery, which holds up to
500 spectators. There are guided
tours of the buildings every
day during the summer and
only at weekends in winter.
Visitors should use the public
entrance at Riksgatan 3A.

From the gallery level is a
striking view from as far as
Gustav Adolfs Torg to Riddarholmen. The main chamber
has benches of Swedish birch
and wall panelling in Finnish
birch, carved in Norway. A
large tapestry, *Memory of a
Landscape* (1983), by Elisabeth
Hasselberg-Olsson, covers
54 sq m (581 sq ft) of wall,
weighs 100 kg (220 lb) and
took 3,500 hours to make.

The old two-chamber
Parliament's beautifully

renovated rooms are now used for meetings of the majority party. The former Upper House has three paintings by Otte Sköld (1894–1958), and in the other chamber there are works by Axel Törneman and Georg Pauli, who realized Törneman's sketches after his death. Between the chambers is a 45-m (148-ft) long hall with an elegant display of coats of arms, paintings and chandeliers. The Finance Committee meets in the old oak-panelled library surrounded by old prints and Jugendstil lamps.

Facing the old entrance at Norrbro, the magnificent stairwell still retains its colouring from 1905. Other impressive survivors from opulent days include eight columns, a floor, steps and balusters all in various types

The chamber where the 349 Members of Parliament meet

of marble. The present entrance was the State Bank's main hall until 1976. It has magnificent columns, too, made from polished granite, and some outstanding paintings from the Parliamentary collection of 3,000 works.

The new Parliament building, with the older building behind

Parliamentary Wanderings

Sweden's first Parliament was opened in the 1860s on Riddarholmen in the combined properties of Fleming House and Hebbe House. From 1835–65, commoners – priests, burghers and farmers – met in Fleming House, which became known as the "House of Commons", while the noblemen sat in nearby Riddarhuset. Situated behind Riddarholmskyrkan at Birger Jarls Torg 5, Fleming House was constructed on the site of the Greyfriars abbey, after the monks were forced to flee due to the Reformation in the 16th century *(see p59)*, and remains of the huge abbey can still be seen in the cellar. A new base for Parliament, adapted for the needs of a two-chamber legislature, was inaugurated on Helgeandsholmen in 1905. When a single chamber was established in 1971, a lack of space meant that Parliament had to move to the newly built Kulturhuset *(see p69)* on Sergels Torg. It returned to Helgeandsholmen in 1983 into an extended and reconstructed Parliament building.

"Mother Svea" above the old Parliament building

⑲ Medeltidsmuseum

Strömparterren, Norrbro.
Map 4 B2. **Tel** 08-508 317 90.
Ⓣ Kungsträdgården. 🚌 43, 62.
Open noon–5pm Tue & Thu–Sun; noon–8pm Wed. 🎫 ♿ 📷 ✉ 📷
🌐 **medeltidsmuseet.stockholm.se**

The fascinating Medieval Museum is built around the capital's archaeological remains, mainly parts of the city wall that date from the 1530s. They were found during intensive archaeological research in 1978–80, which unearthed a number of remarkable finds from Stockholm's medieval history.

Situated, for the most part, below ground level, the museum also includes artifacts from other parts of the city. Among them is the 22-m (72-ft) long Riddarholm ship that was discovered off Riddarholmen in 1930 and dates from the 1520s.

The museum provides a good picture of Stockholm's early days. From the entrance, a 350-year-old tunnel leads into a reconstructed medieval world. There is a pillory in the square and the gallows hill with the tools of the executioner's grisly trade. The old harbour has been rebuilt. Boathouses, complete with salt barrels, seal skins and dried fish, as well as authentic nautical smells, tell the story of fishing and overseas trade. The spruce wreath hanging outside the wine cellar demonstrates that supplies of wine and beer have arrived from the Continent. The large house is built from 6,000 original bricks. The well-tended herb garden includes lavender, roses, tansy and sage. Herbs were important in the Middle Ages for their medicinal qualities as well as their use in food.

The museum runs regular themed exhibitions with a medieval emphasis and holds a programme of lectures and educational activities for children. The shop here sells books on the Middle Ages, plus postcards and jewellery.

CITY

The area known as City today was where, in the mid-18th century, the first stone-built houses and palaces outside Gamla Stan started to appear for Stockholm's burghers and nobility. After World War II, the run-down buildings around Hötorget were demolished to form what is now Sergels Torg; many homes were replaced by rather dreary office blocks.

In recent years the area has been livening up after dark to become the heart and commercial centre of Stockholm. A hub for public transport and banking, City is the place for the best department stores and shopping malls, exclusive boutiques and nightspots. The centre also has some beautiful parks and pleasant squares serving as popular meeting places. The unique landscape surrounding Stockholm permeates even City – here and there appear unexpected glimpses of the water with its bustling boat life and a string of anglers along the embankments.

Sights at a Glance

Museums
4 Dansmuseet
5 Medelhavsmuseet
8 Konstakademien
17 Strindbergsmuseet Blå Tornet
24 Armémuseum
25 Swedish Museum of Performing Arts
28 Hallwylska museet

Squares
1 Kungsträdgården
11 Sergels Torg
12 Hötorget
20 Stureplan

Public Buildings
6 Arvfurstens Palats
7 Rosenbad
10 Kulturhuset and Stockholms Stadsteater
14 Kungstornen

15 Centralbadet
19 Kungliga Biblioteket
26 Hovstallet

Theatres
3 Kungliga Operan
13 Konserthuset
16 Dansens Hus
27 Kungliga Dramatiska Teatern

Churches
2 Jacobs Kyrka
9 Klara Kyrka
18 Adolf Fredriks Kyrka
23 Hedvig Eleonora Kyrka

Markets & Malls
21 Sturegallerian and Sturebadet
22 Östermalmshallen

☐ **Restaurants** pp166–71
1 Belgobaren
2 Cloud Nine
3 Ekstedt
4 Griffins Steakhouse
5 Grill
6 Grodan
7 Hattori Sushi Devil
8 Jamie's Italian
9 Nalen
10 Operakällaren
11 Operakällarens Bakficka
12 PA and Co
13 Riche
14 Rolfs Kök
15 Sturehof
16 Supper
17 Teatergrillen
18 Tjabba Thai
19 Zink Grill
20 Wedholms Fisk

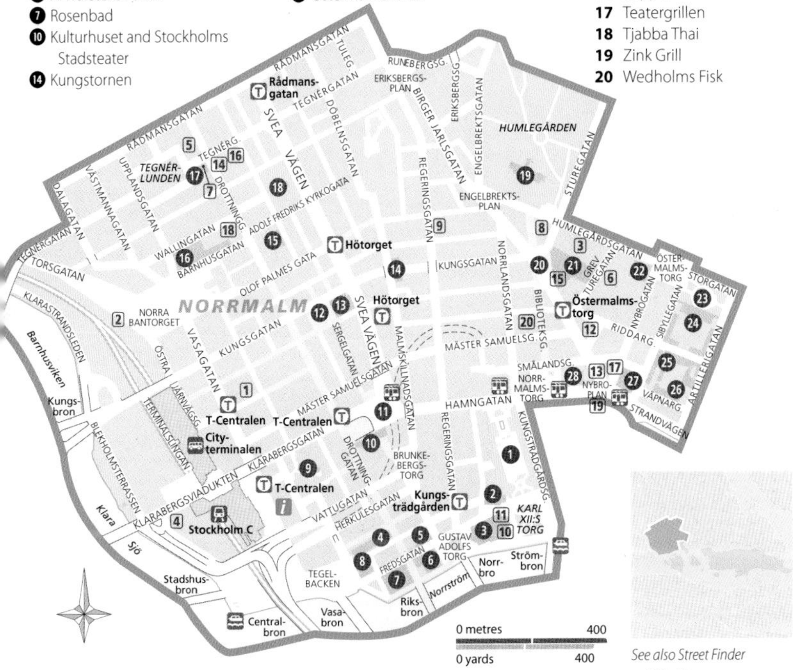

0 metres 400
0 yards 400

See also Street Finder pp206–18

◀ Monument to Gustav II Adolf in Gustav Adolfs Torg

For map symbols see back flap

Street-by-Street: Around Kungsträdgården

With a history going back to the 15th century, the King's Garden (Kungsträdgården) has long been the city's most popular meeting place and recreational centre. Both visitors and Stockholmers gather here for summer concerts and festivals, and in the winter months to make the most of the ice skating rink. Close by is Sweden House, where the tourist office is based, and around the park is a wealth of shops, boutiques, churches, museums and restaurants. A short walk takes you to Gustav Adolfs Torg, flanked by the Royal Opera House and other stately buildings, including the Swedish Foreign Office.

Gustav II Adolf's equestrian statue, designed by L'Archevêque, was unveiled in 1796.

❺ ★ Medelhavsmuseet
This museum near Gustav Adolfs Torg has vast collections from prehistoric cultures around the Mediterranean area.

FREDSGATAN

REGERINGSGATAN

Sagerska Palatset —

STRÖMGATAN

GUSTAV ADOLFS TORG

NORRBRO

STRÖMGATAN

SOPHIA·ALBERTINA ÆDIFICAVIT·

❹ Arvfurstens Palats
The Swedish Foreign Office is based in this palace, built for Gustav III's sister Sofia Albertina in 1794.

Operakällaren
(see p167)

❸ ★ Kungliga Operan
Built in 1898 with a magnificently ornate auditorium, the Royal Opera House replaced an earlier one from the time of Gustav III.

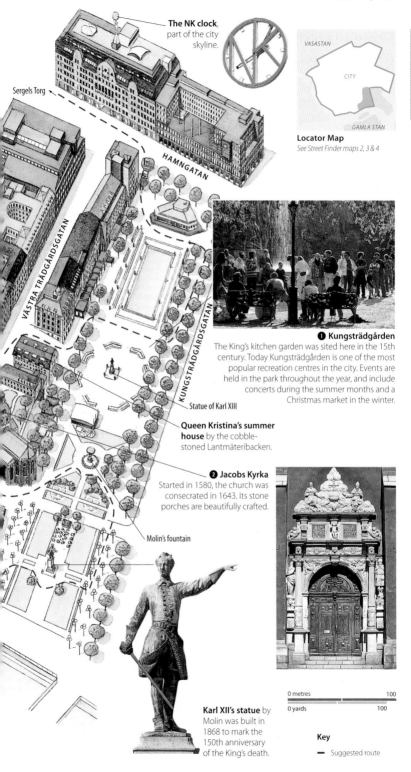

The NK clock, part of the city skyline.

Sergels Torg

HAMNGATAN

VÄSTRA TRÄDGÅRDSGATAN

KUNGSTRÄDGÅRDSGATAN

Locator Map
See Street Finder maps 2, 3 & 4

VASASTAN

CITY

GAMLA STAN

❶ **Kungsträdgården**
The King's kitchen garden was sited here in the 15th century. Today Kungsträdgården is one of the most popular recreation centres in the city. Events are held in the park throughout the year, and include concerts during the summer months and a Christmas market in the winter.

Statue of Karl XIII

Queen Kristina's summer house by the cobble-stoned Lantmäteribacken.

❷ **Jacobs Kyrka**
Started in 1580, the church was consecrated in 1643. Its stone porches are beautifully crafted.

Molin's fountain

Karl XII's statue by Molin was built in 1868 to mark the 150th anniversary of the King's death.

0 metres 100
0 yards 100

Key

— Suggested route

❶ Kungsträdgården

Map 4 B1. Ⓣ Kungsträdgården.
🚌 2, 55, 62, 65, 76.

Once the royal kitchen garden in the 15th century, the "King's Garden" today is a popular meeting place for Stockholmers – with something for everyone all year round. The park, which is Stockholm's oldest, is in the heart of the city and encircled by avenues. At the Strömgatan end of the park is a square, named after Karl XII, with Johan Peter Molin's statue of the warrior king, unveiled in 1868, in the centre. The statue was commissioned to mark the 150th anniversary of the king's death. In Kungsträdgården itself there is a statue of Karl XIII (1809–18) by Erik Göthe. Also here is Molin's famous fountain, made from gypsum in 1866 and cast in bronze seven years later. The fountain is inhabited by mythological characters.

Molin's fountain

During Erik XIV's reign in the 16th century, the kitchen garden was transformed into a formal Renaissance garden, and Queen Kristina had a stone summer house built in it. The 17th-century house still stands at Västra Trädgårdsgatan 2, next to the cobble-stoned Lantmäteribacken.

Each year during the summer months nearly 150 events are staged in Kungsträdgården. The covered, outdoor stage here is the setting for various open-air concerts; Parkteatern, an outdoor theatre group, also puts on shows including musical productions, children's theatre, flamenco and other

dance performances. Many of the events are free and enjoyed by thousands of Stockholmers, who arrive with their picnics and blankets. The park also hosts numerous exhibitions, food festivals, and live street theatre. Local radio stations also hold big festivals featuring a variety of home-grown and international artists. In August, when the annual Gospel Choir Festival takes place, audiences are invited to sing along, whatever their musical abilities. At the garden's centre is a large cirular plaza, and during the winter months this is transformed into a skating rink that attracts children and grown-ups alike. There is also a Christmas market held in the park every weekend throughout December.

Kungsträdgården has several outdoor cafés, art galleries, including the Galleri Doktor Glas, and restaurants at the two ends of the garden.

❷ Jacobs Kyrka

Västra Trädgårdsgatan 2. **Map** 4 B1.
Tel 08-723 30 38. Ⓣ Kungsträdgården.
🚌 2, 55, 62, 65, 76. **Open** 10am–5pm
Mon–Wed; 11am–6pm Thu, Fri & Sun; 10am–5pm Sat. 🚹 (in English)
Sun. Concerts 5pm Fri.
🎧 by arrangement. ♿

Even in medieval times there was a small chapel where Kungsträdgården now lies. Dedicated to St Jacob, the patron saint of wayfarers, the chapel and another modest-sized church in the area were destroyed by King Gustav Vasa in the 16th century. Johan III

wanted to provide two new churches in Norra Malmen, as the area was then called, and work to build the churches of St Jacob and St Klara (see p68) started in 1580. St Jacob's was consecrated first, in 1643. It has been restored several times since then, in some cases rather clumsily. However, several valuable items have been preserved, including a baptismal font from 1634 and some church silver, as well as porches by stonemasons Henrik Blom and Hans Hebel.

The organ's façade was created by the architect Carl Hårleman, and the large painting on the west wall of the southern nave is by Fredrik Westin, Sweden's most distinguished historical painter in the early 19th century.

Altar in Jacobs Kyrka, partly dating from the 17th century

❸ Kungliga Operan

Gustav Adolfs Torg. **Map** 4 B1. **Tel** 08-791 44 00. Ⓣ Kungsträdgården.
🚌 2, 43, 55, 62, 65, 71, 76. Ticket Office **Open** noon–5pm Mon–Fri, noon–3pm Sat. 🎧 by arrangement. ♿
📧 📷 🆆 **operan.se**

Opera has been performed in Sweden since 18 January 1773, when a production was staged at Bollhuset at Slottsbacken. Kungliga Operan (The Royal Opera House) on Gustav Adolfs Torg was inaugurated on 30 September 1782, but by the late 19th century it had become a fire hazard. The architect Axel Anderberg was commissioned to design a new opera house, which was transferred to the State in 1898

View of Kungsträdgården, towards Hamngatan

The 28-m (92-ft) long gold foyer at Kungliga Operan

from a consortium founded by the financier K A Wallenberg.

The colouring of the building in late Renaissance style is in keeping with the Royal Palace and Parliament building, and some details of the architecture are common to all three. The beautiful staircase with ceiling paintings by Axel Jungstedt was inspired by the Paris Opera. The same artist's portrait of Oscar II hangs in the 28-m (92-ft) long gold foyer, where Carl Larsson was responsible for the decorative paintings. The wings at either side of the stage have been kept, as has the width of the proscenium arch (11.4 m/37 ft). Also saved was J T Sergel's group of angels, holding the national coat of arms, above the stage. An angel in Vicke Andrén's ceiling painting is holding a sketch of the Opera House.

Gold ceiling in
Kungliga Operan

❹ Arvfurstens Palats

Gustav Adolfs Torg 1. **Map** 4 B1.
🚇 Kungsträdgården. 🚌 43, 62, 65.
Closed to the public.

Opposite the Royal Opera House, on the other side of Gustav Adolfs Torg, stands Arvfurstens Palats (Prince's Palace), built for Gustav III's sister Sofia Albertina and inaugurated in 1794. She commissioned the architect Erik Palmstedt to carry out the work. He was a pupil of

Carl Fredrik Adelcrantz, designer of the original opera house.

The palace and its decor are shining examples of the Gustavian style, thanks to the contributions of artists and craftsmen such as Louis Masreliez and Georg Haupt and their pupils Gustaf Adolf Ditzinger, Johan Tobias Sergel and Gottlieb Iwersson. In 1906 the building was taken over by the Swedish Foreign Office.

Nearby is the elegant Sagerska Palatset (1894) in French Renaissance style, which is used by the Prime Minister as an official residence.

Arvfurstens Palats (1794), now the Swedish Foreign Office

❺ Medelhavs-museet

Fredsgatan 2. **Map** 4 B1. **Tel** 08-519 550 50. 🚇 Kungsträdgården. 🚌 3, 52, 53, 62, 65. **Open** noon–8pm Tue–Fri, noon–5pm Sat & Sun. 🅿 ♿ 📷 🖼 **w** medelhavsmuseet.se

Gods and people from pre-historic cultures around the

Mediterranean rub shoulders in Medelhavsmuseet (Museum of Mediterranean and Near East Antiquities). Its many treasures include a large group of terracotta figures discovered by archaeologists on Cyprus in the 1930s. Models made of unusual materials, such as cork, show how houses were once constructed, and the museum also has a fascinating gold room. The Islamic collections are complemented by temporary exhibitions.

The museum is housed in a former bank, which was originally built in the 17th century for Field Marshal Gustav Horn, a decorated commander in the Thirty Years' War. The stairwell, dating from 1905, and the peristyles and colonnade around the upper part of the hall are well worth a visit in themselves.

❻ Dansmuseet

Drottninggatan 17. **Map** 4 A1.
Tel 08-441 76 51. 🚇 Centralen, Kungsträdgården. 🚌 52. **Open** 11am–5pm Tue–Fri, noon–4pm Sat & Sun. 🅿 ♿ 📷 🖼 **w** dansmuseet.se

In 2013 the Dance Museum moved into new premises on Drottninggatan, in a former bank with a grand exterior. The museum was originally founded in Paris in 1933 by the Swedish aristocrat and noted art collector Rolf de Maré (1888–1964). He was also the founder and artistic director of the world-renowned Ballets Suédois.

The museum's collection of exhibits reflects all aspects of dance – costumes and masks, scenery sketches, art and posters, books and documents. Temporary displays are organized every year. Apart from the exhibition halls, there is also a Study Centre, which boasts a large collection of books and DVDs. The museum also has a French bistro and a shop, in which Sweden's largest collection of dance DVDs is for sale.

Rosenbad, home of the Government and City Council committees

❼ Rosenbad

Rosenbad 4. **Map** 4 A2.
Ⓣ Kungsträdgården. 🚌 3, 53, 62, 65.
Closed to the public.

Since 1981, the Rosenbad complex – a collection of palatial buildings overlooking the Strömmen channel – has housed the Swedish Government and the Prime Minister's private office in three internally linked sites.

Three of the late 19th century's most notable architects were commissioned to design these buildings. The Venetian-style palace along Strömgatan was the last one to be added, in 1904. Designed by Ferdinand Boberg (1860–1916), it used to house private apartments, a bank and a popular restaurant, traces of which survive in the ornamentation of the open loggia facing the water.

Gustav Wickman (1858–1916) designed the pink sandstone house on the corner of Fredsgatan and Drottninggatan in exuberant, almost Baroque-like, Jugendstil. The Skåne Bank moved into this building in 1900.

The Florentine-style house on Fredsgatan facing Rödbodtorget is three years older. It was designed by Aron Johansson (1860–1936), architect of the old Parliament building on Helgeandsholmen.

Rosenbad got its name from a former 17th-century bathhouse, which offered bathers a choice of a lily bath, a chamomile bath or a rose bath – *rosenbad* in Swedish.

❽ Konstakademien

Fredsgatan 12. **Map** 4 A2. **Tel** 08-23 29 45. Ⓣ T-centralen, T- Kungsträdgården. 🚌 3, 53, 62, 65. **Open** 11am–5pm Tue–Fri, noon–4pm Sat & Sun. ♿ entrance at Jakobsgatan 27C. 🖥

The art collections of Konstakademien (Royal Academy of Fine Arts) reflect more than 250 years of paintings and sculptures, mostly by past and present members. Today the Royal Academy has around 150 members. There are almost 800 sculptures, most of them plaster casts that were once used in drawing classes. They range from Michelangelo's enormous *Moses* to small plant ornaments intended as inspiration for interiors and design.

Between Fredsgatan and Jakobsgatan, the imposing corner house was designed by Tessin the Elder in the early 1670s. The Royal Academy moved in while under the patronage of Gustav III in the late 18th century. It has been rebuilt several times, the latest in

The Fredsgatan entrance of Konstakademien

1897 by the architect Erik Lallerstedt. Its present look ties in with the Royal Opera House (see p66) and the Royal Palace (see pp50–53), whose architect Tessin the Younger had a vision of this area as an extension of his work.

Traces of the older buildings can still be seen. The interior of the small meeting room was designed by Carl Fredrik Adelcrantz around 1780, and two tiled stoves from the same period have been preserved, plus the main porch facing Jakobsgatan.

Interior of Klara Kyrka with decor by Olle Hjortzberg

❾ Klara Kyrka

Klarabergsgatan 37. **Map** 2 C4. **Tel** 08-411 73 24. Ⓣ T-centralen 🚌 52, 59, 65. **Open** 10am–5pm Sun–Fri, 5–7:30pm Sat. 🕊 11am Sun. ♿ 🖥

The convent of St Klara stood on the site of the present church and cemetery until 1527, when it was pulled down on the orders of Gustav Vasa. Later, his son Johan III commissioned a new church, completed in 1590.

The church was ravaged by fire in 1751, and its reconstruction was planned by the period's two outstanding architects, first Carl Hårleman and later C F Adelcrantz. The pulpit was made in 1753 to Hårleman's design, and J T Sergel (see p85) created the angelic figures in the northern gallery. A pair of identical angels adorn the exquisite chancel, based on the sculptor's gypsum originals.

In the 1880s, the 116-m (380-ft) tower was added and for many years could be seen from all over the city. The 20th-century church artist, Olle Hjortzberg, created the vault paintings, dating from 1904.

Edvin Öhrström's glass obelisk in Sergels Torg, with Kulturhuset behind to the left

⑩ Kulturhuset and Stockholms Stadsteater

Sergels Torg 7, Kulturhuset. **Map** 2 C4.
Kulturhuset **Tel** 08-508 315 08.
Stockholms Stadsteater **Tel** 08-506
202 00. Ⓣ T-centralen. 🚌 52, 69.
Open 9am–7pm Mon–Fri, 11am–5pm
Sat & Sun. 🏛 some areas. ♿ ✏ 🖥
📷 🔤 **kulturhusetstadsteatern.se**

Opened in 1974, Kulturhuset is
at the heart of Stockholm's
cultural life. A creation of the
architect Peter Celsing, the
cultural centre is typical of its
era and blends well with
surrounding Sergels Torg. The
building has a façade of glass
all along the southern side of
the square and is a symbol
of Swedish Modernism.

Kulturhuset offers something
for everybody: three galleries
hold regularly changing
exhibitions suitable for all tastes.
Visitors can watch short films,
documentaries and live
broadcast concerts in the
"Klara Cinema". Clubs, concerts
and events are available in
the "Sergels Torg 3" venue; there
is also an open rooftop stage
used during the summer
months. The "Ecoteque" is a
space dedicated to environmental issues, where regular
forums take place. There is
also a coffee shop here and
changing exhibitions. "Lava"
is a meeting place for young
people, where dance, handicraft
and various other workshops
are held.

There are five libraries in the
centre. "Kidszone" caters for
small children with storytelling
and workshops; "TioTretton" is
for children aged 10 to 13;
"Serieteket" is Sweden's only
library for fans of strip cartoons;
the "Plattan Library" is stocked
with international newspapers
and magazines and also has
a bank of computers for
public use; and the "Music and
Film" section has a large archive
of international music that
visitors can listen to.

The centre has a variety of
cafés and eateries as well as
several shops selling items of
contemporary Swedish design.

Kulturhuset also houses
Stockholms Stadsteater
(City Theatre). The theatre
presents a varied programme
of music and other events in its
main auditorium. Here, some
1,400 performances take place
every year for audiences
totalling about 225,000.

⑪ Sergels Torg

Map 2 C4. Ⓣ T-centralen.
🚌 52, 69.

As part of the city centre's
transformation, around 1930
there was a strong lobby in
favour of extending Sveavägen
through to Gustav Adolfs Torg.
But in 1945 it was decided to
end the road at the junction
with Klarabergsgatan and
Hamngatan to form a new square,
Sveaplan. In 1957 a two-level
square was proposed – a lower
level for pedestrians and an
upper level for traffic. The plan
was finalized in 1960, and the
name changed to Sergels Torg.

In 1972 the sculptor Edvin
Öhrström's glass obelisk, *Crystal
Vertical Accent in Glass and Steel*,
was erected in the centre and
now shimmers at night due to
improved lighting.

City's Transformation

During the 20th century Stockholm's population grew from 250,000
to more than 1.6 million. By the 1920s it was obvious that the old
heart of the city did not meet the
future needs of business, public
administration and the growth
in traffic. In 1951 a controversial
30-year programme to transform
the lower Norrmalm city centre
was launched. Slums on 335 of the
600 sites were pulled down, and 78
new houses were built. Two-thirds
of the area's buildings were added
during this period.

The first steps towards a new
Hötorgs City *(see p70)*, 1958

Fresh produce on sale at Hötorget, a marketplace since the 17th century

⓬ Hötorget

Map 2 C4. Ⓣ Hötorget. 🚌 1, 56, 59. 🕐 10am–6pm Mon–Thu, 10am–6:30pm Fri, 10am–4pm Sat.

Tradition is still going strong on Hötorget (Hay Market). Formerly belonging to St Klara convent, in the 1640s the square evolved into an important place for trading in animal fodder, milk, vegetables and meat. Today it is still a lively market for fresh produce.

The buildings around the square are relatively new. The glass-fronted cinema complex opened in 1995, while the PUB department store was added in 1916 and Konserthuset in 1926. On nearby Sergelgatan, where the five high-rises of Hötorgs City were constructed in 1952–6,

there is a reminder of the old city centre. A tablet marks where the renowned sculptor Johan Tobias Sergel (1740–1814) had his studio. A later sculptor, Carl Milles (*see p152*), created the well-noted fountain, *Orpheus*, that stands in front of Konserthuset.

⓭ Konserthuset

Hötorget 8. **Map** 2 C4. **Tel** 08-50 66 77 88. Ⓣ Hötorget. 🚌 1, 56, 59. Ticket Office **Open** 11am–6pm Mon–Fri, 11am–3pm Sat, and 2 hours before a concert. 🎫 ♿ 📷 🏛
🅦 konserthuset.se

A Nordic version of a Greek temple, Konserthuset (the Stockholm Concert Hall) is a masterpiece by the architect Ivar Tengbom (1878–1968) and an outstanding example of the 1920s Neo-Classical style. Tengbom's tradition has been carried on by his son Anders (b. 1911), who was in charge of the hall's renovation in 1970–71,

and his grandson Svante (b. 1942), who had a similar task in 1993–6.

Constructed in 1923–6, the main hall at the outset matched Tengbom's original concept. However, acoustical problems led to major reconstruction work and modernization. Its internal decor is rather frugal, but the Grünewald Hall, by the artist Isaac Grünewald (1889–1946), is more lavish, in the style of an Italian Renaissance palace. The four marble statues in the main foyer are by Carl Milles, creator of the *Orpheus* sculpture group outside. Other artists who have contributed to the decor are Einar Forseth, Simon Gate, Edward Hald and Carl Malmsten.

The Stockholm Concert Hall has been the home of the Royal Stockholm Philharmonic Orchestra since it opened. The orchestra gives some 100 concerts every year, and international star soloists and conductors perform here regularly. It is also the venue for the Polar Music Prize and the Nobel Prize presentations.

⓮ Kungstornen

Kungsgatan 30 and 33. **Map** 3 D4. Ⓣ Hötorget. 🚌 1, 43, 56. **Closed** to the public.

In 1915 the young architect Sven Wallander submitted a sketch showing how Stockholm could be given a modern, USA-inspired main street. His plans were accepted during the 1920s, when a new road was excavated

The Nobel Prizes

Alfred Nobel (1833–96) was an outstanding chemist and inventor, and the prestigious Nobel Prizes – consisting of a monetary award and a medal – have been presented every year since 1901 on 10 December, the date of his death. The ceremony takes place in Konserthuset, where prizes are presented for physics, chemistry, physiology or medicine, and literature. Since 1969 the Bank of Sweden has also given a prize for economic sciences in Nobel's memory. The Nobel Peace Prize is presented in Oslo's City Hall on the same day. In 1901 each prize was worth 150,000 kr, while in 2010 it had increased to 10 million kr. Since 2012, it has been 8 million kr.

The Nobel Medal, awarded annually

The *Orpheus* sculpture group by Carl Milles at Konserthuset

through the Brunkeberg hill linking Hötorget with Stureplan. A bridge was built over what is now Kungsgatan, and a few years later the twin Kungstornen (King's Towers) were added.

Designed in Neo-Classical style by Wallander, the northern tower was originally owned by the sugar company Sockerbolaget. The southern tower was designed by Ivar Callmander and owned by L M Ericsson. Apart from a period when restaurants occupied the top of each one, the towers have been used only as offices. Both are 16 floors high. The northern tower, covering an area of 7,000 sq m (75,350 sq ft), is referred to as the "male", with his more graceful, slightly larger twin, as the "female". At the entrance to the northern tower are some beautiful granite sculptures created by Eric Grate.

The "female" (left) and "male" (right) Kungstornen on Kungsgatan

⑮ Centralbadet

Drottninggatan 88. **Map** 4 C4. **Tel** 08-545 213 00. Ⓣ Hötorget. **Open** 7am–9pm Mon–Fri, 9am–9pm Sat, 9am–6pm Sun. **Closed** public hols. 🅿 🖥 ✎ 🅰 🅆 centralbadet.se

Designed by the architect Wilhelm Klemming in Jugendstil, Centralbadet swimming and fitness centre was completed in 1904. Since then, it has been rebuilt and extended, but the façade remains the same, while the Jugendstil influence continues into the main pool and restaurant.

A protected cultural heritage building, the classic swimming

Centralbadet's characteristic naturalistic Jugendstil façade

centre has a 23-m (75-ft) long pool, bubble and treatment pools, three saunas and skincare and massage sections.

The garden, situated between Drottninggatan and Centralbadet, was originally designed by the prolific 18th-century architect Carl Hårleman. A few of the trees growing there today are thought to date from his era. The garden is a delightful oasis set round an ornamental pool and fountain, and there is also a sculpture showing a Triton riding a dolphin, created by Greta Klemming in the 1920s.

⑯ Dansens Hus

Barnhusgatan 12–14. **Map** 2 C3. **Tel** 08-508 990 90. Ⓣ T-centralen. 🚌 1, 53. Ticket Office **Open** 2–6pm Tue–Fri, three hours before performances Sat & Sun. 🅿 ♿ 🖥 🅰 🅆 dansenshus.se

The most important space for contemporary dance and performance art in the whole of Scandinavia, Dansens Hus has two theatres with a capacity of 750 and 100 seats respectively. Its programme often includes as many as 35 productions a year, and these draw upwards of 60,000 visitors. The artists that have graced these stages range from emerging Scandinavian companies to international established acts. Among them are the Spanish flamenco dancer Israel Galvan, and Virpi Pahkinen, a Finnish choreographer and dancer.

In addition to performances, Dansens Hus arranges seminars, lectures, meet-the-artist sessions and workshops.

⑰ Strindbergsmuseet Blå Tornet

Drottninggatan 85. **Map** 2 C3. **Tel** 08-411 53 54. Ⓣ Rådmansgatan. 🚌 52, 69. **Open** noon–4pm Tue–Sun (Jul & Aug: 10am–4pm Tue–Sun). 🅿 when booked in advance. 🅰 🅆 strindbergsmuseet.se

The world-famous dramatist August Strindberg (1849–1912) had 24 different addresses in Stockholm over the years. He moved to the last of these in 1908, and gave it the name Blå Tornet (The Blue Tower). By this time he had gained international recognition.

The house, now the Strindbergsmuseet, was built with central heating, toilet and lift, but lacked a kitchen. Instead, the writer relied on Falkner's Pension, a hotel in the same building, for food. On his last few birthdays the great man would stand on his balcony and watch his admirers stage a torchlight procession in his honour.

Opened in 1973, the museum includes reconstructions of the author's home with his bedroom, dining room and study, as well as 3,000 books and archives for photographs, press cuttings and posters. In the adjoining premises, a permanent exhibition portrays Strindberg as author, theatrical director, artist and photographer. Temporary exhibitions and other activities are often held here.

Strindberg's desk and writing materials in his study

⓲ Adolf Fredriks Kyrka

Holländargatan 16. **Map** 2 C3.
Tel 08-20 70 76. 🚇 Hötorget. 🚌 52.
Open 1–7pm Mon, 10am–4pm Tue–Sun. 🛐 7pm Mon, 12:15pm Wed & Thu (Mass in English on Thu), 11am Sun. 📷 by appointment. ♿ 🖥 📷

King Adolf Frederik laid the foundation stone of this church in 1768 on the site of an earlier chapel dedicated to St Olof. Designed by Carl Fredrik Adelcrantz, in Neo-Classical style with traces of Rococo, the church has been built in the shape of a Greek cross and has a central dome.

The interior has undergone a number of changes, but both the altar and pulpit have remained intact. The sculptor Johan Tobias Sergel created the altarpiece, which is probably his most important religious work. The memorial to French philosopher Descartes (see p19) is also Sergel's work. The paintings on the dome were added in 1899–1900 by Julius Kronberg.

Memorial to Descartes

More recent items of value include altar silverware by Sigurd Persson.

The cemetery is the resting place of the assassinated Prime Minister Olof Palme, as well as the politician Hjalmar Branting, a key figure of the Social Democratic movement. J T Sergel is also buried here.

The "Devil's Bible" from the early 13th century, stored at Kungliga Biblioteket

⓳ Kungliga Biblioteket

Humlegården. **Map** 3 D3. **Tel** 010-709 30 30. 🚇 Östermalmstorg. 🚌 1, 2, 55, 56, 91, 96. **Open** 9am–7pm Mon–Thu, 9am–6pm Fri, 11am–3pm Sat; 1 Jun–31 Aug: 9am–6pm Mon–Thu, 9am–5pm Fri, 11am–3pm Sat. **Closed** July: Sat 📷 by appointment. ♿ 🖥 🌐 kb.se

This is Sweden's national library and an autonomous Government department in its own right. Ever since 1661, when there were only nine printing presses in Sweden, copies of every piece of printed matter have had to be lodged with Kungliga Biblioteket (the Royal Library). Since 1993 this requirement has also applied to electronic documents. As there are now some 3,000 printers and publishers in Sweden, the volume of material is expanding rapidly. The collection now covers about 4 million books and magazines, more than 14 million ephemera, 500,000 posters, 300,000 maps, 750,000 portraits and 500,000 pictures. The Department of Audiovisual Material (previously the Swedish National Archive of Recorded Sound and Moving Images) is also here and holds a total of 8 million hours of material, including TV and radio

programmes, movies, videos, Swedish music and multimedia recordings. The library has made all of its material available to the public.

The imposing original building, inaugurated in 1878, had to be expanded in the 1920s, and again in the 1990s. This major extension provided an auditorium and, most importantly, two underground book storage areas covering an area in total of 18,000 sq m (193,750 sq ft).

The library is in a beautiful setting in Humlegården, created by King Johan III in the 16th century to grow hops for the royal household. Since the 18th century, the park has been a favourite recreation area for Stockholmers.

⓴ Stureplan

Map 3 D4. 🚇 Östermalmstorg. 🚌 1, 2, 55, 56, 91.

A new town plan for Stockholm towards the end of the 19th century recommended that the Stureplan area should become the capital's new centre. The proposal was accepted, and the

Olof Palme

Olof Palme (1927–86)

On 28 February 1986 the Swedish Prime Minister Olof Palme was killed in a Stockholm street on his way home from a cinema without a bodyguard. The murder happened at the corner of Sveavägen and Tunnelgatan, whose western section was renamed Olof Palmes Gata. A memorial tablet has been placed there. The murder provoked strong reactions but to this day remains unsolved. His grave is in the nearby Adolf Fredrik cemetery.

Stureplan and the circular *Svampen*, one of the city's most popular meeting places

area around *Svampen* (The Mushroom) rain shelter became a popular meeting place, as more and more shops and restaurants opened. However, a new street layout after the introduction of right-hand driving in Sweden in 1967 brought its halcyon days to a close.

But now Stureplan has staged a phoenix-like comeback out of the ashes of a major fire at the Sturebadet swimming pool in 1985. Plans to revamp the area were made: the pool was modernized, and the Sturegallerian shopping mall was built, revitalizing the whole eastern part of the city. Once again Stureplan became one of the capital's most popular meeting places.

㉑ Sturegallerian and Sturebadet

Sturegallerian 36. **Map** 3 D4. Ⓣ Östermalmstorg. 1, 2, 55, 56, 91. Shopping mall **Open** 10am–7pm Mon–Fri, 10am–5pm Sat, noon–5pm Sun. Pool **Tel** 08-545 015 00. **Open** 6:30am–10pm Mon–Fri, 8:30am–10:30pm Sat & Sun; other times by appointment & members only.

The original Sturebadet swimming pool, opened in 1885, was sited within the present-day StureCompagniet complex. Rebuilt on its present site in 1902, it was ahead of its time – even in the 1930s it was offering exercise facilities.

After a disastrous fire in 1985, a sum of 600 million kr was invested, partly to reconstruct the pool according to its original design and partly to develop Sturegallerian, a world-class shopping mall. The architects managed to link the late 19th-century exterior with interiors of modern design using marble, granite, steel, copper, cedar and mahogany.

Indoor streets and squares with some 50 retail outlets have been created, including restaurants, cafés and various services. Today's swimming pool is now the most traditional part of the complex. It has a spa offering luxurious treatments and also has a gym on site.

Painstakingly restored Jugendstil decor at Sturebadet

㉒ Östermalmshallen

Humlegårdsgatan 1–3. **Map** 3 E4. Ⓣ Östermalmstorg. 1, 2, 56, 62. **Open** 9:30am–6pm Mon–Thu, 9:30am–7pm Fri, 9:30am–4pm Sat, 9:30am–2pm Sat in summer. Ⓦ **ostermalmshallen.se**

The temple of gastronomy, this market hall on Östermalmstorg is as far removed from a fast-food outlet as you could imagine. Nowhere else in the city is there such a range of high-quality delicacies under one roof. But it was certainly an example of fast building. Taking only eight months to erect, the hall was opened by King Oscar II in 1888. It is regarded as a fine example of the city's late 19th-century architectural heritage. Construction of a brick building around a cast-iron shell was a novelty in Sweden, and the architects Gustaf Clason and Kasper Sahlin won acclaim for their design, inspired by the arcades of Mediterranean markets. In the early days there were 153 stalls and, after undergoing extensive restoration, there are now 13 larger specialist shops, selling local delicacies, and some popular lunch spots.

㉓ Hedvig Eleonora Kyrka

Storgatan 2. **Map** 3 E4. **Tel** 08-545 675 70. Ⓣ Östermalmstorg. 62. **Open** 11am–6pm daily. 12:15pm Tue & Thu, 7pm Wed, 11am Sun. by appt.

Founded in 1669 to give the Swedish Navy its own place for religious services, the church was not officially opened until 1737. The first plans were drawn up by Jean de la Vallée, but the work was completed with Göran Josuae Adelcrantz as architect. The dome was added in 1866–8. The main bell was cast in Helsingør, Denmark, in 1639 and hung in Kronborg Castle before being seized as a war trophy by General Carl Gustaf Wrangel *(see p58)*.

The church has many valuable artifacts. The altarpiece *Jesus on the Cross* was painted in 1738 by Engelhard Schröder. The designer of the majestic pulpit in Neo-Classical style was Jean Eric Rehn, who saw his work unveiled on Christmas Day in 1784.

The new organ was built in the mid-1970s, but Carl Fredrik Adelcrantz's 1762 organ façade is still in its original state. Included in the silverware is a Baroque chalice from 1650 and a christening bowl dated 1685. The 1678 font is now housed in the baptismal chapel, which was added at the time of the church's restoration in 1944.

Östermalmshallen, a culinary temple inspired by markets in Southern Europe

Armémuseum, with the dome of Hedvig Eleonora Kyrka in the background

❷ Armémuseum

Riddargatan 13. **Map** 3 E4. **Tel** 08-519 56 300. ⓣ Östermalmstorg. 🚍 62, 69, 52, 76. **Open** Sep–May: 11am–8pm Tue, 11am–5pm Wed–Sun; Jun–Aug: 10am–5pm daily. 🎫 🎟 🎫 ♿ 🎭 🎫 🖥 🅦 **armemuseum.se**

The old armoury on Artillerigården has been the home of the Armémuseum (Royal Army Museum) since 1879. During the 1990s the 250-year-old building and its exhibits underwent extensive renovation. It is now one of the capital's best-planned and most interesting museums.

It puts Sweden's history in a 1,000-year perspective, present-ing the information in an exciting and comprehensive way. The march of history is illustrated by life-size settings, and visitors can see many unique objects from the collection of 80,000 exhibits.

Processions for royal visits in the city start from the museum, and during the summer guards-men march from here to the Royal Palace at 11:45am every day for the changing of the guard.

❷ Swedish Museum of Performing Arts

Sibyllegatan 2. **Map** 3 E4. **Tel** 08-519 554 90. ⓣ Kungsträdgården, Östermalmstorg. 🚍 2, 52, 62, 69, 76. **Closed** for renovation until 2016. 🎫 🎟 ♿ 🎭 🎫 🅦 **scenkonstmuseet.se**

Situated in the former royal bakery, an elegant historic building, this museum houses a collection of 50,000 objects relating to the performing arts.

Exhibits include musical instruments, set design models, puppets and costumes, with some pieces dating back to the 16th century.

The museum places a very strong emphasis on interaction, and visitors are encouraged to play with many of the objects on show and participate in performances taking place in the museum.

The museum is currently closed for renovation and will open its doors to visitors in October 2016. Once reopened, there will be a lively programme of temporary exhibitions and events.

❷ Hovstallet

Väpnargatan 1. **Map** 3 E4. **Tel** 08-402 61 05. ⓣ Kungsträd-gården, Östermalmstorg. 🚍 2, 5, 52, 62, 69, 71, 76. **Open** for guided tours. **Closed** public hols. 🎫 1pm Sat (in English). 🎭 🎫 🅦 **royalcourt.se**

Formerly on Helgeandsholmen, Hovstallet (the Royal Mews) moved here in 1893, when the new Parliament building was being constructed. Alongside the Museum of Music, it

Coach and four, with riders on the left-hand horses, at Hovstallet

occupies a site next to the Royal Dramatic Theatre.

The Mews arranges the trans-port for the Royal Family and the Royal Household. It maintains about 40 carriages, a dozen cars and carriage horses, and a few horses used for riding. The royal horses are Swedish half-breeds.

There are many treasures among the carriages, such as the State coach with glass panelling known as a "Berliner", made in Sweden at the Adolf Freyschuss carriage works. It was first seen at Oscar II's silver jubilee in 1897 and is still used on ceremonial occasions.

Incoming foreign ambassadors travel to the Royal Palace for their formal audience with the monarch in Karl XV's coupé. Open carriages from the mid-19th century drawn by two horses are normally used for processions.

❷ Kungliga Drama-tiska Teatern

Nybroplan. **Map** 3 E4. **Tel** 08-667 06 80. ⓣ Kungsträdgården, Östermalm-storg. 🚍 2, 52, 55, 62, 69, 76. Ticket Office **Open** noon–7pm Tue–Sat, noon–4pm Sun. 🎫 🎟 ♿ 🎭 🅦 **dramaten.se**

When plans were drawn up in the early 20th century to build the present Kungliga Dramatiska Teatern (Royal Dramatic Theatre) at Nybroplan, the State refused to give financial aid, so it was funded by lotteries instead. The results exceeded all expectations, giving the architect Fredrik Lilljekvist generous resources, which he used to the full.

The theatre, known as Dramaten, was opened in 1908 after 6 years in construction, and its decor was remarkable for the era.

The Jugendstil façade inspired by Viennese architecture is in costly white marble. Christian Ericsson provided the powerful relief frieze, Carl Milles the centre section, and John Börjesson the bronze statues *Poetry* and *Drama*. These are complemented in the foyer by *Comedy* and *Tragedy* by Gusten Lindberg and Theodor Lundberg respectively.

The lavish design continues inside, both in the choice of materials and in the contributions by leading Swedish artists. The ceiling in the foyer is by Carl Larsson, while the upper lobby's back wall was painted by Oscar Björck, and the auditorium's ceiling and stage lintel by Julius Kronberg. Gustav Cederström provided the central painting in the marble foyer, which also has some fantastic sculptures and busts.

Georg Pauli gave his name to a café, where visitors can see his paintings and enjoy a meal without necessarily attending a performance.

The 805-seat auditorium and revolving stage with a diameter of 15 m (49 ft) have a classic beauty. When Gustav III founded the Royal Dramatic Theatre in 1788, it performed in a building on Slottsbacken. The probable colour scheme there – blue, white and

Courtyard of Hallwylska museet, seen through the gateway arch

gold – was chosen for the new national stage but was changed to the traditional "theatre red" in the 1930s. The auditorium was returned to its original colouring during renovation in 1988.

About 100 actors give some 1,200 performances every year on the theatre's 5 stages to large audiences of over 300,000.

㉘ Hallwylska museet

Hamngatan 4. **Map** 3 D4.
Tel 08-402 30 99. Ⓣ Östermalmstorg, Kungsträdgården. 🚌 2, 55, 62, 69, 76.
📅 Jan–May & Sep–Dec: noon–4pm Tue & Thu–Sun, noon–7pm Wed; Jun: 10am–4pm daily; Jul & Aug: 10am–4pm Tue & Sun, 10am–7pm Wed–Sat. ♿ 📷 📅
🌐 hallwylskamuseet.se

This museum is housed in the elegant 19th-century former residence of Count Walther von Hallwyl and his wife, Wilhelmina. A wealthy heiress, Wilhelmina became one of Sweden's greatest collectors of European and East Asian fine and decorative art.

In 1920, the von Hallwyls donated their Stockholm mansion and its contents to the Swedish State. The terms of the bequest stipulated that the house must remain essentially unchanged.

As a result, the original decor and layout of the rooms has been perfectly preserved. Various styles were adopted throughout. The main salon, for example, pays homage to the late Baroque style. It is built around four grandiose Gobelin tapestries and is finished in 24-carat gold leaf, clearly influenced by Hårleman's work at the Royal Palace *(see pp50–53)*. It is difficult to believe that this was once a room in a private residence.

The museum houses some 50,000 objects amassed by Wilhelmina during her lifetime. These include paintings, porcelain, East Asian sculpture, antique furniture, books and manuscripts, arms and armour, and photographs. Because the house has been preserved exactly as it was when it passed into the hands of the Swedish State, the kitchen utensils, office equipment and personal possessions of the family are also on display. Unusual items include a chunk from the Count's beard and a slice of Walther and Wilhelmina's wedding cake.

Perhaps the most remarkable artifact on display is a Steinway grand piano, dating from 1896, adapted to fit into its majestic setting with a "casing" of hardwood and inlaid wood. In 1990 it was flown to New York in two sections, weighing a total of 900 kg (1,980 lb), for a renovation lasting several months. Visitors strolling through the salon can listen to a recording of music played on this magnificent piano.

Kungliga Dramatiska Teaterns Jugendstil façade in white marble

BLASIEHOLMEN & SKEPPSHOLMEN

Opposite the Royal Palace on the eastern side of the Strömmen channel lies Blasieholmen, a natural springboard to the islands of Skeppsholmen and Kastellholmen.

Several elegant palaces were built at Blasieholmen during Sweden's era as a great power in the 17th and early 18th centuries. But the area's present appearance was acquired in the period between the mid-19th century, when buildings such as Nationalmuseum were erected, until just before World War I. In the early 1900s, stately residences such as Bååtska Palatset became overshadowed by prestigious hotels, lavish banks and

entertainment venues. Blasieholmen is also the place for auction houses, art galleries, antiques shops and second-hand bookshops. The quayside is the departure point for sightseeing and archipelago boats.

Skeppsholmen is reached by a wrought-iron bridge with old wooden boats moored next to it. In the middle of the 17th century the island became the base for the Swedish Navy, and many of its old buildings were designed as barracks and stores. Today they house some of the city's major museums and cultural institutions, juxtaposed with the avant-garde construction of the Moderna museet.

Sights at a Glance

Museums
1. Östasiatiska museet
2. Moderna museet pp82–3
3. ArkDes
7. Nationalmuseum pp84–5

Public Buildings
5. Konsthögskolan

Islands and Squares
6. Kastellholmen
9. Blasieholmstorg
12. Raoul Wallenbergs Torg

Synagogues
10. Synagogan

Hotels and Restaurants
4. af Chapman
8. Grand Hôtel
11. Berns

Concert Halls
13. Musikaliska

See also Street Finder pp206–18

Restaurants pp166–71
1. B.A.R.
2. Hjerta
3. Långa Raden
4. Mathias Dahlgren Matsalen and Matbaren

◄ The af Chapman youth hostel, on a ship moored opposite the Royal Palace

For map symbols see back flap

Street-by-Street: Skeppsholmen

Skeppsholmen has long since lost its importance as a naval base and has been transformed into a centre for culture. Many of the naval buildings have been restored, and traditional wooden boats are moored here, but pride of place now goes to the internationally acclaimed Moderna museet.

The island is ideal for a full-day visit, with its location between the waters of Strömmen and Nybroviken acting as a breathing space in the centre of Stockholm. The attractive buildings, the richly wooded English-style park and the view towards Skeppsbron and Strandvägen also make Skeppsholmen an ideal place for those who would just prefer to have a quiet stroll.

Teater Galeasen is Stockholm's avant-garde theatre for new Swedish and international drama.

Skeppsholmsbron

Blasieholmen

❶ ★ Östasiatiska museet
This porcelain dish with a five-clawed dragon (Ming Dynasty, 1573–1620) is included in a remarkable collection of arts and crafts from China, Japan, Korea and India, covering the period from the Stone Age to the 19th century.

Skeppsholmen Church (1824–42) in well-preserved Empire style.

Salute battery

Admiralty House

SVENSKSUNDSVÄGEN

The Fantastic Paradise (1966), a sculpture group by Jean Tinguely and Niki de Saint Phalle for Montréal's World Exposition, has stood outside the site of the Moderna museet since 1972.

VÄSTRA BROBÄNKEN

Youth Hostel

Swedish Society of Crafts & Design

❺ Konsthögskolan
The first part of the Royal Institute of Art was completed in the 1770s, but it acquired its present appearance in the mid-1990s. This cast-iron boar stands at the entrance.

❹ af Chapman
Built in 1888, the full-rigged former freighter and school ship has served as a popular youth hostel since 1949. Skeppsholmen Church *(left)* and the Admiralty House (1647–50, rebuilt 1844–6) are in the background.

Loading crane built in 1751 – the oldest of its type in Sweden.

The festival area on the quayside below the Moderna museet was provided for the Millennium celebrations. It is the venue for the Stockholm Music and Arts festival.

Locator Map
See Street Finder map 5

❸ ArkDes
ArkDes highlights thousands of years of building, with a collection of models showing the world's architectural masterpieces, for example this model of the Stockholm City Library by Asplund.

❷ ★ Moderna museet
This museum, designed by Rafael Moneo, was opened in 1998, when Stockholm was Cultural Capital of Europe. It has an exciting collection of modern art, and pleasant views from its waterfront location.

ÖSTRA BROBÄNKEN

SVENSKSUNDSV.

AMIRALSVÄGEN

LÅNGA RADEN

SÖDRA BROBÄNKEN

Kastellholmen

Monument commemorating the Battle of Svensksund in 1790 *(see p24)*

Långa Raden is used by the State Board of Culture, and also for exhibitions and as homes. The buildings, dating from about 1700, originally accommodated King Karl XII's bodyguard.

KEY

— Suggested route

0 metres 100
0 yards 100

ArkDes, housed in the Neo-Classical former naval drill hall

❶ Östasiatiska museet

Tyghusplan. **Map** 5 D2. **Tel** 010-456 12 00. Ⓣ Kungsträdgården. 🚌 65. 🚢 Djurgårdsfärja. **Open** 11am–8pm Tue, 11am–5pm Wed–Sun. 📷 🖼 ♿ 🏛 🌐 **ostasiatiskamuseet.se**

It is not unusual for Western capitals to have a museum devoted to art and archaeology from China, Japan, Korea and India. But it is not every museum of Far Eastern antiquities that, like Östasiatiska museet, can claim one of the world's foremost collections of Chinese art outside Asia.

On a visit to the Yellow River valley in China in the early 1920s, the Swedish geologist Johan Gunnar Andersson discovered hitherto unknown dwellings and graves containing objects dating from the New Stone Age.

He was allowed by the Chinese to take a rich selection of finds back to Sweden, and these formed the basis for the museum, founded in 1926. A key figure in its development was the then Crown Prince, later to become King Gustaf VI Adolf,

who was both interested in and knowledgeable about archaeology. He eventually bequeathed to the museum his own large collection of ancient Chinese arts and crafts.

The museum has been on Skeppsholmen since 1963, when it was moved into a restored house that had been built in 1699–1700 as a depot for Karl XII's bodyguard.

❷ Moderna museet

See pp82–3.

❸ ArkDes

Exercisplan. **Map** 5 E3. **Tel** 08-587 270 00. Ⓣ Kungsträdgården. 🚌 65. 🚢 Djurgårdsfärja. **Open** 10am–8pm Tue, 10am–6pm Wed–Sun. 📷 by arrangement (for a fee). 🖼 ♿ 📷 🍴 🛍 🌐 **arkdes.se**

The Swedish Centre for Architecture and Design shares an entrance hall and restaurant with the Moderna museet. It has also taken over its earlier home, the one-time naval drill hall.

In the permanent exhibition, over a hundred models guide visitors through a thousand years of building. These cover categories from the oldest and simplest of wooden houses to the highly varied building techniques and architectural styles of the present day.

It is fascinating to switch from an almost 2,000-year-old longhouse to a Konsum supermarket, encountering in between examples of architecture in Gothenburg dating from the 17th century to the 1930s and the Årsta bridge situated to the south of Stockholm.

Models of historic architectural works worldwide, from 2000 BC up to the present day, are also on show.

The museum offers an ambitious programme – albeit only in Swedish – alongside the permanent and temporary exhibitions, including lectures, study walks around the city, guided tours, school visits and family events on Sunday afternoons.

Head of a woman, dating from the 12th century, at the Östasiatiska museet

The Skeppsholmen Cannons

A salute battery of four 57-mm rapid-fire cannons is sited on Skeppsholmen and is still in use. Salutes are fired to mark national and royal special occasions at noon on weekdays and 1pm at weekends: 28 January – the King's name day; 30 April – the King's birthday; 6 June – Sweden's National Day; 14 July – Crown Princess Victoria's birthday; 8 August – the Queen's name day; 23 December – the Queen's birthday.

The salute battery on Skeppsholmen

❹ af Chapman

Västra Brobänken. **Map** 5 D3. **Tel** 08-463 22 66. Ⓣ Kungsträdgården. 🚌 65. 🚢 Djurgårdsfärja. 🖸 *See Where to Stay p159.*

The sailing ship *af Chapman* is one of Sweden's most attractive and unusual youth hostels and has 136 beds. The hostel also includes the 152-bed building facing the ship's gangway.

Visitors staying in more conventional accommodation can still go on board and enjoy *af Chapman*'s special atmosphere. The three-masted ship was built in 1888 at the English port of Whitehaven and used as a freight vessel. She came to Sweden in 1915 and saw service as a school ship until 1934. The City of Stockholm bought the ship after World War II, and she has been berthed here since 1949. She is named after Fredrik Henrik af Chapman, a master shipbuilder who was born in Gothenburg in 1721.

❺ Konsthögskolan

Flaggmansvägen 1. **Map** 5 E3. **Tel** 08-614 40 00. Ⓣ Kungsträdgården. 🚌 65. 🚢 Djurgårdsfärja. **Open** to the public for special events. 🚻 🖸 8:30am–4:30pm Mon–Fri.

A stroll around Skeppsholmen provides an opportunity to have a closer look at the beautifully restored 18th-century naval barracks, which houses Konsthögskolan (the Royal Institute of Art). At the entrance there are two statues depicting a lion and a boar. "In like a lion and out like a pig" is an old saying among the lecturers and the 200 or so students at this institute, rich in tradition.

The institute started out in 1735 as an academy for painting and sculpture for the decorators working on Tessin's new Royal Palace. Gustav III granted it a royal charter in 1773. Before it moved here in 1995, it was located on Fredsgatan as part of Konstakademien *(see p68),* although since 1978 it had been run independently with departments for painting,

sculpture, graphics, digital media and video, as well as offering courses for architects.

The institute is not normally open to the public, apart from on Skeppsholmsdagen and an "open house" in September. Then visitors can enjoy the beautiful interiors, especially the vaulted 18th-century cellars.

The medieval-style castle on Kastellholmen, built in 1846–8

❻ Kastellholmen

Map 5 F4. Ⓣ Kungsträdgården. 🚌 65. 🚢 Djurgårdsfärja.

Right in the middle of Stockholm, Kastellholmen is a typical archipelago island with granite rocks and steep cliffs. From Skeppsholmen it is reached by a bridge built in 1880. Every morning since 1640 a sailor has hoisted the three-tailed Swedish war flag at the castle. Whenever a visiting naval vessel arrives, the battery's four cannons fire a welcoming salute from the castle terrace.

The charming brick pavilion by the bridge was built in 1882 for the Royal Skating Club, which used the water between the two islands when it froze.

❼ Nationalmuseum

See pp84–5.

❽ Grand Hôtel

Södra Blasieholmshamnen 8. **Map** 4 C1. **Tel** 08-679 35 00. Ⓣ Kungsträdgården. 🚌 55, 59, 62, 65, 76. *See Where to Stay p160 and Where to Eat p168.* 🖳 **grandhotel.se**

Rich in history and tradition, the Grand Hôtel was established in 1874 and occupies a prime location on the city's waterfront. Nobel Prize laureates and their families have all been guests of Grand Hôtel and the list of royalty and artists who have stayed here is impressive. The hotel's interiors are of great historical significance and have been designated as Swedish National Treasures. Most notable are the *Spegelsalen* (Hall of Mirrors), a copy of the one at Versailles, and *Vinterträdgården* (Winter Garden), with a ceiling height of 20 m (66 ft).

In 2007, renowned Swedish chef Mathias Dahlgren opened his eponymous restaurant, Mathias Dahlgren, at the Grand Hôtel.

The other restaurant, called The Veranda, is celebrated not just for its views but also for its traditional *smörgåsbord* and the growing popularity of The Cadier Bar, named after the hotel's founder.

Spegelsalen, the Hall of Mirrors, at the Grand Hôtel, Sweden's first five-star hotel

❷ Moderna museet

The Museum of Modern Art is an airy, contemporary building, designed by the Catalan architect Rafael Moneo in 1998. The museum has a top-class collection of international and Swedish modern and contemporary art, including photography and film, from 1900 to the present day. Built partly underground, the museum includes a cinema, an auditorium and an exhibition gallery. There is an excellent bookshop, and the Restaurangen Moderna Museet has attractive views over the water.

★ **Green Split** (1925)
Painted by Wassily Kandinsky during his time as a teacher at the Bauhaus, this work places an emphasis on geometric shapes.

To ArkDes

Bookshop

Main entrance to both Moderna museet and ArkDes (see p80).

Entrance level

Restaurangen Moderna Museet

Auditorium

★ **Monogram**
This work by Robert Rauschenberg (c.1956) includes an angora goat with painted nose and ears, a white car tyre and a collage with fragments of the word DADA. A self portrait?

Cinema

Middle level

Rafael Moneo

Rafael Moneo (b. 1937) is one of the world's leading contemporary architects. As a young architect he took part in the project to build the Sydney Opera House. His flair for adapting building design to sensitive surroundings was recognized in 1989, when he was chosen out of 211 entries as the winner of the competition to design the Moderna museet.

Luncheon on the Grass (1962) This sculpture group by Picasso, executed in sandblasted concrete by Carl Nesjar, stands in the museum garden.

Moderna museet's northern façade

VISITORS' CHECKLIST

Practical Information
Exercisplan.
Map 5 E3.
Tel 08-520 235 00.
Open 10am–6pm Wed, Thu,
Sat & Sun; 10am–8pm Tue;
6–8pm Fri. **Closed** Mon, 1 Jan,
Easter, midsummer eve, 24–25 &
31 Dec 🟩 Eng: summer. 🔲 ♿
🔲🔲🔲🔲
W modernamuseet.se

Transport
🚌 65. ⛴ Djurgårdsfärja.
🚇 Kungsträdgården.

Gallery Guide

*The large room on the entrance
level is used for temporary
exhibitions. Three rooms on the
same level have alternating
collections from three eras:
1900–45, 1946–70 and 1971–
present. The middle level has an
auditorium, a cinema and an
exhibition gallery. The lowest
level (not shown) has an entrance.*

Key

☐ Museum's own collections
☐ Temporary exhibitions
☐ Non-exhibition space

★ **The Child's Brain** (1914)
The surrealist Giorgio de Chirico
gave his work the title *The Ghost*,
but Louis Aragon renamed it in a
pamphlet about the artist's 1927
retrospective exhibition.

🟡 Blasieholmstorg

Map 4 C1. 🚇 Kungsträdgården.
🚌 2, 55, 62, 65, 76.

Two of the city's oldest palaces
are located in this square,
flanked by two bronze horses.
The palace at No. 8 was built in
the mid-17th century by Field
Marshal Gustav Horn. It was
rebuilt 100 years later, when it
acquired the character of an
18th-century French palace.
Foreign ambassadors and
ministers started to lodge here
when they visited the capital, so
it became known
as the Ministers'
Palace. Later it
became a base for
overseas admin-
istration and soon
earned its present
name of Utrikes-
ministerhotellet
(Foreign Ministry
Hotel). Parts of the
building are now used

**Bronze horse on
Blasieholmstorg**

as offices by the Musical Academy
and the Swedish Institute.

Bååtska Palatset stands
nearby at No. 6. Its restored
exterior dates from 1669 and
was designed by Tessin the
Elder. In 1876–7 it was partly
rebuilt by F W Scholander for
the Freemasons, who still have
their lodge here.

Another interesting complex
of buildings can be found on
the square at No. 10. The façade,
which faces on to Nybrokajen,
along the water's edge, is an
attractive example of the
Neo-Renaissance style of
the 1870s and 1880s.

🔟 Synagogan

Wahrendorffsgatan 3. **Map** 4 C1. **Tel**
08-587 858 00. 🚇 Kungsträdgården.
🚌 7, 55, 62, 65, 76. 🕗 8am Mon,
Thu, Fri; 5:30pm Sat; Hebrew, partly
Swedish. 🟩 15 Jun–4 Sep daily, and
on request. ♿ W jfst.se

It took most of the 1860s to
build the Conservative Jewish
community's synagogue on
what was once the seabed.
When it was inaugurated in
1870, the synagogue was
standing on 1,300 piles, which
had been driven down to a

Monument to the victims of the Holocaust
during World War II

depth of 15 m (50 ft). It is
built in what the architect,
F W Scholander, called "ancient
Eastern style".

Alongside this synagogue,
which can be visited on
guided tours during
the summer, is the
congregation's
assembly room and
library. Outside is a
monument erected in
1998 to the memory
of 8,000 victims of the
Holocaust whose
relations had been rescued
and taken to Sweden during
World War II.

There is also an Orthodox
synagogue in the city centre,
reached through the Jewish
Centre (Judiska Centret) on
Nybrogatan at No. 19.

🔴 Berns

Berzeli Park, Nackströmsgatan 8.
Map 3 D4. **Tel** 08-566 322 00. 🚇
Kungsträdgården, Östermalmstorg.
🚌 2, 55, 62, 65, 76. ♿ W berns.se
See also Where to Stay p159.

This has been one of Stockholm's most legendary
restaurants and entertainment
venues since 1863. Both salons,
with their stately galleries,
magnificent crystal chandeliers
and elegant mirrors, were
restored to their original
splendour by the British
designer Sir Terence Conran
to mark the new millennium.

Berns is one of Stockholm's
biggest restaurants, with
seating for 400 diners.
The gallery level, with its
beautifully decorated dining
rooms, was made famous by
August Strindberg's novel
The Red Room (1879).

❼ Nationalmuseum

The Nationalmuseum is a landmark on the southern side of Blasieholmen. The location by the Strömmen channel inspired the 19th-century German architect August Stüler to design a building in the Venetian and Florentine Renaissance styles. Completed in 1866, the museum houses Sweden's largest art collection, with 16,000 paintings and sculptures. In addition there are around 500,000 drawings and graphics from the 15th century to the early 20th century. Other treasures include a 500-year-old tapestry, and Scandinavia's largest collection of porcelain. The Nationalmuseum is currently closed for restoration work and is expected to reopen in 2018. Until then, items from the museum's collection will be making appearances at temporary exhibitions around the city.

The Love Lesson *(1716–17)*
Antoine Watteau is renowned for his so-called *fêtes galantes*, depicting young couples in playful mood.

★ The Conspiracy of the Batavians under Claudius Civilis
(1661–62) Originally intended for Amsterdam, Rembrandt depicts the Batavians' conspiracy against the Romans, symbolizing the Dutch liberation campaign against Spain.

Level 2

Atrium through levels 1 and 2

Chest of Drawers *(1780)*
This impressive piece of furniture was created by Georg Haupt, who was one of the foremost Swedish cabinet-makers of the 18th century.

Gravure gallery

Entrance

Entry for wheelchairs

David and Bathsheba *(1490)*
This tapestry from Brussels is created in the decorative medieval style, with pomegranates, faces and hands forming an exquisite work.

★ The Lady with the Veil
Alexander Roslin's elegant portrait (1769) is often considered a symbol for 18th-century Sweden.

The Upper Staircase
At the back is Carl Larsson's monumental mural *The Entry of King Gustav Vasa of Sweden in Stockholm 1523*. On the opposite wall is his *Midwinter Sacrifice*.

Level 1

Auditorium

Entrance level

Key to Floorplan
- Painting and sculpture
- Applied art and design
- Temporary exhibitions
- Non-exhibition space
- No admission

Amor and Psyche *(1787)*
Johan Tobias Sergel was the foremost sculptor of the Gustavian era. Inspired by Greek mythology, this piece shows a scene from the story of Amor and Psyche.

Gallery Guide
The Nationalmuseum is undergoing extensive renovations aimed at creating larger public spaces, and will be closed until 2018. During this time, a number of artworks from the Nationalmuseum's collections will be on display in rotating temporary exhibitions at the Royal Academy of Fine Arts (Konstakademien) at Fredsgatan 12. In addition, some other works from the collection will appear at other museums in the city. Check the website for more details.

⑫ Raoul Wallenbergs Torg

🚇 Östermalmstorg.
🚌 2, 55, 62, 65, 76.

This square is dedicated to Raoul Wallenberg (1912–unknown), who during World War II worked as a diplomat at the Swedish Embassy in Budapest. By using Swedish "protective passports" he helped a large number of Hungarian Jews to escape deportation to the Nazi concentration camps.

In 1945, when Budapest was liberated, he was imprisoned by the Soviets and, according to Soviet sources, he died in Moscow's Lubianka prison in 1947. His fate, however, has never really been satisfactorily explained.

The small square adjoins Berzelii Park and Nybroplan and faces the Nybrokajen waterfront. The definitive design of the square has been hotly debated because it is set in a sensitive architectural environment, but great efforts have been made to ensure that it remains a worthy memorial to Raoul Wallenberg.

⑬ Musikaliska

Nybrokajen 11. **Map** 4 C1. **Tel** 08-545 703 00. 🚇 Kungsträdgården, Östermalmstorg. 🚋 7. 🚌 2, 52, 62, 69, 76, 97. 🚢 Djurgårdsfärja.
Open for concerts (phone for details). ♿ **W** musikaliska.com

Constructed in the 1870s, this building facing the waters of Nybroviken once housed the Musical Academy. Its concert hall, opened in 1878, was the first in the country, and was used for the first presentations of the Nobel Prize in 1901. Designed in Neo-Renaissance style with cast-iron pillars, the hall has a royal box and galleries, and can seat up to 600 people.

After extensive restoration, it is now run by the state musical organization Rikskonserter, which has provided a much-needed concert stage for chamber, choral, jazz and folk music *(see p177)*.

DJURGÅRDEN

Once a royal hunting ground, Djurgården is an island right in the centre of Stockholm covered by a natural park. It has very few buildings with only around 800 permanent residents and forms part of Stockholm's Royal National City Park, the only one of its type in the world (see p123).

From 1580 parts of Djurgården were a royal animal reserve, where Johan III kept reindeer, red deer and moose. A century later the area was fenced off by Karl XI to be used for hunting. It developed into a popular recreational park during the 18th century, and in the time of troubador Carl Bellman (see p98) many inns appeared. The Gröna Lund funfair was established just a few decades before Artur Hazelius founded the fascinating outdoor museum of Skansen and Nordiska museet in around 1900. Today, there is a wealth of museums on Djurgården offering a mixture of nature, culture and entertainment. A royal connection survives in the beautiful Rosendal Palace, which has magnificent Empire-style decor.

Sights at a Glance

Museums & Galleries
2 Junibacken
3 *Nordiska museet pp92–3*
5 Spritmuseum
6 *Vasamuseet pp94–6*
7 Museifartygen
8 Biologiska museet
9 Liljevalchs Konsthall
10 ABBA Museum
13 *Skansen pp100–101*
15 Waldemarsudde
16 Thielska Galleriet

Historic Areas
12 Djurgårdsstaden & Beckholmen
14 Rosendals Slott & Trädgårdar

Memorials
4 Estoniaminnesvården

Bridges
1 Djurgårdsbron

Amusement Parks
11 Gröna Lund

Restaurants pp166–71
1 Hasselbacken
2 Solliden Skansen
3 Spritmuseum Restaurant
4 Ulla Windbladh
5 Villa Godthem

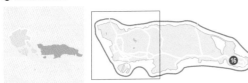

See also Street Finder pp206–18

0 metres 500
0 yards 500

◀ Reindeer at Skansen

For map symbols see back flap

Street-by-Street: Around Lejonslätten

Lions were kept for animal-baiting up to 1792 on the spot where Nordiska museet now stands, hence the name of this area – Lejonslätten (The Lion Plain). Today visitors can safely stroll along the waterfront, look at the boats and take in the panorama across to Nybroviken, Skeppsholmen and the heights of Södermalm.

This area also offers several sights of cultural interest. The majestic Nordiska museet, built in Neo-Renaissance style, reflects Swedish cultural history over almost 500 years. In Vasamuseet lies the beautifully restored 17th-century warship, while two more vintage ships are moored outside. Nearby, Junibacken brings Pippi Longstocking and other favourite children's book characters imaginatively to life.

❷ Junibacken
This fun place for children is dedicated to the author Astrid Lindgren. It also features characters from stories by other authors.

❻ ★ Vasamuseet
The royal warship *Vasa* was salvaged after 300 years in the depths of Stockholm's harbour. It is now housed in Stockholm's most popular museum.

LADUGÅRDSLANDSVIKEN

GALÄRPARKEN

❼ Museifartygen
Alongside Vasamuseet are two faithful vessels: the ice-breaker *Sankt Erik* and the lightship *Finngrundet*.

| 0 metres | 100 |
| 0 yards | 100 |

Key

— Suggested route

❹ Estoniaminnesvården
Near the Galär cemetery, a national memorial has been erected to the 852 people who lost their lives in the *Estonia* ferry disaster on the night of 27–28 September 1994. The ferry sank on its way from Tallinn to Stockholm.

❶ Djurgårdsbron
There has been a bridge to Djurgården since 1661. The current bridge was built in 1896 to mark the Stockholm Exhibition the following year.

Locator Map
See Street Finder maps 5, 6 & 7

Blå Porten is a copy of one of the many blue-painted gateways once set in a 20-km (12-mile) fence around the former royal hunting reserve.

Strandvägen

DJURGÅRDSBRUNNSVIKEN

Kaptensudden

Lejonslätten

DJURGÅRDSVÄGEN

Djurgårds-brunnsbron

ROSENDALSVÄGEN

DJURGÅRDSVÄGEN

Spritmuseum

Galärkyrkogården
(cemetery)

❸ ★ Nordiska museet
Artur Hazelius, creator of Skansen, also founded Nordiska museet, which portrays Swedish cultural history from the 1520s to the present day.

Villa Lusthusporten
was built in the Italian style during the 1880s.

❽ Biologiska museet
Swedish fauna is shown in realistic natural settings in this charming old museum.

Karl XV's equestrian statue
by Charles Friberg was erected in 1909. The king (1826–72) was a great patron of the arts.

A colourful scene from one of Astrid Lindgren's stories, seen from the mini-train

❶ Djurgårdsbron

Map 3 F4. 🚌 44, 69, 76. 🚋 7.
🛳 Djurgårdsfärja.

The Djurgården bridge came into use a few days before the major Art and Industrial Exhibition opened in Stockholm in May 1897. Made at the Bergsund plant in Södermalm, the bridge is richly ornamented with cast-iron railings in the form of stylized water plants. At that time Sweden was in union with Norway, and King Oscar II's monogram and motto "The sister nations' wellbeing" can be seen on the central span. The capital's patron saint, Erik, is depicted on the pillar supports among sea gods and water lilies.

Wrought-iron lamps and sculptures portraying mytho-logical gods, created by Rolf Adlersparre, adorn the four granite pillars at either end. On the Strandvägen side, the pillars show Heimdal, the watchman, and Frigga, the wife of Oden. On the opposite side are Thor, with his hammer,

and Freja, the goddess of love and fertility.

The gate of Blå Porten, just to the left on the Djurgården side, recalls the time during the 17th century when the island was a royal hunting ground, and the surrounding fence was punctuated by blue-painted wooden gateways. This gate, decorated with Oscar I's monogram, was made from cast iron in 1849.

❷ Junibacken

Galärvarvsvägen. **Map** 5 F1.
Tel 08-587 230 00. 🚌 44, 69. 🚋 7.
🛳 Djurgårdsfärja. **Open** Jan–Apr: 10am–5pm Tue–Sun; May–Aug: 10am–5pm daily; Sep–Dec: 10am–5pm Tue–Sun. 🅿 ♿ ⚗
🅿 📷 🌐 junibacken.se

You can find them all here – Pippi Longstocking, Mardie, Karlsson on the Roof, Emil, Nils Karlsson Pyssling, Ronja the robber's daughter, the Lionheart Brothers and many more characters from Astrid Lindgren's children's books. In accordance with the popular novelist's wishes, visitors can also meet the creations of other

Swedish children's authors. When she heard about Staffan Götestam's project for a children's cultural centre she was adamant it should not be just an Astrid Lindgren museum.

Nevertheless Junibacken is still something of a tribute to the much-loved author. It was officially opened by the Royal Family in the summer of 1996 and has become one of the city's most popular tourist attractions. A mini-train takes visitors from a mock-up of the station at Vimmerby (the author's home town) to meet some of her characters, finishing with a visit to Pippi's home in Villekulla Cottage, where children can play in the different rooms. There is also a well-stocked children's bookshop and a restaurant.

❸ Nordiska museet

See pp92–3.

❹ Estonia-minnesvården

Galärkyrkogården. **Map** 5 F2. 🚌 44.
🛳 Djurgårdsfärja.

On the night of 27–28 September 1994 the ferry MS *Estonia* sank in the Baltic on its journey from Tallinn to Stockholm with the loss of 852 lives. The deceased came from many countries including Sweden, Estonia, Latvia, Russia, Finland, Norway, Denmark, Germany, Lithuania, Morocco, the Netherlands, France, the

Astrid Lindgren and Pippi Longstocking

Astrid Lindgren wrote around 100 children's books, which have been translated into 74 languages, making her one of the world's most-read children's authors. Publishers turned down her first book about Pippi Longstocking, but she went on to win a children's book competition with it two years later, in 1945. Her headstrong and tough character Pippi soon won the hearts of children worldwide.

Following Lindgren's death in 2002, the Swedish government created the world's largest prize for children's literature in her name.

Astrid Lindgren

One of the beautifully decorated pillars supporting Djurgårdsbron

Museifartygen: the lightship *Finngrundet* and ice-breaker *Sankt Erik* outside Vasamuseet

United Kingdom, Canada, Belarus, Ukraine and Nigeria. Their names and their fate will never be forgotten.

So reads the inscription on this national memorial to the victims of the *Estonia* disaster adjoining the cemetery of Galärkyrkogården. It was designed by the Polish artist Miroslaw Balka (b. 1958), who created it together with the two landscape architects Anders Jönsson and Thomas Andersson.

Unveiled on 28 September 1997, the memorial is made of blasted granite and forms a roofless, triangular room with 11-m (36-ft) long sides and a height of 2.5 m (just over 8 ft). The exact position of where the ferry sank is given on a metal ring around a tree in the triangle. With relatives' consent, the names of most of the dead have been carved in the walls.

❺ Spritmuseum

Galärskjulen, Djurgården, Djurgårdsvägen 38. **Map** 6 A3. **Tel** 08-121 313 00. Ⓣ Karlaplan. Spårvagn City. **Open** 10am–6pm daily in summer; 10am–5pm daily in winter. 🔲 🔲 🔲 🔲
W spritmuseum.se

The Museum of Spirits looks at the unique history of alcoholic beverages in Sweden. Spanning two floors, the museum is the only one of its kind in the country

and boasts an impressive array of exhibits. The highlight of the museum is the Absolut Art Collection, which includes over 800 works by famous international artists such as Andy Warhol, Keith Haring, Damien Hirst and Louise Bourgeois. The works were produced in conjunction with the advertising campaigns that helped make Absolut one of the best-known brands in the industry. It is the first time these works have been united under one roof.

The museum is housed in Stockholm's historic Galärskjulen, or "galley sheds", which date from the 18th century. The sheds were modelled on a Venetian design and were built for the galleys of the Royal Navy, which were stored on land in these buildings. Visitors can dine at the museum's elegant fine dining restaurant, which serves dishes made from seasonal, locally sourced organic produce.

❻ Vasamuseet

See pp94–6.

Snaps label, Spritmuseum

❼ Museifartygen

Galärvarvet. **Map** 5 F2. **Tel** 08-519 549 00. 🚌 44. 🚊 7 ⛴ Djurgårdsfärja. **Open** 22 May–30 Aug: 11am–6pm daily; also during various public holidays, ring for details. 🔲 🔲 🔲
W sjohistoriska.se

The two vintage ships moored alongside Vasamuseet are both fine examples of the ships built to handle various tasks in Swedish waters during the early 20th century. The lightship *Finngrundet*, built in 1903, used to be anchored during the ice-free season on the Finngrund banks in the southern Gulf of Bothnia. In the 1960s lightships started to be replaced by permanent automatic lighthouses, so *Finngrundet* was withdrawn from service and became a museum ship. At 31 m (102 ft) long and 6.85 m (22 ft 6 in) wide, with a draught of 3.1 m (10 ft 2 in), she was designed for a crew of eight. The light had a range of 11 nautical miles.

Built in 1915, *Sankt Erik* was Sweden's first seagoing ice-breaker. This classic Baltic model slides up over the ice and crushes it. She also has a system that enables the ship to be rocked sideways to loosen the ice and widen the channel. One of the two three-cylinder engines is Sweden's largest working marine steam engine. The ice-breaker is 60 m (197 ft) long and 17 m (56 ft) wide and needs a crew of 30.

❸ Nordiska museet

Resembling an extravagant Renaissance castle, Nordiska museet portrays everyday life in Sweden from the 1520s to the present day. It was created by Artur Hazelius (1833–1901), who was also the founder of Skansen (see pp100–101). In 1872, he started to collect objects that would remind future generations of the old Nordic farming culture.

The present museum, designed by Isak Gustaf Clason, was opened in 1907. Today it has more than 1.5 million exhibits in its collection, with everything from luxury clothing and priceless jewellery to everyday items, furniture and children's toys, and replicas of period homes.

The Proposal
This painting in the Homes and Interiors section, is by Knut Ekwall (1843–1912) and depicts a town flat in the 1880s. The room is heavily decorated with objets d'art, ornaments and textiles.

Level 3

Corridor to staircase

Level 2 (Main Hall)

State Bedchamber from Ulvsunda Castle
At the end of the 17th century, the lord of the manor at Ulvsunda accommodated prominent guests in this prestigious bedchamber.

Ground floor

Key to Floorplan

- ☐ Folk art
- ☐ Small Objects 1700–1900
- ☐ Homes and Interiors
- ☐ Table Settings, Traditions
- ☐ Strindberg Collection
- ☐ Jewellery
- ☐ Sápmi exhibition
- ☐ Photographic exhibition
- ☐ Temporary exhibitions
- ☐ Non-exhibition space

Obelisk with an inscription meaning: "The day may dawn when not even all our gold is enough to form a picture of a bygone era."

Main entrance

Entrance

Gallery Guide

The museum has four floors. From the entrance, stairs lead up to the temporary exhibitions in the Main Hall. On the ground level is the Reference Room. Level 3 has the Strindberg Collection, Jewellery, Table Settings and Traditions. Sections on Folk Art, Homes and Interiors, Small Objects, and the Sami (Sápmi) People and Culture are on Level 4.

★ Table Settings
In the mid-17th century, table settings were a feast for the eyes. A swan is the centrepiece at this meal.

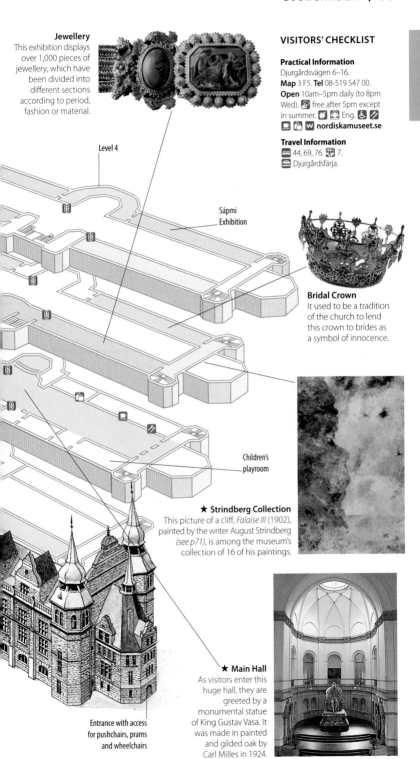

Jewellery
This exhibition displays over 1,000 pieces of jewellery, which have been divided into different sections according to period, fashion or material.

Level 4

Sápmi Exhibition

VISITORS' CHECKLIST

Practical Information
Djurgårdsvägen 6–16.
Map 3 F5. **Tel** 08-519 547 00.
Open 10am–5pm daily (to 8pm Wed). 🆓 free after 5pm except in summer. 🎟 📷 Eng. ♿ 🚻
📱 🎁 🌐 **nordiskamuseet.se**

Travel Information
🚌 44, 69, 76. 🚊 7.
⛴ Djurgårdsfärja.

Bridal Crown
It used to be a tradition of the church to lend this crown to brides as a symbol of innocence.

Children's playroom

★ Strindberg Collection
This picture of a cliff, *Falaise III* (1902), painted by the writer August Strindberg (*see p71*), is among the museum's collection of 16 of his paintings.

★ Main Hall
As visitors enter this huge hall, they are greeted by a monumental statue of King Gustav Vasa. It was made in painted and gilded oak by Carl Milles in 1924.

Entrance with access for pushchairs, prams and wheelchairs

❻ Vasamuseet

After a maiden voyage of just 1,300 m (4,265 ft) in calm weather, the royal warship *Vasa* capsized in Stockholm's harbour on 10 August 1628. About 30 people went down with what was supposed to be the pride of the Navy, only 100 m (330 ft) off the southernmost point of Djurgården. Most of the guns were salvaged from the vessel in the 17th century, and it was not until 1956 that a marine archaeologist's persistent search led to the rediscovery of *Vasa*. After a complex salvage operation followed by a 17-year conservation programme, the city's most popular museum was opened in June 1990, less than a nautical mile from the scene of the disaster.

Gun-Port Lion
More than 200 carved ornaments and 500 sculpted figures decorate *Vasa*.

★ Lion Figurehead
King Gustav II Adolf, who commissioned *Vasa*, was known as the Lion of the North. So a springing lion was the obvious choice for the figurehead. It is 4 m (13 ft) long and weighs 450 kg (990 lb).

Emperor Titus
Replica carvings of 20 Roman emperors stand on parade on *Vasa*.

Entrance

KEY

① Information desk

② To the restaurant

③ **The main mast** was originally 52 m (170 ft) high.

④ **Reconstruction** of the upper gun deck

⑤ **A model** of the Vasa to a scale of 1:10

⑥ Main film auditorium

Bronze Cannon
More than 50 of *Vasa*'s 64 original cannons were salvaged already in the 17th century. Three 11-kg (24-lb) bronze cannons are on display in the museum.

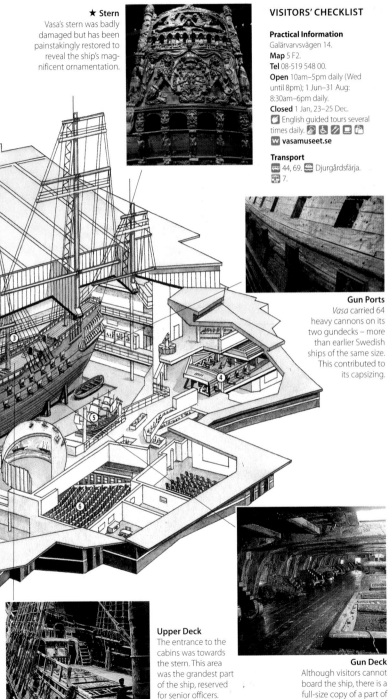

★ Stern
Vasa's stern was badly damaged but has been painstakingly restored to reveal the ship's magnificent ornamentation.

VISITORS' CHECKLIST

Practical Information
Galärvarvsvägen 14.
Map 5 F2.
Tel 08-519 548 00.
Open 10am–5pm daily (Wed until 8pm); 1 Jun–31 Aug: 8:30am–6pm daily.
Closed 1 Jan, 23–25 Dec.
🎧 English guided tours several times daily. 🧱 ♿ 🚻 🖥 📷
W vasamuseet.se

Transport
🚌 44, 69. 🚢 Djurgårdsfärja.
🚋 7.

Gun Ports
Vasa carried 64 heavy cannons on its two gundecks – more than earlier Swedish ships of the same size. This contributed to its capsizing.

Upper Deck
The entrance to the cabins was towards the stern. This area was the grandest part of the ship, reserved for senior officers. Part of the original mainmast can be seen on the right.

Gun Deck
Although visitors cannot board the ship, there is a full-size copy of a part of the upper gun deck, which gives a good idea of what conditions were like on board.

Exploring the Vasamuseet

The Royal Warship *Vasa* has been restored to 98 per cent of its original appearance. The low salt content of the water saved the ship's timber – which came from thousands of oaks – from attacks by shipworms. The hull was all present, but fitting the 13,500 loose pieces together was like doing a jigsaw puzzle without a picture, as there were no detailed designs to follow. The salvage operation produced more than 700 sculpted figures and carved ornaments, as well as many everyday items.

A sailor's simple belongings found on *Vasa*

Carved soldiers on *Vasa*'s stern

The Ship

In 1628 *Vasa* was potentially one of the world's mightiest ships. It was able to carry 64 cannons and 300 soldiers (out of a total 450 men on board). *Vasa* was equipped for both traditional close combat and for artillery battles. From its high stern it would have been possible to fire down on smaller ships. The musketeers had shooting galleries for training, and on the upper deck were so-called "storm pieces", erected as protection against musketry fire.

All this may appear very impressive, but it is uncertain exactly what the ship's role would have been if it had survived. The main task of the Swedish navy at that time had been to transport weapons and soldiers as well as to protect shipping or block harbours. It seems doubtful that *Vasa* would have been suitable for these roles.

The Imagery of Power

The warship's many figures and elaborately carved ornaments formed an important part of that era's language of power and were designed as a type of war propaganda. Many of the builders and carpenters who worked in the shipyard that built *Vasa* came from Holland, while most of the sculptors, whose work was typical of the late Renaissance and early Baroque eras, came from Germany. The German woodcarver Mårten Redtmer made most of the ship's larger sculptures. Created out of oak, pine and lime wood, the figures were inspired mainly by Greek mythology, as well as the Bible and 17th-century Swedish royal personalities.

Life on Board

Vasa's first destination on its maiden voyage, with about 150 people on board, was intended to be the Älvsnabben naval base in the southern Stockholm archipelago, where 300 soldiers were to embark. The ship was fully equipped, and the divers were able to recover many everyday items, including food and drink. But when the chief diver, Per Edvin Fälting, tasted the 333-year-old butter from a tub made of wood and tin, sores erupted around his mouth.

The museum has full-scale models of a part of *Vasa*'s upper gun deck and the Admiral's cabin. The sailors and soldiers had to eat and sleep on deck among the cannons. No wonder that in the 17th century more died from illness than in battle.

In a fascinating exhibition of original artifacts, you can see the medical equipment that was used, an officer's backgammon game, some of the sailors' wooden spoons and plates and the officers' dinner service in pewter and earthenware. The divers also found about 4,000 coins, made mainly from copper, and a chest still neatly packed with hats, clothing and other personal belongings. Replicas of some of these artifacts are on sale in the museum shop.

The Salvage Operation

The marine archaeologist Anders Franzén had been looking for *Vasa* for many years. On 25 August 1956 his patience was rewarded, when he brought up a piece of blackened oak on his plumb line. From the autumn of 1957, it took divers 2 years to clear tunnels under the hull for the lifting cables. The first lift with six cables was a success, after which *Vasa* was lifted in 16 stages into shallower water. Thousands of plugs were then inserted into holes left by rusted iron bolts. The final lift started on 24 April 1961, and on 4 May *Vasa* was finally towed into dry dock.

Vasa in dry dock after being salvaged between 1956 and 1961

8 Biologiska museet

Lejonslätten. **Map** 6 A3. **Tel** 08-442 82 15. 🚌 44. 🚋 7. ⭕ Apr–Sep: 11am–4pm daily; Oct–Mar: noon–3pm Tue–Fri, 11am–3pm Sat & Sun. 📷 by arrangement. 🎨 📷
🌐 **biologiskamuseet.com**

The architect Agi Lindegren, commissioned to design the Museum of Biology in the 1890s, based his plans on the simple lines of the medieval Norwegian stave churches.

The man behind the museum was the zoologist, hunter and conservationist Gustaf Kolthoff (1845–1913). In 1892, he persuaded the industrialist C F Liljevalch – who later financed the nearby art gallery – to form a company whose aim was to "maintain a biological museum to include all the Scandinavian mammals and birds as stuffed specimens in natural surroundings". The result was the world's first museum of its type. Many of the creatures are shown against a diorama background, with about 300 species of Scandinavian birds and land mammals in their respective biotypes.

9 Liljevalchs Konsthall

Djurgårdsvägen 60. **Map** 6 A3. **Tel** 08-508 313 30. 🚌 44, 47. 🚋 7. 🚢 Djurgårdsfärja. **Open** 11am–8pm Tue & Thu, 11am–5pm Wed & Fri–Sun. **Closed** Mon. 📷 2:15pm Mon–Fri. 🎨 ♿ 📷 📷
🌐 **liljevalchs.se**

Constructed thanks to a donation from the industrialist Carl Fredrik Liljevalch, this heritage building is regarded as one of northern Europe's most attractive art galleries. It was

designed by the architect Carl G Bergsten and built in 1913–16 in Neo-Classical style.

Liljevalch's bust, sculpted in granite by Christian Eriksson, is set in the northern wall of the building. On a high column outside the entrance is Carl Milles' sculpture *The Archer*.

The gallery features Liljevalch's collections of Swedish, Nordic and international art from the 20th century, as well as handicrafts dating from the same period. Every year, four or five major exhibitions are staged, including the Spring Salon, a major attraction for Stockholm art-lovers. The exhibitions are complemented by guided tours, lectures, debates and concerts. Children and young people have a special section, where they can create their own works of art from various different types of materials.

10 ABBA Museum

Djurgårdsvägen 68. **Map** 6 A3. 🚌 44. 🚋 7. 🚢 Djurgårdsfärja. **Open** 30 Apr–30 Aug: 10am–8pm daily. Last slot 6:30pm; 31 Aug–13 Dec: 10am–6pm Mon–Tue. Last slot 4:30pm. 10am–8pm Wed–Thu. Last slot 6:30pm; 14 Dec–31 Dec: 10am–6pm Mon–Sun; Fri–Sun 10am–6pm. Last slot 4:30pm. 🎨 📷
📷 📷 ♿ 🌐 **abbathemuseum.com**

This museum is dedicated to ABBA, Sweden's best-known pop band. In addition to stage costumes, gold records and an audio guide with fascinating insights into life as a band, the museum delivers a delightfully interactive experience. Visitors can audition to be ABBA's fifth member at a perfect replica of the band's Polar Studio and record a music video. There is also a piano that is connected to Benny Andersson's

Gröna Lund funfair seen from Kastellholmen

own piano; when the composer tinkles the ivories, the museum piano also starts playing.

11 Gröna Lund

Lilla Allmänna Gränd 9. **Map** 6 A4. **Tel** 010-708 91 00. 🚌 44. 🚋 7. 🚢 Djurgårdsfärja. **Open** late Apr–mid-Sep: opening hours vary. 🎨 ♿ 📷 📷 🌐 **gronalund.com**

A tavern called Gröna Lund (Green Grove) existed on this site in the 18th century, and it was one of the haunts of the renowned troubadour Carl Michael Bellman *(see p98)*. Jakob Schultheis used the tavern's name for the modest-sized funfair that he opened here in 1883 with a two-level horse-drawn roundabout as the main attraction. Today Gröna Lund is Sweden's oldest amusement park, with 30 rides ranging from child-friendly to thrillingly fast.

The 130-day season is short but hectic. However, Gröna Lund draws about 1.4 million visitors each year. Its exciting attractions include a haunted house, a ghost train and an 80-m (262-ft) free-fall tower. There is also a wooden roller coaster that is said to be the best of its type in the world.

The amusement park boasts 13 restaurants and cafés, three stages, a cabaret restaurant with space for 600 guests, and a 200-seat theatre. The main stage has hosted world stars such as Bob Marley, who, in 1980, played to a record audience of 32,000.

Liljevalchs Konsthall's spacious main exhibition hall

⑫ Djurgårdsstaden & Beckholmen

Map 6 A4. 🚌 44. 🚋 7. 🚢 Djurgårdsfärja.

Behind Gröna Lund amusement park lies Djurgårdsstaden, a tranquil oasis of wooden houses, providing flats for about 200 people. The area was originally developed from a town plan drawn up around the Admiralty churchyard in 1736, to house workmen at the nearby Johan Lampas shipyards.

When the Djurgården shipyard took over this area in 1768, the carpenters were given the opportunity to buy their homes. The company then erected the majestic two-storey stone building at Lilla Allmänna Gränd 15–17 with offices, employees' homes and a chapel.

Other buildings on this street also date from the 18th century such as Apotekshuset, the shipyard manager's residence, and Mjölnargården, now belonging to the amusement park. Several two-storey wooden houses were built on the churchyard, which had fallen into disuse in the 19th century.

At the junction of Östra Varvsgränd and Breda Gatan is the house of the ship's carpenter Sven Månsson. Enlarged in 1749, the building still looks much as it did then, with original tiled stoves and wood fires. It is now used by the Djurgården Local Culture Society.

Lying just to the south of Djurgårdsstaden is the island of Beckholmen, which, during the

Well-preserved wooden homes in Djurgårdsstaden

The Karl Johan-style Rosendals Slott on Djurgården

17th century, was used as a warehouse for commercial goods. It was also used to store tar and pitch. The fire hazard meant that such dangerous items could not be stored any closer to the city centre.

In 1848 the Wholesalers' Society decided to build a shipping repair yard on the island, and two docks were blasted out of the solid rock on the southern side. They were later widened to accommodate more wharves. In 1917 another large dock was opened, named after King Gustaf V, and the two were used by the Navy and the Finnboda shipbuilding firm.

Door lintel, Rosendals Slott's Gold Room

The fleet moved to the island of Muskö in 1969, and Finnboda remained until 1982. The docks and houses form an unusual industrial setting. The 18th-century tar inspector's residence, the dockmaster's 19th-century home, and workmen's cottages from the 1890s are well preserved.

⑬ Skansen

See pp100–101.

⑭ Rosendals Slott & Trädgårdar

Rosendalsvägen. **Map** 6 C3. 🚋 7. Palace **Tel** 08-402 61 30. **Open** for guided tours Jun–Aug: Tue–Sun; 1 Sep–27 Sep every hour (noon–3pm Sat & Sun). 📷 every hour noon–3pm. ♿ 🅿 Gardens **Open** all year. 📷 ♿ summer. 🌐 **royalcourt.se**

What was considered elsewhere as Empire style was named Karl Johan style in Sweden after King Karl XIV Johan (1818–44). One of the best examples is Rosendal Palace, built as a summer retreat for the king. Constructed in the 1820s and designed by Fredrik Blom, a prolific architect of the era, the palace was one of Sweden's first prefabricated homes. In 1913, it was opened to the public as a museum devoted to the life and times of Karl XIV Johan and represents a pioneering work of historic restoration.

The decor is magnificent, with Swedish-made furniture and lavish textiles in wonderful colours. The carpeting and curtains are worth a visit in themselves. The dining room is fitted out in heavily woven

An Immortal Troubadour

Carl Michael Bellman (1740–95) was a much-loved troubadour. Gustav III gave him a job as secretary of a lottery, but he was best known around Stockholm's many taverns – particularly on Djurgården. His works about the drunken watchmaker Jean Fredman and his contemporaries (*Fredman's Epistles and Fredman's Songs*) have never lost their popularity and form part of Sweden's musical heritage. A bust of Bellman was unveiled on Djurgården in 1829 in the presence of Queen Desideria.

Bust of Bellman by J N Byström (1829)

fabric to create the impression of being in a tent. Tiled stoves are everywhere, along with some grandiose artifacts and delightful details. In front of the palace is a large bowl made in porphyry from Karl XIV Johan's own workshops at Älvdalen in central Sweden.

Close to the palace is Rosendals Trädgårdar, a biodynamic market garden managed by a foundation since 1984. Its aim is not just to use biodynamic cultivation methods but also to run courses, lectures and exhibitions. Plants are available to buy at the shop, and there is a café.

⓯ Waldemarsudde

Prins Eugens Väg 6. **Map** 6 C4.
Tel 08-545 837 00. 🚌 7. **Open** 11am–5pm Tue–Sun. 🌐 📷 ♿ 📷 🖥 📷 **w** waldemarsudde.se

Prince Eugen's Waldemarsudde, which passed into State ownership after his death in 1947, is one of Sweden's most visited art museums. The prince was trained as a military officer but became a successful artist and was one of the leading landscape painters of his generation. He produced monumental paintings for Kungliga Operan, Kungliga Dramatiska Teatern and Rådhuset. Among his own works hanging in Waldemarsudde, his former home, are three of his most prized paintings: *Spring* (1891),

The Old Castle (1893) and *The Cloud* (1896).

Based on works by his contemporaries, the collection represents early 20th-century Swedish art with names such as Oscar Björck, Carl Fredrik Hill, Richard Bergh, Nils Kreuger, Eugène Jansson, Bruno Liljefors and Anders Zorn.

Prince Eugen was a generous patron to the next generation – for example, the group known as "The Young Ones" – so works by younger artists including Isaac Grünewald, Einar Jolin, Sigrid Hjertén and Leander Engström are also in the collection. Sculptors of the same era are well represented, particularly Per Hasselberg whose works can be seen in the gallery and the park.

Along with the architect Ferdinand Boberg, Prince Eugen drew up the sketches for the house, completed in 1905. The same architect was called in later to plan the gallery, which was finished in 1913. This now includes parts of the collection of some 2,000 works, as well as the Prince's own paintings.

The guest apartments remain largely unchanged to this day, and the two upper floors with the Prince's studio at the top are used for temporary exhibitions.

Hornsgatan (1902) by Eugène Jansson, in Thielska Galleriet

⓰ Thielska Galleriet

Sjötullsbacken 6–8. **Map** 7 F4.
Tel 08-662 58 84. 🚌 69. **Open** noon–5pm Tue–Sun (to 8pm Thu). 🌐 by appt. 📷 🖥 **w** thielska-galleriet.se

When the magnificent apartments of the banker Ernest Thiel (1860–1947) on Strandvägen started to overflow with his excellent collection of contemporary paintings, he commissioned the well-known architect Ferdinand Boberg to design a dignified villa on Djurgården.

However, during World War I Thiel lost most of his fortune. In 1924, the State bought his collection, mostly covering Nordic art from the late 19th and early 20th centuries, and opened Thielska Galleriet in his villa two years later.

Thiel was regarded as something of a rebel in the banking world and he was particularly fond of works by painters in the Artists' Union, which had been formed in 1886 to counter the influence of the traditionalist Konstakademien (*see p68*).

There are paintings by all the major Swedish artists who formed an artists' colony at Grèz-sur-Loing, south of Paris, such as Carl Larsson, Bruno Liljefors, Karl Nordström and August Strindberg. And there are paintings by Eugène Jansson, Anders Zorn and Prince Eugen, as well as wooden figures by Axel Petersson and sculptures by Christian Eriksson. Thiel also acquired works by foreign artists, not least his good friend Edvard Munch.

Prince Eugen's Waldemarsudde, seen from the water

⑬ Skansen

The world's first open-air museum, Skansen was opened by Artur Hazelius in 1891 to show an increasingly industrialized society how people once lived. About 150 houses and farm buildings were assembled from all over Sweden, portraying the life of both peasants and landed gentry, as well as Lapp *(Same)* culture. The Town Quarter has wooden urban dwellings and crafts including glass-blowing and printing. Nordic flora and fauna feature every-where, with bears, wolves and moose in natural habitat enclosures and more exotic creatures in the Aquarium. Many festivals are celebrated in Skansen *(see pp28–31).*

★ Älvros Farmstead
The living room in this 500-year-old wooden cottage from Härjedalen shows the tools for daily tasks.

Swedenborg's Pavilion
Set in the rose garden is the pavilion that used to belong to the philo-sopher and scientist Emanuel Swedenborg (1688–1772).

★ Town Quarter
Original Stockholm wooden town houses replicate a medium-sized 19th-century town. Glass-blowers, bakers and other craftsmen demonstrate their traditional skills in restored workshops.

KEY

① Skansen Aquarium

② Solliden stage

③ Hazelius Entrance

④ **A cable car** runs from the Hazelius Entrance.

⑤ **Tingsvallen/Bollnästorget** is the venue for the Christmas market and Midsummer celebrations.

⑥ Wolves

⑦ Skåne farmstead

⑧ **Skogaholm Manor** The main building in this Carlovingian manor estate (1680) comes from the Skogaholm ironworks village in central Sweden.

Main entrance

**Vastveit
Storehouse**
This storehouse from
eastern Norway was
built in the 14th cen-
tury and is Skansen's
oldest building.

VISITORS' CHECKLIST

Practical Information
Djurgårdsslätten 49.
Map 6 B3.
Tel 08-442 80 00.
Open 10am–5pm daily (to 8pm
in summer). **Closed** 24 Dec.
Seglora Church 11am Sun.
Jun–Aug. **skansen.se**

Transport
44. 7. Djurgårdsfärja.

★ Bear Pit
Skansen's brown bears are firm
favourites, not least in April,
when the new cubs emerge.

Seglora Church
This shingle-roofed wooden church
was built in 1729–30 in western
Sweden and has an interesting
interior decor with a pulpit that
is even older than the church itself.
It is popular for weddings.

Hornborga Cottage
A timber cottage with a
straw and peat roof from
western Sweden shows
how poorer people lived
in the 19th century.

| 0 metres | 100 |
| 0 yards | 100 |

MALMARNA & FURTHER AFIELD

As Stockholm started to grow, the heart of the city, Gamla Stan, became cramped and building spread out to the surrounding areas, known as "Malmarna" (the "ore hills"). Parts of these now make up present-day Stockholm.

Södermalm came into the ownership of the city in 1436. Much of Stockholm's old charm can still be found in the areas around Fjällgatan, Mosebacke and Mariaberget. To the north, the Norrmalm area expanded rapidly and became known as Stockholm's northern suburb in the 17th century. Much of Vasastan is a residential area, but in recent years it has become popular because of its wide choice of restaurants. The once-rural Östermalm was transformed in the late

19th century into an affluent residential area with grand, wide boulevards, contrasting with the 1930s Functionalist style of the adjoining Gärdet district. This is the location of some of Stockholm's most important museums, including Historiska museet, with its impressive Gold Room, and Folkens Museum Etnografiska.

To the west is Kungsholmen, the centre for local government, with distinguished buildings such as Stadshuset (the City Hall) and Rådhuset (the Law Court). The Royal National City Park (Ekoparken), the first of its kind in the world, is a green area of ecological and cultural interest surrounding the city and reaching into its central districts.

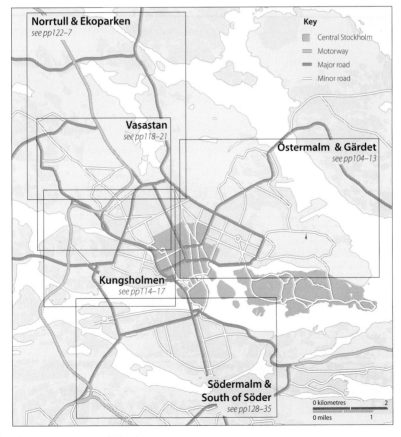

Norrtull & Ekoparken
see pp122–7

Key

  Central Stockholm
  Motorway
  Major road
  Minor road

Vasastan
see pp118–21

Östermalm & Gärdet
see pp104–13

Kungsholmen
see pp114–17

Södermalm & South of Söder
see pp128–35

0 kilometres 2
0 miles 1

◀ Picturesque night-time view of Södermalm

Östermalm & Gärdet

The four wide boulevards, Strandvägen, Karlavägen, Narvavägen and Valhallavägen, were created around 1870–80 as part of the development of Östermalm into one of the city's most affluent residential districts, adjoining the extensive green area of Ladugårdsgärde. In addition to embassies and the headquarters of Swedish Radio and TV, four leading museums are located in this green oasis, as well as Kaknästornet. The area between Östermalm and the former military exercise grounds was developed in the 1930s with housing in the clean lines of the Functionalist style typical of the period.

Housing at Karlaplan, built in the late 19th century

Sights at a Glance

1. Strandvägen
2. *Historiska museet (see pp106–7)*
3. Karlavägen
4. Sveriges Radio och TV
5. Berwaldhallen
6. Diplomatstaden
7. Sjöhistoriska museet
8. Tekniska museet
9. Gärdet
10. Etnografiska museet
11. Kaknästornet
12. Ladugårdsgärde
13. Filmhuset
14. Tessinparken
15. Försvarshögskolan
16. Stadion
17. Tekniska Högskolan
18. Engelbrektskyrkan

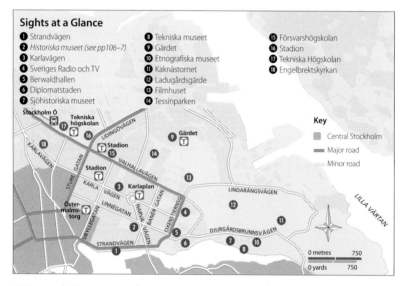

Key

▓ Central Stockholm
▬ Major road
··· Minor road

0 metres 750
0 yards 750

❶ Strandvägen

Map 5 E1. 🚌 69, 76. 🚇 Östermalmstorg, Karlaplan. 🚊 7.

In the early 1900s Stockholm's ten richest citizens lived in palatial new houses along Strandvägen. Seven of them were wholesale merchants. Up to 1897's major exhibition on Djurgården, the hilly and muddy former Ladugårdslands Strandgata had been moving towards the goal of becoming "a street, the like of which will not be found anywhere else in Europe". It was a long process. Even after all the stately buildings had been completed, the wooden quay erected in the 1860s was something of an eyesore. It was still used up to the 1940s by boats bringing fire wood from the archipelago islands.

All the same, Strandvägen and its three rows of lime trees soon became the elegant boulevard envisaged and, then as now, it was a popular place for admiring the elegant façades, watching the boats and to see and be seen.

The financiers behind the housing projects of the early 1900s were wealthy and called on the best architects, including I G Clason (1856–1930). Clason was influenced by Italian and French Renaissance styles for his work on No. 19–21 (Thaveniuska Huset) and No. 29–35 (Bünsowska Huset), where he designed gateways made of ship's timbers. No. 55 (Von Rosenska Palatset) was also created by him.

Strandvägen with stately houses and boats along the quayside

❷ Historiska museet

See pp106–7.

❸ Karlavägen

Map 3 E3. Ⓣ Karlaplan, Stadion.
🚌 1, 42, 44.

Until 1885 Karlavägen was
known as Esplanaden, a 42-m
(138-ft) wide avenue planted
with lime trees and flower beds.
Towards the end of the 19th
century several impressive
houses were built there, many
in Neo-Renaissance style. The
street has retained its character
as a grand boulevard despite a
lot of building and the arrival of
shops and offices.

A major development was
undertaken in the 1960s, when
the central section of the road
was gradually converted into
an open-air sculpture gallery.
At the crossroads with Engel-
brektsgatan is *The City* by Lars
Erik Husberg; at Villagatan a
female figure by the French
sculptor Paul Cornet; at
Floragatan Gunnar Nilsson's
Mimi, which can also be seen
at other places in the city; at
Sturegatan *Living Iron* by Willy
Gordon, a gift from the LKAB
mining company, whose head
office at No. 45 acquired a
façade relief by Eric Grate in
1970. Also situated at the
crossroads with Sturegatan is
Scatola by the Italian sculptor
Arnoldo Pomodoro.

At Nybroplan is *Man – Horse –
Carriage* by Asmund Arle; at
Sibyllegatan *Woman with Hand
Mirror* by Ebba Ahlmark-Hughes;
in front of Östra Real a bust of the
author August Blanche (1811–68)
by Aron Sandberg – the

secondary school
building was designed
by Ragnar Östberg
with sculptures by Carl
Eldh; at Grevgatan is
Incoming Sea by
Håkan Bonds; at
Karlaplan a marble
sculpture by Gert
Marcus; at Tysta Gatan
Jeanette by Curt
Thorsjö; and at
Banérgatan is *Urn* by
Hedy Jolly-Dahlström.
Finally, at No. 100, is the long
Garrison administration building
with a sculpture group at the
entrance, a work in glazed
stoneware by Gustav Kraitz.

The fountain and round pond
at Karlaplan were added in 1929.
The Aviator is by Carl Milles and
was unveiled two years later.

Fountain on Karlaplan, on the tree-lined
Karlavägen

Swedish Television's main building, next to Swedish
Radio's headquarters

❹ Radio-och TV-husen

Oxenstiernsgatan 20 & 34. **Map** 6 A1,
A2, B1. Ⓣ Karlaplan. 🚌 4, 56, 76. SR
Tel 08-784 50 00. 🎫 by appt. ♿
🌐 sr.se SVT **Tel** 08-784 00 00.
🎫 by appt. ♿ 🌐 svt.se

The headquarters of Swedish
Radio (SR) and Swedish
Television (SVT) take up a
12 ha (30 acres) site alongside
Ladugårdsgärde. The area's long
history as a military training
depot is reflected by several old
buildings once used for stores.
Now it is the site not just of the
modern radio and TV buildings
(designed by the architects Erik
Ahnborg and Sune Lindström),
but also of three old buildings
with military connections: the
gunpowder cellar from 1717,
the old stone coach-house
from 1750, and the Karl Johan
storehouses from 1820. Both
architects also designed
Berwaldhallen *(see p108)*, a
concert hall, which is linked
to SR and SVT by a tunnel.

Swedish Radio started its
transmissions from Malm-
skillnadsgatan on 1 January
1925. It moved to No. 8
Kungsgatan in 1928 and into
its new premises in 1961.

SVT started transmissions from
the Svea Artillery Regiment's old
premises on 24 October 1954. In
1969 it moved into the new TV
building in the former barracks
area, where an office block was
added 4 years later. Additions in
1983–7 included a building for
news broadcasts. SVT now
covers an area of 51,600 sq m
(555,220 sq ft) with eight
studios, three of which are used
for news programmes.

Boats along Strandvägen

Until the 1940s sailing vessels used to carry firewood from Roslagen
on the Baltic coast to the quayside at Strandvägen. This trade had
lost its importance by the 1950s, and boating enthusiasts started
buying up these old vessels.
Some were renovated and sailed
to the Caribbean, others became
illegal drinking or gambling clubs
on Strandvägen. New harbour
regulations led to the formation
of two associations to administer
the boats. About 40 have
survived and are owned by
people who want to preserve a
piece of cultural heritage. By
every boat there is a sign
describing its history.

Old wood-carrying boats along the
Strandvägen quay

❷ Historiska museet

Sweden's Historiska museet (History Museum) was opened in 1943. It was designed by Bengt Romare and Georg Sherman. Sculptor Bror Marklund was responsible for the decoration around the entrance and the richly detailed bronze gateways depicting events in early Swedish history. The museum originally made its name with its exhibits from the Viking era, as well as its outstanding collections from the early Middle Ages. Contemporary church textiles are also on show. Many of Historiska museet's gold treasures have been gathered together to form one of Stockholm's most remarkable sights, Guldrummet (the Gold Room).

Upper floor

Bronze Age Find
This Bronze Age artifact, thought to be a percussion instrument, was discovered in a bog in southern Sweden in 1847.

Courtyard

Ground floor

★ The Alunda Elk
This 21-cm (8-inch) stone axe, discovered in 1920 at Alunda in central Sweden, resembles an elk's head. It is a ceremonial axe, probably made in Finland or Karelia in around 2000 BC.

Rosengården

The Bäckaskog Woman
The 1.5-m (5-ft) long Bäckaskog woman lived around 5000 BC. She died at the age of 40–50 and was buried sitting in a cramped pit.

Key

☐ Prehistoric Era
☐ Middle Ages and Baroque
☐ Temporary exhibitions
☐ Non-exhibition space

The Viking Era
This eventful era is represented by exhibits including a Viking sword with artistic embellishments, and ornaments in the shape of Nordic animals.

The Skog Tapestry
This once hung in the wooden church at Skog in northern Sweden. It is one of the museum's oldest textile treasures.

VISITORS' CHECKLIST

Practical Information
Narvavägen 13–17.
Map 3 F4. **Tel** 08-51 95 56 00.
Open Jun–Aug: 10am–6pm daily;
Sep–May: 11am–5pm Tue–Sun,
11am–8pm Wed. **Closed** 24, 25 &
31 Dec. 🅿 ♿ ✉ The Gold
Room. 🖥 📷 ⓦ **historiska.se**

Transport
Ⓣ Karlaplan; Ⓣ Östermalmstorg,
🚊 7 to Djurgårdsbron. 🚌 Hop-
on-hop-off.

Baroque Hall

★ **Maria from Viklau**
This Madonna figure on the upper floor is the best-preserved example from Sweden's early medieval period. The colourful wooden sculpture is richly gilded.

Gallery Guide

The exhibitions are divided chronologically on two floors with the prehistoric section on the ground floor and the Middle Ages on the upper floor, where there is also a Baroque Hall. In the basement, reached by a staircase from the entrance hall, is the Gold Room with priceless exhibits from prehistoric times to the medieval period.

History of Sweden

Stairs descending to the Gold Room

Main entrance

★ The Gold Room

Since the early 1990s the museum's many priceless gold artifacts have been on show in Guldrummet (the Gold Room), a 700-sq m (7,550-sq ft) underground vault built with 250 tons of reinforced concrete to ensure security. The room is in two circular sections. The inner section houses the main collection, with 50 kg (110 lb) of gold treasures and 250 kg (550 lb) of silver from the Bronze Age to the Middle Ages.

The Elisabeth Reliquary was origi-nally a drinking goblet, which was mounted with gold and precious stones in the 11th cen-tury. In about 1230 a silver cover was added to enclose the skull of St Elisabeth. In 1631 it was seized as a trophy for Sweden during the Thirty Years' War.

The Gold Collars were found between 1827 and 1864; the three-ringed collar in a stone quarry in eastern Sweden, the five-ringed in a ditch on the island of Öland, and the seven-ringed in a mound of stones in the county of Västergötland.

The underground Gold Room in Historiska museet

Berwaldhallen – the concert hall is home to the Swedish Radio Symphony Orchestra

❺ Berwaldhallen

Dag Hammarskiölds väg 3.
Map 6 A2. **Tel** 08-784 18 00.
Karlaplan. 4, 42, 56, 69.
Open noon–6pm Mon–Fri.
berwaldhallen.se

On 30 November 1979 the Swedish Radio Symphony Orchestra and the Radio Choir acquired their own concert hall, Berwaldhallen. Since then the hall has become a national showcase for Swedish music. It is named after Franz Berwald (1796–1868), one of Sweden's greatest composers. The architects Erik Ahnborg and Sune Lindström won an award for their "wonderful and sensitively designed concert hall". Hans Viksten, Hertha Hillfon and other artists undertook the decoration of the foyer. Nature has made its own contribution in the form of untouched areas of rock, which were blasted out to accommodate two-thirds of the six-sided building.
    The Swedish Radio Symphony Orchestra and Radio Choir give approximately 100 concerts per year in the hall, which has contributed to establishing this venue as an internationally renowned concert stage, attracting audiences of 150,000 a year. In late August the hall hosts the annual Baltic Sea Festival, a classical music festival that presents world-class musicians from around the world.

❻ Diplomatstaden

Map 6 A2. Karlaplan. 56, 69,76.

The elegant villas that gave the area of Diplomatstaden its name stretch along Nobelgatan and the eastern part of Strandvägen (from No. 74). The first house for a foreign diplomat was built in the 1910s, when the British ambassador moved into Nobelgatan 7. Nearby is Engelska Kyrkan (the English Church), which was built in the city centre in the 1860s but was moved to the diplomatic quarter in 1913. In the 1980s the church was finally completed with the addition of an octagonal parish hall. Villa Bonnier at No. 13 was designed by Ragnar Östberg and was a gift to the State by a prominent publishing family. It is now used by the Government for official functions.
    The embassies of Hungary, Turkey, South Korea, Norway, Germany, the UK and USA are all located in or near the area.

Nobelparken, the park adjoining the embassies, is named after the scientist Alfred Nobel (1833–96). In the early 20th century plans for a Nobel Palace in the park were drawn up by the architect Ferdinand Boberg, but the project never came to fruition. On the north side of Strandvägen is the Törner Villa, a heritage wooden house built in 1880. The villa is named after a firemaster at Nobel's gunpowder factory.

❼ Sjöhistoriska museet

Djurgårdsbrunnsvägen 24. **Map** 6 C2.
Tel 08-519 549 00. 69. **Open** 10am–5pm Tue–Sun.
sjohistoriska.se

The National Maritime Museum's architectural design and location on Djurgårdsbrunnsviken are worthy of a country with a long coastline and numerous archipelagos and lakes. Sjöhistoriska museet focuses on shipping, shipbuilding and naval defence, and there are fascinating exhibits, both permanent and temporary, on these themes.
    There are some 100,000 exhibits, including more than 1,500 model ships. The oldest ship was built in the 17th century, and the oldest Swedish ship is a reproduction of the so-called "Cathedral ship" from the early 1600s. The collections include every conceivable type of ship – from small coasters and Viking longboats to oil tankers, coal vessels, dinghies, full-riggers and submarines. A series of models on a scale

Majestic buildings in the diplomatic quarter at Djurgårdsbrunnsviken

of 1:200 show the development of ships in Scandinavia from the Iron Age to the present day.

There are also full-scale settings, which give a good idea of life on board the ships. Among them are the beautiful original cabin and elegant stern from the royal schooner *Amphion*. The ship was built at the Djurgården shipyard and designed by the leading shipbuilder F H Chapman. It was Gustav III's flagship in the 1788–90 war with Russia. Contrasting with this is the cramped and damp-preserved forecastle from the schooner *Hoppet*, where four crew members ate, slept and spent their time off watch.

The galley *Lodbrok*, one of many maritime models at Sjöhistoriska museet

The museum has some notable examples of ship decoration from the late 17th century. They include part of the national coat of arms recovered by divers in the 1920s from the stern of the *Riksäpplet*, which sank at Dalarö in 1676. When *Carolus XI*, an 82-cannon ship, was launched from the shipyard in Stockholm in 1678 the stern had a large relief portrayal of Karl XI on horseback. The relief was possibly removed some years later, when the ship was renamed *Sverige*, but it was saved and is now in the museum. There are many fine figureheads in the collection, including one depicting Amphion, the son of Zeus, playing his lyre, which once adorned the schooner of the same name.

Linked to the museum is the Swedish Marine Archaeology Archive, which contains a mass of information, including a complete listing of shipwrecks with 10,000 entries from 1720 to the present day. The ship-design archive has documents covering most eras of maritime history and is used extensively

Figurehead, about 1850

by researchers. The photographic collection has 300,000 pictures, while the library covers all aspects of seafaring and war at sea. There is a special children's section with a workshop that is open on Saturdays, Sundays and during school holidays. During the summer a dinghy-sailing school is arranged for children aged 8–14. The attractive museum building was one of the architect Ragnar Östberg's last works and was opened in 1938. On the gable facing Djurgårdsbrunnsviken is *The Sailor*, a monument to the victims of naval war by Nils Sjögren.

❽ Tekniska museet

Museivägen 7. **Map** 6 C2. **Tel** 08-450 56 00. 🚌 69. **Open** 10am–5pm Mon–Tue, Thu–Fri, 11am–8pm Wed, 11am–5pm Sat & Sun. 📷 by appointment. ♿🅿🅟📷🚫📖 Ⓦ tekniskamuseet.se

Anyone planning to visit the Museum of Science and Technology should allow plenty of time. Throughout the 20th century it accumulated a wealth of exhibits connected with Sweden's technical and industrial history. It has 12,000

sq m (129,000 sq ft) of well-stocked exhibition space plus a library with 50,000 volumes and a large collection of technical magazines. It is also the home of Sweden's first Science Centre, Teknorama, with many "hands-on" experiments aimed particularly at children and young people.

The machinery hall is the largest exhibition area with many powered machines from different eras. Among them is the country's oldest preserved steam engine, built in 1832 and once used in a coal mine in southern Sweden. The classic T-Ford is there, too, as well as early Swedish cars from Volvo, Scania and Saab.

The museum also has sections on the history of telecommunications and the computer, electric power, book-printing and the Swedish forestry industry. The mining and processing of iron and steel is also highlighted.

Ericsson telephone made in 1903 for Czar Nicholas II

❾ Gärdet

Rindögatan. Ⓣ Gärdet.
🅦 **housingprototypes.org**

Gärdet, one of the largest residential neighbourhoods in Stockholm, was built as the result of a design competition in the late 1920s, at a time when the Swedish Modern Movement was in full swing. The competition was won by the architect Arvid Stille, and this area exhibits the graceful form of Functionalism for which Sweden became known at the time, and which continues to exert a strong influence to this day. One characteristic of Swedish architecture from that period was the emphasis it placed on decoration whilst still adhering to the basic principles of Functionalist ideology.

The individual buildings in Gärdet were designed and built between 1935 and 1939 by a variety of architects, including Sture Fröhlén, Albin Stark, Ernst Grönwall, Wolter Gahn, Björn Hedvall and Sven Wallander, all within Stille's overall plan.

❿ Etnografiska museet

Djurgårdsbrunnsvägen 34.
Map 6 C2. **Tel** 010-456 12 00. 🚌 69.
Open 11am–5pm Tue–Sun (to 8pm Wed). 🅲 🅿 ♿ 🗑 🅿 📷
🅦 **varldskulturmuseerna.se/ etnografiskamuseet**

The National Museum of Ethnography is a showcase for the collections brought home to Sweden by travellers and scientists from the 18th century to the present day. The imaginative displays are intended to offer visitors not only a better understanding of the unknown or unfamiliar from around the world, but also of the cultural connections between such far-off places and Sweden through explaining how and why the objects came into the museum's collection.

The explorer Sven Hedin (1865–1952), who was the last Swede to be ennobled (in 1902), contributed many exhibits, including Buddha figures and Chinese costumes, as well as Mongolian temple tents donated by leaders of the Kalmuck people in western China to King Gustav V.

A Japanese tea house, built by 15 Japanese craftsmen to a design by Professor Masao Nakamura, was opened in 1990. It is a work of art in itself, offering a space for reflection and meditation within a traditional setting. During the summer months visitors can take part in tea ceremonies, while at other times the house can be viewed from outside.

Another section of interest is dedicated to the native peoples of North America. Here, there are masks, textiles and ceramics from various tribes.

Closer to home, the museum also reflects upon the multicultural influences on Sweden brought about by

Religious mask from British Columbia

the large-scale immigration into the country in the late 20th century.

Alongside the permanent displays, the museum puts on a changing series of temporary exhibitions highlighting different aspects of the collection. There is also a good reference library.

The museum also houses an unusual but well-regarded restaurant, Matmekka. It is renowned for using top-quality organic ingredients and seasonal, locally grown produce to create an appealing menu that combines traditional Swedish cuisine with exotic influences from all around the world.

⓫ Kaknästornet

Ladugårdsgärdet. **Map** 7 D1. **Tel** 08-667 21 80. 🚌 69, 69K. **Open** Jun–Aug: 9am–10pm Mon–Sat, 9am–6pm Sun; Sep–May: 10am–9pm Mon–Sat, 10am–6pm Sun. 🅲 by appointment.
🅰 🅿 ♿ 🗑 🗑 📷

Anchored by 72 steel poles, each one driven 8 m (26 ft) into the rock, the 34-storey Kaknästornet soars to a height of 155 m (508 ft). The tower, designed by the architects Bengt Lindroos and Hans Borgström, was opened in 1967. It was erected as a centre for the country's television and radio broadcasting and also contains technical equipment to conduct conferences by

The Japanese tea house in the gardens of the Etnografiska museet

Kaknästornet, with the Sjöhistoriska, Tekniska and Etnografiska museums in the foreground

satellite between European cities. Five dishes to the left of the tower – the largest of which has a diameter of 13 m (43 ft) – relay signals to and from satellites. The main hall containing the transmitters and receivers has been blasted out of the rock below the dishes.

The observation points on levels 30 and 31 provide a spectacular view of the city, and the restaurant on the 28th floor has panoramic windows. It is reached by two lifts, travelling at 18 km/h (11 mph). The restaurant also runs a busy tourist information office at the entrance level, selling souvenirs and maps. Decorative features include a wall relief by Walter Bengtsson, who was inspired by the tower's daunting technology.

⑫ Ladugårdsgärde

Map 6 C1. 🚌 1, 69, 76.

As early as the 15th century there was a royal farm on the site where the Nobel Park now stands. After 250 years it had outlived its usefulness and for a few centuries it was used as a training area for the Stockholm garrison. Between Kungliga Borgen (Royal Fortress) and Hakberget are the remains of Karl XI's fort (dating from 1672), which was largely rebuilt in time for the World Equestrian Championships, held here in 1990. During the 20th century what became known simply as Gärdet lost

its military role. In the early 1900s the area was used for May Day processions, and car races were staged here around 1920.

The fortress of Kungliga Borgen is a relic of the military training era, and it was from here that Karl XIV Johan used to watch his troops manoeuvring. He rode from here to Rosendal Palace on Djurgården *(see p98)* via a pontoon bridge near the present-day National Maritime Museum. The fortress was badly damaged by fire in October 1977, but it has since been rebuilt to its original appearance. A restaurant is open during the summer.

Something is always going on in Gärdet. It is the starting point for major fun runs and the venue for kite-flying festivals, and is used by the city's balloonists. It is also a favourite place to exercise horses and dogs.

Ingmar Bergman

The playwright and producer Ingmar Bergman was born in Uppsala in 1918. His long series of masterly films made him world-famous,

Ingmar Bergman (1918–2007)

but he started his career in the theatre. From 1960–6 he was Managing Director of Kungliga Dramatiska Teatern (the Royal Dramatic Theatre), where he remained a guest producer. He created more than 100 theatrical productions. His most acclaimed are *Smiles of a Summer Night* (1955), *The Seventh Seal* (1957) and his final film *Fanny and Alexander* (1982), which won him four Oscars. He will also be remembered for his problematic private life, which his films often depicted.

⑬ Filmhuset

Borgvägen 1–5. **Map** 6 B1. **Tel** 08-665 11 00. 🚇 Karlaplan. 🚌 1, 4, 56, 72, 76. **Open** 8am–6pm Mon–Thu, 8am–5pm Fri. Film club, library & archives: ring for details. ♿ 🚻 🎁 📷 **w** **sfi.se/filmhuset**

The production of quality Swedish films is supported by the Swedish Film Institute. The institute also acts as guardian of the country's cinematic heritage and promotes Swedish films both at home and abroad. From 1971, all its activities were brought under one roof in Filmhuset, a Modernist structure by Peter Celsing.

Cinema screenings are held six days a week at the internationally acclaimed Cinematheque. It showcases movies from all over the world, ranging from silent picture shows with live music to more contemporary films. Filmhuset also houses Sweden's largest public library specialising in all things film. There is also a popular weekday-lunch restaurant and a café-bar.

Filmhuset, home of the Film Institute and Cinematheque

Tessinparken, surrounded by Functionalist-style housing dating from the late 1930s

⓮ Tessinparken & Nedre Gärdet

Map 3 F2. Ⓣ Karlaplan, Gärdet.
🚌 1, 4, 72.

Three generations of the Tessin family of architects *(see p38)* have given their name to this park opened at Lower Gärdet in 1931. Tessinparken runs from north to south and is attractively designed with lawns, play areas, paths and ponds. The adjoining houses, built between 1932 and 1937, have their own gardens and blend in such a way that they give the impression of being part of the park itself.

The earliest houses, nearest to Valhallavägen, still show signs of 1920s Neo-Classicism, although Gärdet's real hallmark is Functionalism *(see p39)*. The lower white houses along Askrikegatan are Functionalist in style and noticeably different from other buildings in Gärdet. They mark the northern boundary of the park. Some 60 different architects were involved in designing the Gärdet development, including Sture Frölén.

A granite statue of a woman with a suitcase, *Housewife's Holiday*, stands in the part of Tessin Park adjoining Valhallavägen. It was made by Olof Thorwald Ohlsson in the 1970s. At the other end of the park is a colourful concrete statue, *The Egg*, by Egon Möller-Nielsen.

⓯ Försvars-högskolan

Valhallavägen 117. **Map** 3 E2. 🚌 4, 62, 72. Ⓣ Stadion. **Closed** to the public.

Two decorative cannons, an aircraft propeller and an 18th-century anchor guard the entrance to Försvarshögskolan (the Military Academy). The building has been sympathe-tically renovated and appears to be lower than it really is, because the adjoining Valhallavägen was built at a higher level.

It was originally the base for the Svea Artillery Regiment and is one of many notable military buildings designed by the architect Ernst Jacobsson. After Nybrogatan was blasted out through the Tyskbagar-bergen hill, the regimental

building provided a backdrop to the newly extended street.

The regiment moved out in 1949 to make way first for Swedish Radio and later for the Military Academy, in whose present gym Swedish TV was born. A plaque reads: "From this building the first regular television programme was transmitted on 24 October 1954."

⓰ Stadion

Lidingövägen 1–3. **Map** 3 E2. **Tel** 08-508 283 51. Ⓣ Stadion. 🚌 4, 55, 72, 73. **Open** 15 Apr–15 Oct. 🅿 during events. ♿ 🚻 ▣

A new main arena was built for the 1912 Olympic Games in Stockholm. The architect of Stadion, Torben Grut (1871–1945), followed the National Romantic influences of the day. His design was based on his own interpre-tation of the commission to build a stadium "using modern construction methods adapted from traditional medieval brick-building techniques". It is no coincidence that the arena, which is the world's oldest Olympic stadium still in use, is often known as the "Stadium Fortress".

In addition to the 1912 Olympics, the stadium has also been the venue for ice hockey and bandy (a type of hockey) championships, the European Athletics Championships in 1958, and the World Equestrian Championships in 1990. The stadium is renowned for athletics events, and stages an international athletics gala every summer.

Stadion is listed as a heritage building, and its twin towers are a familiar landmark. The complex is richly decorated. The

The restored façade of Försvarshögskolan (Military Academy) on Valhallavägen

clock tower has
two figures by Carl
Fagerberg, *Ask
and Embla*, the
counterparts of Adam
and Eve in Nordic
mythology. There are
also busts of Victor
Balck, the man behind
the 1912 Olympics;
P H Ling, the father of
Swedish gymnastics;
and Edwin Wide,
the "flying teacher",
who was a leading
opponent of the Finnish master-
athlete Paavo Nurmi in long-
distance races during the 1920s.

Four notable sculptures were
added in the 1930s. The artist and
gymnast Bruno Liljefors (best
known for his wildlife paintings)
created *Play* at the main entrance,
Carl Eldh made *The Runners*, and
Carl Fagerberg provided *Relay
Runners* and *The Shot-Putter*.

Bruno Liljefors's statue *Play* outside Stadion

⑰ Tekniska Högskolan

Valhallavägen 79. **Map** 3 D1.
Tekniska högskolan. 4, 72, 73.

The renowned higher education
establishment, Tekniska
Högskolan, accounts for one-
third of Sweden's technical
research and engineering
education at university level.
It has 15,000 students, 1,000
active research students and a
staff of 2,500. It was founded in
1827, and since 1917 its campus
has been housed in heritage
buildings on Valhallavägen,
as well as in the suburbs of

Haninge and Kista, and outside
Stockholm in Södertälje, Gävle
and Visby.

The main building on
Valhallavägen was designed by
Erik Lallerstedt, and its opening,
in October 1917 was a
milestone in Sweden's
technological development.

The architect commissioned
several contemporary artists to
decorate the austere technical
environment, so it has become
something of an artistic treasure
trove. The sculptors and painters
whose works adorn the
buildings included Einar
Forseth, Olle Hjortzberg, Georg
Pauli, Ivar Johnsson, Axel
Törneman, Hilding Linnqvist
and Carl Milles. The latter artist
was also responsible for the
fountain sculpture, *The Industrial
Monument*, which rests on a
marble base in the courtyard
facing Valhallavägen.

Early in the 20th century the
main building underwent a
painstaking renovation. The
surrounding park was also
restored to its original state.

⑱ Engelbrektskyrkan & Lärkstaden

Östermalmsgatan 20. **Map** 3 D2.
Tekniska högskolan. 1.
Engelbrektskyrkan. **Tel** 08-406 98 00.
Open 11am–3pm Tue–Sun. 11am
Sun, 11:30am Thu.

One of Sweden's leading
Jugendstil architects, Lars Israel
Wahlman, designed the
Engelbrekt Church as a result
of winning an architectural
competition in 1906. The church
was opened on 25 January 1914
in the presence of King Gustaf V.

Engelbrektskyrkan gives the
appearance of thrusting out
from the rocks, and it dominates
the surrounding area with its
slender brick tower. In the
chancel, the monumental
paintings are by Olle Hjortzberg
(1872–1959). The sculptor
Tore Strindberg (1882–1968)
was commissioned for the
stucco reliefs both in the
chancel and above the main
entrance. Filip Månsson
executed the frescoes in the
west portico and elsewhere.
The nave is the highest in
Scandinavia, and the arches
inside the church are supported
by eight granite pillars.

Engelbrektskyrkan is located
in Lärkstaden, a quarter that was
developed around 1910 and is
characterized by dark red
façades and tiled roofs that blend
in well with the church. The area
has winding streets and natural
differences in level – inspired
partly by Austrian patterns.

Engelbrektskyrkan, dominating the
surrounding area of Lärkstaden

Arena for Records

No other athletics arena can compete with Stockholm's Stadion
when it comes to world records. The 1912 Olympics gave the
statistics a flying start with 11 of them. The
gold medallist Ted Meredith's time of 1
min 51.9 sec in the 800-m event can be
compared with Wilson Kipketer's 1997
time of 1 min 41.73 sec over the same
distance – the last world record set at
Stadion. It has recorded a total of 83 world
records. London is second with 68, and
Los Angeles is third with 66. The top
Swedish runner of the 1940s, Gunder
Hägg, set seven world records and the
Finn, Paavo Nurmi, had six.

Running track at Stadion

Kungsholmen

Once best known for its handicrafts and small industries, Kungsholmen changed in the late 19th century with the emergence of new apartment blocks and institutional buildings. By the early 1900s the area had a different status, exemplified by Ragnar Östberg's Stadshuset (City Hall) – Stockholm's most notable architectural project of the 20th century – and Carl Westman's majestic Rådhuset (Law Court). These were followed by the elegant waterfront houses along Norr Mälarstrand. The area has a high concentration of government buildings, but it also offers many venues for entertainment and nightlife.

Stately buildings on Norr Mälarstrand line the Riddarfjärden waterfront

Sights at a Glance

1. Stadshuset
   (see pp116–17)
2. Rådhuset
3. Norr Mälarstrand
4. Rålambshovsparken
5. Västerbron
6. Marieberg

Key

■ Central Stockholm
= Motorway
■ Major road
Minor road

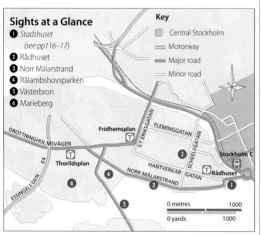

0 metres 1000
0 yards 1000

❶ Stadshuset

See pp116–17.

❷ Rådhuset

Scheelegatan 7. **Map** 2 A5.
Ⓣ Rådhuset. 🚌 40, 52.

In the early 20th century, the intention was to build a combined city hall and law court, but the plans changed when two separate architectural competitions were launched. The winning entry for Rådhuset (the law court), was a design by Carl Westman (1866–1936), who became a leading exponent of the National Romantic School along with Ragnar Östberg (1866–1945), architect of Stadshuset. Building began in 1911, and Rådhuset was opened in December 1915. In

Rådhuset, exterior detail

his design, Westman drew inspiration from the Vasa Renaissance of the 16th century and was probably influenced by Vadstena Castle in southern Sweden. Rådhuset, with its prominent tower, is one of the best examples of the National Romantic style, but its solid scale also shows Jugendstil influences.

The sculptors Christian Eriksson and the brothers Aron and Gustaf Sandberg were responsible for the decoration, which also includes paintings by Olle Hjortzberg and scene-paintings by Filip Månsson and his workshop. Beside the staircase on the fifth floor is a copy of *Kopparmatte*, the pillory that once stood on Stortorget in Gamla Stan. The original pillory is at Stockholms Stadsmuseum (see p129).

❸ Norr Mälarstrand

Map 1 C3. Ⓣ Rådhuset, Fridhemsplan. 🚌 40, 52.

When industries including textiles and dyeing left Norr Mälarstrand in the early 20th century, work began on exploiting Kungsholmen's attractive location along the bay of Riddarfjärden. Gradually an exclusive residential area emerged. During World War II a sculpture park was developed along the waterfront, where the excursion boats and vintage coasters are moored today. Willow, poplar, alder and birch trees thrive along the shoreline. A pavilion with a summer café stands on pillars above the water. It was designed by Erik Glemme, assistant to the city's master gardener Holger Blom (b. 1906).

The architect of Stadshuset, Ragnar Östberg, designed Norr Mälarstrand 76. Cyrillus Johansson, Sven Wallander and J Norberg were the architects of Nos. 26, 28 and 30, where the figures on the gables above the steps were created by the metal craftsman Ragnar Myrsmeden. There is much to see in the small side streets, including the façades of No. 5 Jacob Westins Gata (architect Harald Wadsjö) and No. 9 Skillinggränd. The original service-flat building at No. 6 John Erikssongatan was designed by Sven Markelius, who was influenced by the ministerial couple Gunnar and Alva Myrdal. It is the first residential building in the Functionalist style typical of the 1930s to be listed as a heritage site.

❹ Rålambshovs-parken

Map 1 B3. 🚇 Fridhemsplan. 🚌 1, 4, 40, 56, 57, 62, 74. 🚤

Rålambshovsparken was created in 1935, when the Västerbron was built. It adjoins other green areas, including Smedsudden and Marieberg and Fredhäll parks. These open spaces attract joggers and sun-bathers. In summer it is possible to swim from the beach at Smedsudden or the cliffs at Fredhäll.

When the city celebrated its 700th anniversary in 1953, an amphitheatre was opened in Rålambshovsparken, and a paddling pool and playgrounds were added. The park has been enhanced with Elli Hemberg's sculpture *The Butterfly*, Eric Grate's *Monument to an Axeman*, *Judgement* by Egon Möller-Nielsen and Lars Erik Falk's *Colour Tower*.

Rålambshovsparken on the north side of Västerbron

❺ Västerbron

Map 1 B4. 🚌 4, 40, 74.

As Stockholm expanded and car use increased in the 1920s, it became necessary to build an additional bridge between the northern and southern shores

of Lake Mälaren. German experts dominated the architectural competition launched in 1930, but their plans were implemented by Swedish architects and engineers, and the bridge was completed in 1935.

The attractive design blends well with the landscape. The bridge is built in two spans of 168 m (551 ft) and 204 m (669 ft) with a vertical clearance of 26 m (85 ft). It is used by an average of 12,000 vehicles daily. A walk to the centre of Västerbron is rewarded with a magnificent view of central Stockholm.

❻ Marieberg

Map 1 A3. 🚇 Thorildsplan. 🚌 1, 49, 56, 62. Riksarkivet **Tel** 010 476 71 00.

The area at the northern end of Västerbron, Marieberg, was once known for its porcelain factory and military installations. But since the early 1960s it has become the city's main newspaper district and the home of three of the four Stockholm dailies.

The architect Paul Hedqvist's 98.6-m (323-ft) high building for *Dagens Nyheter* and *Expressen* is one of the city's landmarks. The neon sign that tops the building at Gjörwellsgatan 30 was designed by P O Ultvedt, who also created the relief at the entrance. Works of art include Lennart Rodhe's walls made from glazed stoneware, *Day and Night*, and Arne Jones' sculpture *Nova*. Some older works of art were brought from the papers' original building in the central Klara district, including Stig Blomberg's

The Orb (1970) by Elli Hemberg in front of Riksarkivet

copper sculpture, *Freedom our Watchword*, made in 1951.

The offices of *Svenska Dagbladet* are not as richly decorated as their neighbours', but they are no less interesting architecturally. The building was inspired by Pirelli's high-rise offices in Milan and designed by Tengbom Architects in 1960–2.

The third interesting building in Marieberg is Riksarkivet, the state archive. It was built in 1968 by architects Åke Ahlström and Kjell Åström. Riksarkivet is one of Sweden's oldest public bodies, dating from the Middle Ages. At the entrance is Elli Hemberg's iron sculpture, *The Orb*. The main hall, which has 56 seats for researchers and 18 individual study rooms, is dominated by Lennart Rodhe's tapestry, *Symbol in the Archive*, created by the Friends of Handicrafts. In an adjoining room the public has access to archive documents, microfilm and microfiche.

Among the archives is one of the world's largest books – the accounts for the province of Östergötland dating from 1813. It has 12,390 pages, weighs 42 kg (93 lb) and is 1.13 m (3 ft 8 inches) wide.

Guided tours of Riksarkivet can be arranged.

Meaning "The Western Bridge", Västerbron opened in 1935 to link Kungsholmen with Södermalm across Lake Mälaren

❶ Stadshuset

Probably Sweden's biggest architectural project of the 20th century, the City Hall was completed in 1923 and has become a symbol of Stockholm. It was designed by Ragnar Östberg (1866–1945), the leading architect of the Swedish National Romantic style, and displays influences of both the Nordic Gothic and Northern Italian schools. Several leading Swedish artists contributed to the rich interior design. The building contains the Council Chamber and 250 offices for administrative staff. The annual Nobel Prize festivities take place in the Blue Hall and the Golden Hall.

★ **The Golden Hall**
The Byzantine-inspired wall mosaics by Einar Forseth (1892–1988) have 19 million fragments of gold leaf. The theme of the northern wall is Queen of Lake Mälaren.

KEY

① **The Blue Hall** contains the banqueting room, made from hand-shaped dark bricks. The name comes from the original plan to use polished blue-painted bricks.

② **Norra Trapptornet** is a tower crowned by a sun.

③ **Courtyard**

④ **Marriage room**

⑤ **Engelbrekt the Freedom Fighter** by Christian Eriksson (1858–1935).

★ **The Prince's Gallery**
A fresco, *The City on the Water*, in the Prince's Gallery, was painted by Prince Eugen *(see p99)*, who donated it to the City Hall.

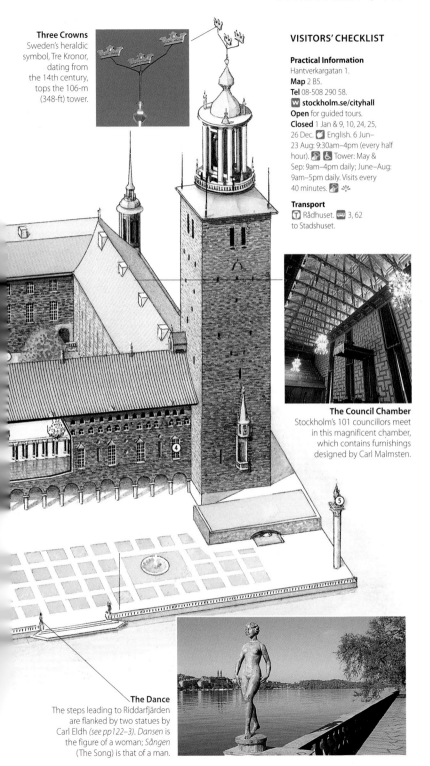

Three Crowns
Sweden's heraldic symbol, Tre Kronor, dating from the 14th century, tops the 106-m (348-ft) tower.

The Council Chamber
Stockholm's 101 councillors meet in this magnificent chamber, which contains furnishings designed by Carl Malmsten.

The Dance
The steps leading to Riddarfjärden are flanked by two statues by Carl Eldh *(see pp122–3)*. *Dansen* is the figure of a woman; *Sången* (The Song) is that of a man.

Vasastan

Building started in Vasastan, the most northerly part of Norrmalm, in the 18th century. Today it is both a residential area, with houses built around 1900 for manual workers and craftsmen, and a lively part of the city with a wide choice of bars and restaurants. The area also includes some of Stockholm's most agreeable green open spaces, including Vasaparken and Vanadis-lunden. Stadsbiblioteket, the city library, is one of Stockholm's most distinctive buildings, and there are several architecturally outstanding churches.

Sights at a Glance

1. Schefflelerska Palatset
2. Observatoriemuseet
3. Handelshögskolan
4. Stadsbiblioteket
5. Gustav Vasa Kyrka
6. Judiska museet
7. Vasaparken
8. Rörstrandsgatan
9. Karlbergs Slott
10. Röda Bergen
11. Vanadislunden

Key

- Central Stockholm
- Motorway
- Major road
- Minor road

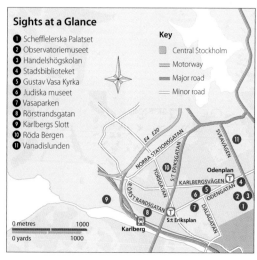

The old observatory (1748–53) at the top of the Observatory hill

❷ Observatorie-museet

Drottninggatan 120. **Map** 2 B2.
Ⓣ Odenplan/Rådmansgatan. 🚌 2, 4, 40, 42, 65, 72. **Open** Café Himlavalvet: 7 Apr–30 Sep: 11am–5pm daily (to 6pm Sat & Sun); 1 Oct–6 Apr: 5pm Sat & Sun. **Closed** to the public. 🅿️ ♿ 📷 🅦 observatoriet.kva.se

A number of institutions connected with science and education can be found on and around the hill of Brunkeberg. The oldest is the former observatory designed by Carl Hårleman for the Royal Swedish Academy of Sciences and opened in 1753. In 1931 its astronomical research was moved to Saltsjöbaden in the Stockholm archipelago. The building has since become Observatoriemuseet (the Observatory Museum).

The grove, which surrounds the old observatory, began to take shape in the 18th century. It is an idyllic enclosed area, which was first opened to the public in the 20th century.

On top of Brunkeberg is Sigrid Fridman's statue *The Centaur*. A park stretches down to Sveavägen, where a large pond is fed by water from a stream running down the hillside. The statue *Dancing Youth* is by Ivar Johnsson. At the southern entrance of the park is Nils Möllerberg's sculpture *Youth*.

Although the observatory is currently closed to the public, the on-site restaurant, Café Himlavalvet, is still open.

❶ Schefflelerska Palatset

Drottninggatan 116. **Map** 2 B3.
Ⓣ Rådmansgatan. 🚌 52.

Until about 1900 the most northerly section of Drottninggatan formed the main road into the city from the north. Here is Schefflelerska Palatset (the "haunted palace"), built in the grand style popular during Sweden's time as a great power, thus dating it to around 1700. It has been suggested that it was designed by Tessin the Elder, but it is more likely that it was by his stepson, Abraham Winantz, who was ennobled in 1693 for his services as

an architect. On show in the palace is Stockholm University's collection of 370 paintings from the 16th to the 19th century, and the Hellner collection of 700 pieces made at the Orrefors glassworks. Pehr Hilleström's painting *With the Fortune Teller* is included in the collection, but the emphasis is on foreign works such as *The Assault*, attributed to Pieter Bruegel the Elder (1567), and *Danae Banquet* and *Cleopatra's Banquet* by Tiepolo. The property was acquired in 1925 by the College of Higher Education, later Stockholm University, which handed it over to the State in 1960. Legend has it that the house has a ghost.

Orrefors bowl by Simon Gate, 1925

❸ Handels-högskolan

Sveavägen 65. **Map** 2 C2. **Tel** 08-736 90 00. Ⓣ Rådmansgatan. 🚌 59.

When the architect Ivar Tengbom (1878–1968) designed Handels-högskolan, Stockholm School of Economics (SSE), in the early 1920s he was inspired mainly by the Renaissance and Neo-Classical styles. Tengbom himself took charge of the construction, and the building was officially opened in 1926 in the presence of King Gustav V. The façade has stone reliefs and a gilded Mercury – the god of commerce – all by Ansgar Almquist, who also contributed a stucco relief with a lion gate based on the one in ancient Mycenae in Greece.

SSE is one of the leading business schools in Northern Europe. For more than a century, the school has educated men and women for leading positions in the business and public sectors.

Entrance of Handelshögskolan, the Stockholm School of Economics

Gunnar Asplund

Gunnar Asplund (1885–1940) was the dominant figure among Swedish architects between the two world wars. His first major commission was the chapel at the Skogskyrkogården Cemetery, designed in National Romantic style. His last work was Heliga Korsets Kapell, the cemetery's crematorium (1935–40). Regarded as a masterpiece in the Functionalist style, it has earned a place on the UNESCO World Heritage list (*see p135*). Asplund also designed Stadsbiblioteket (City Library, 1920–28). He pioneered the Functionalist style as chief architect for the Stockholm Exhibition in 1930.

Stockholm Exhibition, by Gunnar Asplund, 1930

The Stadsbiblioteket, Stockholm's main library

❹ Stadsbiblioteket

Sveavägen 73. **Map** 2 B2. **Tel** 08-508 310 60. Ⓣ Rådmansgatan. 🚌 4, 42, 46, 52, 53, 72. **Open** mid-Jun–mid-Aug: 9am–7pm Mon–Fri, noon–4pm Sat; mid-Aug–mid-Jun: 9am–9pm Mon–Thu, 9am–7pm Fri, noon–4pm Sat & Sun. ♿ 🖥

Gunnar Asplund's master work, Stadsbiblioteket (City Library), is one of the capital's most architecturally important buildings (*see pp38–9*). Asplund, the champion of the Functionalist style prevalent in the 1930s, designed a library dominated by the ideals of Nordic Classicism. It was opened in 1928.

Internally, the furnishings and many of the lightfittings were designed by Asplund himself. In the entrance hall are Ivar Johnsson's stucco reliefs with themes from Homer's *Iliad*. The sparkling mural painting in the children's section, *John Blund*, is by Nils Dardel, and the depiction of the stars in the heavens by Ulf Munthe. The door lintels, fine door handles and drinking fountains are by Nils Sjögren. Hilding Linnqvist was responsible for the giant-sized tapestry, and also for four mural paintings using ancient fresco techniques.

The library lends more than a million books every year.

❺ Gustav Vasa Kyrka

Odenplan. **Map** 2 B2. **Tel** 08-508 886 00. Ⓣ Odenplan. 🚌 4, 40, 42, 46, 53, 69, 72. **Open** 11am–6pm Mon–Thu, 10am–6pm Fri, 11am–3pm Sat & Sun; Jun–Aug: 11am–6pm daily. ✝ noon Mon & Fri, 8:30am Wed, 6pm Thu, 11am Sun, in Swedish. ♿ 🖵 **gustafvasa.nu**

Sweden's largest Baroque sculpture forms the altar in Gustav Vasa Kyrka, which was opened in 1906. The piece, by the court sculptor Burchardt Precht (1651–1738), was made for Uppsala Cathedral, from where it was removed in the late 19th century. It was bought by the Gustav Vasa parish congregation, whose church immediately gained a notable attraction.

The architect Agi Lindegren designed the central part of the church in Italian Neo-Baroque style with a 60-m (197-ft) high dome. Lindegren himself designed the marble pulpit and the font was created by Sigrid Blomberg. The baptismal chapel there is a 15th-century painting by an unknown Dutch artist. The paintings on the dome are by Vicke Andrén, who also portrayed the four evangelists in the transepts. The organ was built with the help of the composer Olle Olsson, the church organist for 50 years.

An eight-stemmed *chanukiah* (candlestick) in the collection of Judiska museet

❻ Judiska museet

Hälsingegatan 2. **Map** 2 A2. **Tel** 08-557 735 60. 🚇 Odenplan. 🚌 4, 72. **Open** noon–4pm Mon–Fri & Sun. 📷 in English by appointment. 📱 ♿ 📷 💻 📺 judiska-museet.se

In 1774 Aaron Isaac became the first Jewish immigrant to settle in Stockholm and practise his religion. Half of Sweden's Jewish population of around 18,000 live in the Stockholm area. Judiska museet depicts the history of the Swedish Jews from Isaac's time up to the present day. It focuses on Judaism as a religion, its integration into Swedish society and also the Holocaust. A comprehensive collection of pictures and other items provide an insight into Jewish life in Sweden with its important traditions and customs. The beautiful *Torah* (the five books of Moses) and the collection of eight-stemmed *chanukiot* (candlesticks) are just some of the museum's remarkable spiritual artifacts.

❼ Vasaparken

Map 2 A3. 🚇 S:t Eriksplan. 🚌 3, 4, 72.

Vasaparken dates from the early 20th century. It was typical of parks of its time with its emphasis on sport exemplified by the inclusion of a spacious grass sports field. During World War I the field was used for growing potatoes. A playground area was added in 1911.

It is a leafy and pleasant park. With few exceptions the trees were planted when the park was opened, but a lime tree in the shape of a candelabra is

believed to be more than 200 years old. During a major facelift in the 1940s, the appearance of the section along Torsgatan was changed. Three terraced gardens were added with granite and concrete walls and reliefs. Gottfrid Larsson's bronze statue *The Workman* has stood in this part of the park since 1917. On the opposite side of the park is *Romeo and Juliet*, a small granite sculpture by Olof Thorwald Ohlsson.

Vasaparken, a green lung in the built-up area of Vasastan

❽ Rörstrandsgatan

Map 1 C1. 🚇 S:t Eriksplan. 🚌 3, 4, 42, 57, 72.

This street takes its name from the no-longer-existing Rörstrand palace, built in the early 1630s. In the summer of 1726 the manufacture of Delft-style porcelain started in the building. Two hundred years later the now-famous Rörstrand porcelain factory was moved to the Gothenburg area and then

to its current home at Lidköping in south-west Sweden.

Rörstrandsgatan was the site of one of the city's first Chinese restaurants, and today the many outdoor cafés give the street a colourful atmosphere during summer. The area around Rörstrandsgatan and Odengatan has several nice shops, bars and restaurants.

❾ Karlbergs Slott

Map 1 B1. **Tel** 08-734 20 00. 🚌 42, 72 to the station of Karlberg, then 15 min walk. 📷 groups only, by appointment.

Admiral Karl Karlsson Gyllenhielm started to build Karlbergs Slott in the 1630s, during the Thirty Years' War. From 1670 the palace was extended and rebuilt by Magnus Gabriel de la Gardie, with Jean de la Vallée as his architect. When Karlberg became royal property in 1688, it was one of Sweden's most majestic palaces. It was where the "hero king", Karl XII (1682–1718), grew up, and it was here that he lay in state after his death at the Battle of Fredrikshald (*see p21*).

In 1792 the architect C C Gjörwell converted the property into the Royal War Academy, which later became the Karlberg Military School, and since 1999 it has been one of the country's military academies.

Cadet balls at Karlberg are unforgettable experiences, not least because of the magnificent setting. The interior

Rörstrandsgatan, a popular area for restaurants and pubs

Karlbergs Slott, a palace dating from the 1630s – now one of Sweden's military academies

decorations include Carl Carove's magnificent stuccowork, which can be seen in the grand hall. The palace church has been renovated, but the 17th-century lamps are original. De la Gardie's "Rarities Room" is now the sacristy but once housed his collection of valuables.

⑩ Röda Bergen

Map 2 A2. Ⓣ S:t Eriksplan. 🚌 3, 42, 57, 69.

Turning off from Sveavägen into Vanadisvägen, one soon reaches Matteus Kyrka, which dates from 1902–3. This church was designed by Erik Lallerstedt, who 20 years later undertook its renovation. The figure of St Matthew at the entrance, as well as the reredos figures, are the work of Ivar Johnsson. The mural paintings are by the artist Olle Hjortzberg.

The Röda Bergen ("Red Mountains") district starts at Vanadisplan with a sculpture made from reinforced plastic – *Transformation*, by Chris Gibson (1984). The area is a typical 1920s garden city where, as in Lärkstaden *(see p113)*, the architects abandoned the normal rigid road layout and allowed the street plan to follow the terrain. After the rose gardens of Rödabergsbrinken, flanked by the parkland

oases of Hedemora and Sätertäppan, comes Rödabergsgatan, an avenue of horse chestnut trees typical of the area. A Modernist sculpture in steel has sneaked in here – Björn Selder's *1 1/2 Spheres* (1979). In the background is a playground with Bo Englund's sculpture *Genesis* (1984).

⑪ Vanadislunden

Map 2 B1. 🚌 2, 40, 52. Vanadisbadet **Tel** 08-30 23 00. **Open** mid-May–Sep: 10am–7pm daily. 🐾 ♿ 🚽 📷
W **vanadisbadet.nu**

Many places in Vasastan are named Vanadis, which derives from Norse mythology. It was not until the late 19th century that the area around the northern end of Sveavägen started to be developed. In the 1880s a park was laid out on the nearby hillside with cultivated areas created from

a landfill site. A chapel, Stefanskapellet, at the southern end of the park, was opened in 1904. It was designed by Carl Möller, who was the architect responsible for the Johannes Kyrka. During a renovation in 1925–6 the chapel acquired its painted altar by Einar Forseth depicting the Passion.

It took almost a half-century to complete Vanadislunden. The Vanadisbadet, an outdoor swimming pool, was opened in 1938. Above the pool the sculpture *Girl in the Evening Sun* by Anders Jönsson looks out over Vasastaden. This is the highest part of Vanadislunden, and the streets around here have attractive black-and-white paving stones.

At one time there were numerous suburban mansions in the area. One of them, Cederdals Malmgård, can still be seen towards the northern end of the park.

Houses in Röda Bergen built in typical warm colours

Norrtull & Ekoparken

Large parts of the Royal National City Park (Ekoparken) are spread around the Brunnsviken inlet, only a few kilometres north of the city centre. The English-style park, Hagaparken, with its 18th-century buildings, extolled by the poet Carl Bellman *(see p98)*, is located in this oasis. To the north lies the majestic Baroque Ulriksdals Slott. In stark contrast, to the south, visitors come abruptly to the inner city's built-up area at the old Norrtull gateway. The area has several museums, including Naturhistoriska Riksmuseet, Sweden's largest museum building.

The Wenner-Gren Center's main building, called Pylonen

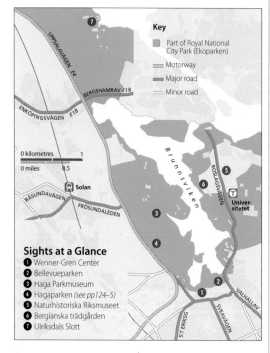

Key

▮ Part of Royal National City Park (Ekoparken)

▬ Motorway

▬ Major road

— Minor road

0 kilometres 1
0 miles 0.5

Sights at a Glance

❶ Wenner-Gren Center
❷ Bellevueparken
❸ Haga Parkmuseum
❹ Hagaparken *(see pp124–5)*
❺ Naturhistoriska Riksmuseet
❻ Bergianska trädgården
❼ Ulriksdals Slott

❶ Wenner-Gren Center

Sveavägen 166. **Map** 2 B1. 🚌 2, 40, 52, 69.

The industrialist Axel Wenner-Gren (1881–1961) had an almost religious faith in the potential of science. "Let us use science to solve mankind's problems" is an expression attributed to him. During the 1920s he launched products including vacuum cleaners and refrigerators through his company, Electrolux, which he founded in 1919. His name is preserved in three foundations and in the Wenner-Gren Center,

whose 24-storey headquarters, Pylonen, stands like an excla-mation mark at the northern end of Sveavägen.

It was opened in 1962, but Wenner-Gren lived only long enough after that to see the topping-out ceremony in 1961. In the semi-circular Helicon building are 155 apartments for the use, at subsidized rents, of foreign scientists undertaking long-term research in Sweden.

The Wenner-Gren Foundation was set up to encourage scientific exchanges between Sweden and other countries. About 250 scientists take part every year, and international symposiums are arranged.

❷ Bellevueparken

South of Brunnsviken lake, Ekoparken 11346. 🚌 2, 40, 53. Carl Eldhs Ateljémuseum Lögbodavägen 10, Bellevueparken. **Tel** 08-612 65 60. **Open** May–Aug: noon–4pm Tue–Sun; Sep–Oct: 11am–4pm Sat & Sun. 📷 1:30pm in English. 🏛♿📷📷📷☀

Bellevue Park is part of the Royal National City Park (Ekoparken). Built by architect Fredrik Magnus Piper, who also planned Haga Park *(see pp124–5)*, Bellevue offers winding paths, groves, tree-lined avenues and open green areas. The park also boasts 200-year-old lime trees and rare medicinal plants. The name "Bellevue", French for "beautiful view", was given to the park by Baron Carl Sparre who purchased a villa here on Bellevue Hill in 1782. The villa was built in 1757 by court painter John Pasch and today is used as a conference centre.

On Bellevue Hill is the Lögbodavägen viewpoint. The site is not easy to locate, but those who do find it are richly rewarded. The point looks out over the Brunnsviken inlet and is close to the monument *The Young Strindberg in the Archipelago* by Carl Eldh (1873–1954). The sculptor's studio, now preserved as the Carl Eldhs Ateljémuseum, is only a few metres from Lögbodavägen. The sheltering environment and panoramic view of Brunnsviken and Haga were important factors in Eldh's decision to locate his studio here. The sculptor was able to benefit from the northern light, and the garden belonging to the studio made it possible for Eldh to work in the open air. Today, the area exudes calm, and it is easy to see why the artist chose to settle here.

In his time Carl Eldh was one of Sweden's most prolific sculptors. Like his colleague Carl Milles, he lived in Paris for several years and was influenced by Rodin's Impressionist style. Later his works were characterized by a more robust Realism. Eldh's sculptures can be seen at 30 public sites in Stockholm. The plaster casts of these works are on show in the studio. Examples include *The Branting Monument* at Norra Bantorget, the statue of Strindberg in Tegnérparken, and *The Runners* at Stadion

Carl Eldh's Ateljémuseum containing plaster cast originals of his works

(see pp112–13). Also here are drawings, tools and other personal belongings of the artist. The unusual wooden building that housed the artist's studio was built in 1919 and was designed by the City Hall's architect, Ragnar Östberg.

❸ Haga Parkmuseum

Mellersta Koppartältet, Hagaparken. **Tel** 08-27 42 52. 🚇 Odenplan then bus. 🚌 515. **Open** Oct–May: 10am–3pm Fri & Sun, May–Sep: 11am–5pm daily. 💻
w hagaparkmuseum.se

This museum is housed in the largest of the three copper-clad "tents" situated in the northwest corner of Hagaparken. It is dedicated to the history of the park and includes exhibits on the plans for its original design, its unusual collection of buildings, and the people associated with them, from the time of Gustav III to the present.

Originally built in 1787–90 as an open stable yard, the building housing the museum was completely destroyed by fire in 1953. The tent-like façade was restored to its former glory in the 1960s, including the painted copper cladding, but it was not until the 1970s that the stables behind were rebuild as a covered structure, in keeping with the original design.

The museum has its own café, whilst the "tents" on either side contain their own restaurant and accommodation. The large rolling lawn in front of the museum is popular with locals for sunbathing and picnics in summer.

The Royal National City Park (Ekoparken)

The Royal National City Park (Ekoparken) was established by the Swedish Parliament in 1995. This has enabled the capital to safeguard the ecology of its "green lung", a 27-sq-km (10.5-sq-mile) area for recreation and outdoor activities in an urban setting. In fact, the park covers an area that is as large as Stockholm's inner-city. The National City Park includes central districts such as Skeppsholmen and the southern part of Djurgården, and continues northwest to northern Djurgården, Hagaparken, Brunnsviken and Ulriksdal. Much of the park was a royal hunting ground as early as the 16th century, scattered with beautiful palaces and other sights. The archipelago is represented with the Fjäderholmarna islands in the south.

There are no gates around the Royal National City Park, so you may enter it without realising. Guided boat tours are available around Brunnsviken, with stops at some of the more important sights. For more information on the Royal National City Park and bookings enquiries, call 08-587 140 40.

The Royal National City Park (Ekoparken) has habitats that support rich bird-life, including breeding herons

❹ Hagaparken

In the mid-18th century King Gustav III decided to create a royal park in the popular Haga area. The king's vision was realized by the fashionable architect Fredrik Magnus Piper (1746–1824) with the help of leading architects and decorators, and the result was an English-style park with some unusual buildings. A royal palace inspired by Versailles in France was also planned, but construction halted after the king's death and it remained unfinished. Today Hagaparken is part of the Royal National City Park (Ekoparken; *see p123*), the world's first national city park – an oasis of nature and culture in the city centre.

Gustav III's Pavilion, painted in 1811 by A F Cederholm

Fjärils- & Fågelhuset
Hundreds of exotic butterflies and birds fly freely around the greenhouses containing humid tropical rainforest with waterfalls and luxuriant growth at a temperature of 25°C (77°F).

★ Koppartälten
These "Roman battle tents" designed by Louis Jean Desprez were completed in 1790. They were originally used as stables and accommodation, but now house a restaurant, café and the Haga Parkmuseum.

KEY

① Haga Parkmuseum

② **Ruined remains** of Gustav III's unfinished royal palace.

③ Royal Cemetery

④ Old Haga

⑤ Turkish Pavilion

Stora Pelousen
The lawns stretching down from Koppartälten to Brunnsviken are popular with Stockholmers for sunbathing and picnics in the summer, and skiing or sledging in the winter. At the rear is Gustav III's Paviljong.

Haga Slott
Built in 1802–4 for Gustav IV Adolf, the palace was the childhood home of the present monarch, Carl XVI Gustaf. It is now the residence of Crown Princess Victoria, Prince Daniel and family.

VISITORS' CHECKLIST

Practical Information
4 km (2 miles) N of Stockholm. Gustav III's Paviljong: **Tel** 08-402 61 30. ▢ hourly Jun–Aug: noon–3pm Tue–Sun. Haga Parkmuseum: **Tel** 08-27 42 52. **Open** 15 May–30 Sep: noon–5pm Tue–Sun; 1 Oct–14 May: 10am–3pm Thu–Sun. Fjärils- & Fågelhuset: **Tel** 08-730 39 81. **Open** Apr–Sep: 10am–5pm Mon–Sun; Oct–Mar: 10am–3pm Tue–Fri, 11am–4pm Sat & Sun. **Closed** 24, 25 & 31 Dec. ▢ ✎
W hagaparkmuseum.se

Transport
🚌 515 from T-Odenplan.
⛴ Royal Haga (in summer).

Ekotemplet
This building designed by Louis Jean Desprez in the 1790s was a royal summer dining room. The acoustics made it possible to eavesdrop on secret conversations.

| 0 metres | 200 |
| 0 yards | 200 |

Kinesiska Pagoden
With the 18th century's fascination for anything Chinese, this pagoda was a natural part of Piper's plans for the park.

★ Gustav III's Paviljong
Olof Tempelman designed this Gustavian masterpiece, and Louis Masreliez undertook the interior decoration. The magnificent hall of mirrors is particularly worth seeing.

Polar bear in a natural setting at Naturhistoriska Riksmuseet

❺ Naturhistoriska Riksmuseet

5 km (3 miles) N of Stockholm.
Tel 08-519 540 00. Ⓣ Universitetet.
🚌 40, 540. **Open** 10am–6pm Tue–Fri,
11am–6pm Sat & Sun. 📷 by
appointment. 🅿 ♿ 📷 ▯ 🔍
🆆 nrm.se

Completed in 1916, the vast Naturhistoriska Riksmuseet (Natural History Museum) was designed by Axel Anderberg and decorated by Carl Fagerberg. The museum is a venerable institution, founded in 1739 by Carl von Linné (1707–78) as part of Vetenskaps-akademien (the Academy of Science). It is one of the ten largest museums of its kind in the world. Over the centuries, the number of exhibits has risen to about 17 million.

During the 1990s it was modernized with the aim of providing "experience-based knowledge". There are permanent collections, such as "Treasures from the Earth's Interior" and "The Human Journey", along with temporary exhibitions. In "4.5 Billion Years" visitors can get acquainted with the dinosaurs and the earliest human beings. "Life and Water" presents both the smallest creatures and the giants of the sea, while penguins, sea lions and polar bears await visitors in "The Polar Regions".

During the 1980s the restau-rant and museum courtyard were given an artistic facelift by Nils Stenqvist, Gunnar Larsson and Pål Svensson, and a major extension was added in the early 1990s. This also saw the opening of Cosmonova, which is both a planetarium and an IMAX cinema. The architects were Uhlin & Malm. The dome-shaped cinema screen is 25 times the size of a normal screen. It is largely due to Cosmonova that the museum is now a major visitor attraction.

The *Vega Monument* was erected in front of the museum in 1930 to mark the 50th anniversary of explorer Adolf Erik Nordenskiöld's first voyage through the North-East Passage in his ship *Vega*. Designed by Ivar Johnsson, it is an obelisk in dark granite topped with a copper ship.

Mola Mola,
Naturhistoriska
Riksmuseet

❻ Bergianska trädgården

3 km (2 miles) N of Stockholm.
Tel 08-545 917 00. Ⓣ Universitetet.
🚌 40, 540. Edvard Anderson
Conservatory: **Open** Apr–Sep:
11am–5pm daily; Oct–Mar:
11am–4pm Mon–Fri, 11am–5pm
Sat & Sun. Victoria House: **Open** May–
Sep: 11am–4pm Mon–Fri; 11am–5pm
Sat & Sun. 🅿 📷 ♿ 🏠 ▯
🆆 bergianska.se

Bergianska trädgården (Bergius Botanic Garden) features plants from all over the world in beautiful natural settings, and provides an attractive display throughout the year. The garden consists of different areas such as the systematic section, the Japanese pond, the orchard and the wetland. There is a kitchen garden in the shade of 100-year-old spruce hedges, and an area for spices and medicinal plants. The Italian terrace has been one of the outlooks of the garden ever since it was founded at the end of the 19th century. From the end of May until the middle of June, visitors can enjoy the wonderful flowering of rhododendrons in the valley leading down to Brunnsviken.

The Victoria House (1900) houses tropical water plants, utility plants and epiphytes. The Edvard Anderson Conservatory (1995) has large sections for Mediterranean and tropical plants.

Bergianska trädgården's Edvard Anderson Conservatory, featuring Mediterranean and tropical plants

Ulriksdals Slott with its magnificent 18th-century Baroque exterior, seen from the palace park

❼ Ulriksdals Slott

7 km (4 miles) N of Stockholm.
Tel 08-402 62 60. 🚌 503. 🚌 Royal
Haga (summer). Palace, Orangery &
Coronation carriage: **Open** mid-Jun–
mid-Aug: noon–4pm daily; May–mid-
Jun & mid-Aug–Oct: noon–4pm Sat &
Sun. Also available for pre-booked
groups year-round. 🖼️ 🖼️ ♿ 📷 📷
💻 🌐 **kungahuset.se/royalpalaces**

Ulriksdals Slott is situated
between the two main roads
in the northern outskirts of
Stockholm – the E4 and
Norrtäljevägen. The palace
sits on a headland in the bay
of Edsviken. Its attractive
buildings and lush and leafy
surroundings are well worth
a visit. At the entrance to the
grounds is one of Stockholm's
best-known restaurants,
Ulriksdals Wärdshus.

The original palace was built
in the 1640s and designed by
Hans Jakob Kristler in German/
Dutch Renaissance style. The
owner, Marshal of the Realm
Jakob de la Gardie, named the
palace Jakobsdal. It was bought
in 1669 by the Dowager Queen
Hedvig Eleonora. When she had
a grandson, Ulrik, 15 years later
she donated the palace to
him as a christening gift, and
it was renamed Ulriksdal.

Around this time the architect
Tessin the Elder *(see p38)* suggested some rebuilding work, but
only a few of his proposals saw
the light of day. However, the
stucco work by Carlo Carove in
the southern wing can still be
seen. In the 18th century the
palace acquired its Baroque
exterior. After being a popular
place for festivities in the time
of Gustav III (1746–92), it began
to lose its glamour and at one
time was used as a home for
war invalids.

Interest in the palace was
revived under Karl XV (1826–72),
and furnishings and handicrafts
many hundreds of years old are
on show in his rooms. The living
room of Gustav VI Adolf (1882–
1973) in the rebuilt Knights' Hall,
contains furnishings by the
great architect and designer
Carl Malmsten. The suite was a
gift from the Swedish people
in 1923 to the then Crown
Prince when he married Louise
Mountbatten. A staircase was
built at the same time to
designs, that Tessin the Elder
had suggested 250 years earlier.

The park was laid out in
the mid-17th century. It has
300-year-old lime trees, as
well as one of Europe's most
northerly beechwoods. Carl
Milles's two sculptures of wild
boars stand by the pool in front
of the palace. A stream is
crossed by a footbridge, which
is supported by Per Lundgren's
Moors Dragging the Nets. More
art can be seen in the orangery,
designed by Tessin the Elder in
the 1660s and rebuilt in 1705. It
now houses a sculpture museum.

The palace chapel, a popular
place for weddings, was
designed by F W Scholander
and built in 1865 in Dutch
Neo-Renaissance style. It
has some notable medieval
stained-glass windows.

It was from Ulriksdal that
Queen Kristina's Coronation
procession departed in 1650.
Legend has it that by the time
the queen reached the city, some
of her retinue had still not left
Ulriksdal. In one of the stables
there is a replica of Kristina's
carriage. A riding school, built
in 1671, was converted into a
theatre by Carl Hårleman and
C F Adelcrantz in the 1750s.
Performances are staged in the
theatre, named Confidencen,
every summer.

Sculpture on display in the 17th-century orangery at Ulriksdals Slott

Södermalm & South of Söder

The Södermalm area, generally known as "Söder", rises steeply from the water and is something of a city in itself with its own character, charm and dialect. The slopes are lined with old wooden cottages with an unrivalled view of Stockholm. The dramatic topography has provided some hilly parks, and allotments are scattered among the built-up areas. The area has plenty of shops, bars and restaurants and a lively nightlife, as well as the latest in modern architecture. South of Söder is Globen, a spectacular indoor arena, and Skogskyrkogården Cemetery, which is on the UNESCO World Heritage list.

The towers of Mariaberget on a steep hillside close to Slussen

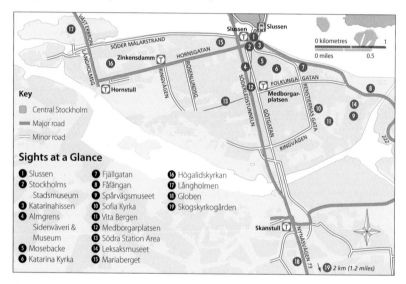

Key

- ▓ Central Stockholm
- ▬ Major road
- ═ Minor road

Sights at a Glance

1. Slussen
2. Stockholms Stadsmuseum
3. Katarinahissen
4. Almgrens Sidenväveri & Museum
5. Mosebacke
6. Katarina Kyrka
7. Fjällgatan
8. Fåfängan
9. Spårvägsmuseet
10. Sofia Kyrka
11. Vita Bergen
12. Medborgarplatsen
13. Södra Station Area
14. Leksaksmuseet
15. Mariaberget
16. Högalidskyrkan
17. Långholmen
18. Globen
19. Skogskyrkogården

❶ Slussen

Map 4 C4. Ⓣ Slussen. ▤ 2, 3, 43, 53, 55, 59 76. ▤ Djurgårdsfärja.

Steadily increasing traffic in the early 1900s turned the narrow road between Södermalm and Gamla Stan into a bottleneck. All the boats sailing between Lake Mälaren and the Baltic had to pass through the locks here, and land traffic was confined to a narrow bridge. The congestion was eased in 1928, when some of the boat traffic was transferred to a new canal, but the problem needed a more radical solution. This took the form of a clover-leaf system of roundabouts devised by Tage William-Olsson and Gösta Lundborg. It was opened in 1935 and was so well designed that it was able to cope with the change to right-hand driving in 1967.

At Slussplan, facing Söder-malm and the lock that bears his name, is Bengt Fogelberg's bronze statue of Karl XIV on horseback, unveiled in 1854 by Oscar I on the 40th anniversary of the union between Sweden and Norway (1814–1905). Around the same time, the locks were rebuilt. New machinery devised by the inventor Nils Ericsson was installed. Today the locks are used mostly by pleasure boats, whose erratic manoeuvres provide enter-tainment for onlookers.

Although the construction of Västerbron and Söderleden have eased the traffic burden, Slussen is still a busy junction and is in need of a thorough facelift.

Slussen's intricate traffic system, opened in 1935

❷ Stockholms Stadsmuseum

Ryssgården. **Map** 4 B5. **Tel** 08-508 316 00. 🚇 Slussen. 🚌 2, 3, 43, 53, 55, 76. **Closed** for renovation until autumn 2017 🎫 📷 ♿ 📷 🏪 🌐 **stadsmuseet.stockholm.se**

Hemmed in between the traffic roundabouts of Slussen and the steep hill up to Mosebacke Torg is Stockholms Stadsmuseum (City Museum). It is housed in a late 17th-century building originally designed by Tessin the Elder as Södra Stadshuset (Southern City Hall). After a fire, it was completed by Tessin the Younger in 1685. It has been used for various purposes over the centuries, including law courts and dungeons, schools and city-hall cellars, theatres and churches. It became the city museum in the 1930s.

The museum, which is closed for renovation until autumn 2017, documents the history of Stockholm. During the renovation period it is organising daily city walks (most in Swedish). The city's main stages of development are described in a permanent exhibition, and there are also regular temporary exhibitions.

The library has a large archive of pictures and a documentary room. There are also children's activities, concerts and lectures.

The museum's Stieg Larsson Millennium Tour visits the world

of Larsson's best-selling Millennium books (*The Girl with the Dragon Tattoo* series), which are set in Södermalm. The tours are 2 hours long and start at Bellmansgatan 1, home of character Mikael Blomkvist. Tours in English take place on Saturdays at 11:30am even during the renovation period. Tickets must be bought online in advance.

❸ Katarinahissen

Stadsgården. **Map** 4 C5. 🚇 Slussen. 🚌 2, 3, 43, 53, 55, 76. **Closed** to the public. 🚷 ♨

Katarinahissen is the oldest of Stockholm's "high-rise" attractions. The 38-m (125-ft) high lift was opened to the public in March 1883 and is still a prominent silhouette on the Söder skyline. The first Swedish neon sign was erected here in 1909 – a legendary advertisement for Stomatol tooth-paste. Since the 1930s, the sign has been placed on a nearby rooftop.

Stomatol neon sign on Katarinahissen

The original lift was driven by steam, but it switched to electricity in 1915. In the 1930s it was replaced by a new lift, when the Cooperative Association (KF) built its large office complex at Slussen. In its first year the lift was used by more than a million passengers, but its record year was 1945,

Almgrens Sidenväveri (silk mill), now a museum with working 19th-century looms

when it carried 1.8 million people between Slussen and Mosebacke Torg.

The lift is now closed to the public; however, there is a modern lift to reach the restaurant and the veranda at the top of the building, from where amazing views can still be enjoyed.

❹ Almgrens Sidenväveri & Museum

Repslagargatan 15a. **Map** 9 D2. **Tel** 08-642 56 16. **Open** 10am–4pm Mon–Fri, 11am–3pm Sat (25 Jun–6 Aug: 11am–3pm Mon–Fri). 🎫 1pm Mon, Wed & Sat. 📷 🏪 🌐 **kasiden.se**

Karl August Almgren was the founder of Almgren's silk-weaving mill, now a museum, in 1833. While on a study tour to Lyon and Tours in France in 1825, Almgren learned about the punch-card system, which was one of the secrets of France's dominance in the silk business. Armed with this information, he returned to Sweden with designs for modern looms and opened his own mill. It soon became a leader in the market, which in the 1700s had seen the establishment of more than 30 silk-weaving mills in Stockholm.

The Almgren family continued the business until 1974, when the mill finally closed. Everything was left intact, and the mill took on a new role in 1991 as a living museum. In the weaving room there is a museum shop selling textiles. The area where the old steam-driven machinery stood is now used as a banqueting room with well-preserved 19th-century decorations.

Katarinahissen with Stockholms Stadsmuseum in the background

❺ Mosebacke

Map 9 D2. 🅣 Slussen, then a short walk. 🚌 59, then a short walk. ✻

The district of Mosebacke, with its distinctive atmosphere, got its name from a miller and landowner, Moses Israelsson, the son-in-law of Johan Hansson Hök, who managed two mills on the hilltop plateau in the 17th century.

In the mid-19th century Mosebacke became increasingly attractive to Stockholmers as a centre for entertainment. A theatre was built in 1852. However, it was destroyed by fire soon after and replaced in 1859 by a new building, Södra Teatern, designed by Johan Fredrik Åbom. The gateway leading to Mosebacke Terrass and its spectacular panoramic views of the city was added at the same time.

Södra Teatern is a classic among Stockholm's stages. Around 1900 the auditorium was enhanced with a ceiling painting by Vicke Andrén. In the 1930s murals were added, some by Isaac Grünewald. Carl Eldh's bronze bust, *The Young Strindberg*, placed on the theatre's terrace in 1975, shows the author looking across to the city from this very terrace, recalling the character of Arvid Falk in the beginning of Strindberg's novel *The Red Room* (1879).

Nils Sjögren's sculpture *The Sisters* stands behind railings on Mosebacke Torg. Attractive steps lead up to Fiskargatan. At No. 12 is an experimental

Katarina Kyrka (1695) after its extensive restoration due to a devastating fire in 1990

fireproof-gable design, *Morning Light*, an *al secco* painting on limestone plaster.

❻ Katarina Kyrka

Högbergsgatan 13. **Map** 9 D2. **Tel** 08-743 68 00. 🅣 Medborgarplatsen, then 3 min walk. 🚌 2, 3, 53, 76. **Open** 11am–5pm Mon–Sat, 10am–5pm Sun (Oct–Mar: Tue–Sun only). 📷 by appointment. ✝ noon & 6pm Wed, 11am Sat, 11am Sun. ♿ 📷

The buildings on Katarina-berget date partly from the 18th century and surround a hilltop, where various churches have been sited since the late 14th century. The earlier chapels were replaced in the 17th century by a more impressive and appropriate building, Katarina Kyrka, designed by one of the era's greatest architects, Jean de la Vallée (1620–96). King Karl X Gustaf was also deeply involved in the project, and he insisted that the church should have a central nave with the altar and pulpit right in the middle. The church was founded in 1656, although it was not completed until 1695. In 1723 it was badly damaged by fire, but it was restored over the next couple of decades. Major restoration was also carried out in the 20th century, and a new copper roof was added in 1988. Two years later, on the night of 16 May 1990, there was another fire and, apart from the outer walls, the church and virtually all its fittings were destroyed.

The architectural practice of Ove Hidemark was commissioned to design a new church, which, as far as possible, would be a faithful reconstruction of the original. It was not just the outer shell of the building that had to undergo detailed restoration. In order to make the best use of the surviving walls, it was necessary to adopt 17th-century building techniques throughout the new building. Experts and craftsmen managed to join heavy timbering on to the central dome in the traditional way, and the collapsed central arch was rebuilt with specially made bricks in 17th-century style.

In 1995, the church was reconsecrated, more beautiful than ever in the view of many people, with the altar sited exactly where it was originally planned.

The reconstruction cost 270 million kronor, of which 145 million kronor were covered by insurance. Such was the popularity of the project that the rest was raised through public donations.

Mosebacke Torg with Södra Teatern in the background

❼ Fjällgatan

Per Anders Fogelström (1917–98), probably Söder's best-known author, wrote: "Fjällgatan must be the city's most beautiful street. It's an old-fashioned narrow street which runs along the hilltop with well-maintained cobble-stones… and with street lights jutting out from the houses. Then the street opens up and gives a fantastic view of the city and the water…" This area offers an experience of the authentic Söder and its unique atmosphere.

The Heights of Söder
With its 300-year-old houses and terraced gardens, the Söder hilltop stands like a giant stage-set behind Stadsgården harbour.

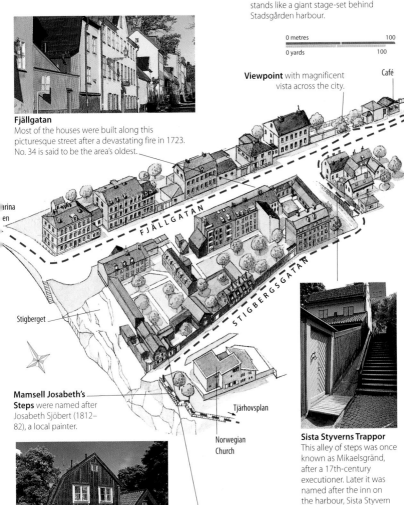

| 0 metres | | 100 |
| 0 yards | | 100 |

Viewpoint with magnificent vista across the city.

Café

Fjällgatan
Most of the houses were built along this picturesque street after a devastating fire in 1723. No. 34 is said to be the area's oldest.

FJÄLLGATAN

STIGBERGSGATAN

arina
en

Stigberget

Mamsell Josabeth's Steps were named after Josabeth Sjöbert (1812–82), a local painter.

Tjärhovsplan

Norwegian Church

Sista Styverns Trappor
This alley of steps was once known as Mikaelsgränd, after a 17th-century executioner. Later it was named after the inn on the harbour, Sista Styvern ("The Last Penny").

Söder Cottages
Typical well-preserved cottages can be found along Stigbergsgatan. No. 17 was the house of the blockmaker Olof Krok during the 1730s.

Key
▬ Suggested route

❽ Fåfängan

Map 6 A5. 🚌 53. 🚇 ☀️

Fåfängan, at Södermalm's most easterly point, provides a grandstand view of the boats sailing in and out of Stockholm's harbour. In the 1650s, Field Marshal Erik Dahlberg made full use of its strategic location on a hilltop to build a defensive fortress. Some relics of this period can still be seen.

The hill and its park were given the name Fåfängan in the 1770s. The wholesale merchant Fredrik Lundin owned the area at that time, and he built a pavilion, which still stands on the hilltop in a square garden filled with flowerbeds. The word "Fåfängan" ("Vanity") originally denoted an area of land that was not worth using. But in Stockholm it has a special meaning: "The pavilion on the hilltop with a marvellous view." It is a delightful place for a coffee break while exploring Söder.

❾ Spårvägsmuseet

Tegelviksgatan 22. **Map** 9 F3.
Tel 08-686 17 60. 🚌 53, 55, 66.
Open 10am–5pm Mon–Fri,
11am–4pm Sat & Sun. 📷 by appt. 🅿️
♿ 🏠 🚇 🌐 **sparvagsmuseet.sl.se**

The Tram Museum, Spårvägsmuseet, covers the development of the Stockholm public transport system, SL, from the horse-drawn buses of the 19th century to the high-tech underground trains of today. Visitors can try out old and new trams and buses for comfort and can experience a driver's-eye view of the city traffic on film.

Horse-drawn tram from the 1890s on display in Spårvägsmuseet

Sofia Kyrka and Vita Bergen park with its 18th-century cottages

The museum has three permanent exhibitions covering 5,000 sq m (53,800 sq ft). One shows the history of public transport with the help of some 50 vehicles. Another section traces technical developments from different eras. The third section focuses on the artistically decorated underground stations (see p202). There is also a library and archive. On Saturdays and Sundays for most of the year visitors can take two free round trips on a vintage bus.

❿ Sofia Kyrka

Vitabergsparken. **Map** 9 F3.
Tel 08- 615 31 00. 🚌 3, 4, 76.
Open 11am–5pm daily. 🕊 6:30pm
Thu, 11am Sun. 📷 by appt. ♿
🏠 Concerts 3pm Sat.
🌐 **svenskakyrkan.se**

High up on Vita Bergen, surrounded by a leafy green park, is Sofia Kyrka, named after Oscar II's consort and built in 1902–6.

The 35-year-old architect Gustaf Hermansson, who had already designed several churches, including Oscarskyrkan at Östermalm, created a monumental design with both National Romantic and Gothic influences and tall spires, the highest reaching 78 m (256 ft).

Three windows by Olle Hjortzberg are all that remain of the original decorations. The early 1950s saw the addition of the large altar fresco by Hilding Linnqvist with themes from the Old and New Testaments. The interior acquired its present appearance as part of a major renovation in the early 1980s, when the layout of the church was radically altered.

⓫ Vita Bergen

Map 9 F3. 🚌 2, 3, 66, 76.

Vita Bergen (White Mountains) is best known as a park, largely because of Swedish TV broadcasts from its open-air theatre. But it is more than just a park. Houses for workers at Söder's harbours and factories were built on and around the hilltop in the 18th century. They were simple homes, often with a small garden and surrounded by a fence. In 1736 the building of new wooden houses was forbidden because of the fire risk, but the slum districts were exempted. As a result, areas such as Bergsprängargränd still have houses that have retained their original character and give a good idea of life in bygone days.

Around 1900, when Sofia Kyrka was built, the area was turned into a leafy hillside park. This was complemented to the east by an area of allotment-garden cottages. Towards Malmgårdsvägen is the 300-year-old Werner Groen Malmgård (suburban mansion). The park has a bronze statue, *Elsa Borg* (1972), by Astri Bergman Taube, wife of the great troubadour Evert Taube (see p59).

⓬ Medborgar-platsen

Map 9 D3. Ⓣ Medborgarplatsen.
🚌 59, 66.

Södermalm's natural centre is Medborgarplatsen. The square had been called Södra Bantorget for more than 100 years, but in 1939 it was renamed Medborgarplatsen (Citizen's Square) on completion of Medborgarhuset. The building, designed by Martin Westerberg in Functionalist and Neo-Classical styles, contains an auditorium, gym, swimming pool and library.

On the west side of the square is Söderhallarna, a complex of restaurants, delicatessens and a cinema. In 1984 the Göta Ark offices, designed by Claes Mellin and Willy Hermansson, were added on the northwest side.

Alongside the stairway to Södra Station is the Södertorn apartment block designed by the Danish architect Henning Larssen. At the entrance is *Nana's Fountain* by Niki de Saint-Phalle, who also created a large sculpture group *(see p78)* at the Moderna museet *(see pp82–3)*. The western corner of Medborgarhuset features a 17th-century gateway. Closer to Götgatan is Gustaf Nordahl's *The Source of Life* (1983).

Göran Strååt's sculpture *Kasper* can be seen at the 17th-century Lillienhoffska Palatset. Stefan Thorén's sculpture *Dawn* in welded iron is a dominant feature on the square outside.

The lofty Södertorn and Ricardo Bofill's curved building near Södra Station

⓭ Södra Station Area

Map 8 C3. Ⓣ Medborgarplatsen or Mariatorget, then a short walk. 🚌 43, 55, 66.

In the mid-19th century Fatburen lake existed to the west of Medborgarplatsen. It was filled in, and in the 1860s a train station – Södra – was opened nearby. In the 1980s the track site was transformed into a new residential area with approximately 3,000 apartments.

The district became a test-bed for the design concepts of the 1980s and was shaped by architects' efforts towards Stockholm's urban renewal. The most interesting additions were by the Spanish architect Ricardo Bofill. He designed the tower blocks near to the station building as well as the curved residential building – the area's most impressive Neo-Classical feature – which adjoins Fatbur Park.

The park has an open section close to Bofill's curved building, with a wooded area further away. It is crossed by a path, which links Medborgarplatsen with Söder-malmsallén and the rail-shuttle station. A 200-m (660-ft) long avenue with 16 sculptures cuts diagonally across the park, with a fountain and pool in the middle. In the northern part of the park a flower garden has been named after the Swedish composer Johan Helmich Roman (1694–1758). The arches of Bofill's curved building shelter some interesting works of art.

⓮ Leksaksmuseet

Tegelviksgatan 22. **Map** 8 F3. **Tel** 08-641 61 00. Ⓣ Slussen. 🚌 2, 55, 66. **Open** 10am–5pm Mon–Fri, 11am–4pm Sat & Sun. 📷 by appt. 🐾 ♿ 🏠 💻 🌐 **leksaksmuseet.se**

Toys, which have delighted children and adults alike over the past century, are on show at Leksaksmuseet (the Toy Museum). The museum was opened in 1980, and the main exhibition changes continuously as new toys are added to the collection.

One section features musical instruments, including musical boxes, barrel organs and accordions. Another area is devoted to mechanical toys, models and dioramas. A third section has dolls, dolls' houses, wooden toys, steam engines, and several working model railways. Private collections are also on show. There is a playroom and children's theatre.

Medborgarplatsen, central Södermalm, with Lillienhoffska Palatset, once a poorhouse

Bastugatan, one of Mariaberget's well-preserved 18th-century streets

⓯ Mariaberget

Map 8 C2. Ⓣ Mariatorget. 🚌 43, 55.

A fire in 1759 destroyed the old buildings of Mariaberget. The area was rebuilt according to a 1736 law forbidding the construction of wooden houses in this part of Söder. The result of this purposeful 18th-century town planning remains intact. Mariaberget's stone buildings on the slopes down towards Riddarfjärden are among Stockholm's most distinctive, and the character of the steep winding streets and alleys has been well preserved.

Towards the end of the 20th century a conservation programme was implemented to safeguard the area's cultural heritage, including the view over Riddarfjärden. Near Bastugatan, an attractive promenade, Monteliusvägen, has been built along the rock's edge. A new flight of steps leads down to the Söder Mälarstrand quayside.

The author Ivar Lo-Johansson (1901–90) lived in this area for more than half a century. A small park with a bust of the artist bears his name. The 18th-century poet C M Bellman (see p98) was born at Mariaberget, although he is more usually associated with Haga and Djurgården.

Mariaberget presents a pleasant contrast to the busy traffic artery of Hornsgatan. When the street was widened and levelled in 1901, a number of 18th-century buildings came into view. The area now features galleries and antiques shops. On the opposite side of Hornsgatan is Maria Magdalena Kyrka, on a site where there have been religious buildings since the 14th century. The predecessor of the present building was constructed in 1634. It burnt down in 1759 and was rebuilt four years later.

⓰ Högalidskyrkan

Högalids Kyrkväg. **Map** 1 C5. **Tel** 08-616 88 00. Ⓣ Hornstull. 🚌 4, 66, 74. **Open** 9am–noon & 1–3pm Mon, Tue, Thu, Fri, 9am–noon Wed, 10am–4pm Sat & Sun. ✝ noon Wed, 1pm Thu, 11am Sun. ♿ 📷

The octagonal twin towers of Högalidskyrkan make the church easy to identify from many parts of the city. The impressive brick building in National Romantic style was completed in 1923. It was designed by Ivar Tengbom. He also put his mark on the interior decoration, which involved a number of leading artists and craftsmen.

Tengbom was enlisted to design the columbarium, which was added in 1939. The most prolific artist was Gunnar Torhamn, who provided the Crucifix – the largest in

The distinctive twin towers of Högalidskyrkan, built in 1923

Scandinavia – as well as the frescoes in the baptismal chapel and the decoration of the pulpit and organ loft. Erik Jerke created the reredos in Byzantine style. In the cemetery chapel below the chancel, Einar Forseth designed an apse mosaic using the same techniques he employed for Gyllene Salen (the Golden Room) in Stadshuset (see pp116–7).

By no means everything in the church is new. The font is from the 16th century, and the seven-stemmed candlestick on the altar dates from the 18th century.

Exercise yard in the former royal prison on Långholmen

⓱ Långholmen

Map 1 B5. Ⓣ Hornstull, then 3 min walk. 🚌 66. 🚢

Below the majestic Västerbron (see p115) is the island of Långholmen, which is linked to Södermalm by two bridges. Långholmen is best known for the various prisons, which have been located here since 1724. During the 20th century the prison here was the largest in Sweden, housing 620 inmates. When the prison closed in 1975, the island became a popular recreational area.

The prison buildings were demolished in 1982, but the old royal jail dating from 1835 remains. The one-time cells now form part of a hotel, as well as a prison museum. There is also a youth hostel and an excellent restaurant, as well as a small museum to the poet C M Bellman (see p98) with a café in the gardens, which run down towards Riddarfjärden.

Långholmen's park has an open-air theatre, and offers excellent swimming both from the beaches and the rocks.

⓲ Globen

3 km (2 miles) S of Stockholm.
Ⓣ Globen. **Tel** 08-50 83 53 00.
Open during events. 🔑 by appt.
♿ 🖥 📷 🌐 **globen.se**

The Globen, or Ericsson Globe, is Sweden's national indoor arena. Built to represent the Sun in the Swedish Solar System, the unusual structure took two and a half years to build and opened in 1989. It is the world's largest hemispherical building and seats up to 16,000 spectators.

The Globen is primarily used for ice hockey, and is home to the Swedish national team. The arena has also been used for major cultural events. In 1989, Pope John Paul II held Mass at the Globen – the first ever Mass to be conducted by a pope in Sweden. The Dalai Lama and Nelson Mandela are among the many influential figures who have given speeches here. The arena is also a popular venue for concerts, and has hosted international artists such as U2, the Rolling Stones and Beyoncé.

Visitors can take in sweeping views of Stockholm from SkyView, an inclined lift on the exterior of the building. Two specially designed glass gondolas, each carrying 16 passengers, take visitors to the apex of the globe, which is 130 m (425 ft) above sea level. There are often long queues for SkyView, especially at weekends and during school holidays, so it is advisable to book your slot well in advance.

Chapel of the Holy Cross by Gunnar Asplund at Skogskyrkogården

⓳ Skogskyrko-gården

6 km (4 miles) S of Stockholm.
Tel 08-508 317 30. Ⓣ Skogskyrko-gården. 🚌 183 (weekends only).
📅 Jul–Sep: 10:30am Sun (in English).
♿ 🖥 🌐 **skogskyrkogarden.se**

Nature and the splendid buildings have combined to provide a harmonious setting, which has placed Skogskyrko-gården Cemetery on the UNESCO World Heritage list. It is sited amid pinewoods, which provide a justly sombre framework for the chapels and crematorium.

The winners of a competition to design the cemetery in 1914 were Gunnar

Epitaph to Gunnar Asplund

Asplund (see p119) and Sigurd Lewerentz, whose proposals were considered the most likely to safeguard the area's special character. Asplund's first significant work, Skogskapellet (Woodland Chapel), with its

steep shingled roof, was opened at the same time as the cemetery in 1920. This was followed 5 years later by Uppståndelsekapellet (Resurrection Chapel), designed by Lewerentz.

In 1940 Asplund's last great work, Skogskrematoriet (Woodland Crematorium), was opened, along with its three chapels representing Faith, Hope and the Holy Cross. They are sited along Korsets Väg. John Lundqvist's The Resurrection stands in the pillared hall of Heliga Korsets Kapell – the largest of the three. Adjoining the chapel is Asplund's black granite cross.

A memorial park was added in 1961 to the north-west of the chapel. The Hill of Meditation lies to the west. The chapel has been decorated by artists including Carl Milles, Sven Erixson and Gunnar Torhamn.

Skogskyrkogården is the last resting place of both the unknown and the celebrated, among whom is Greta Garbo.

Greta Garbo

The legendary Greta Garbo, one of the 20th century's outstanding film stars, was born in 1905 in a humble part of Södermalm. At the age of 17 she joined the theatre academy of Dramaten and made her film debut in Peter the Tramp. Her breakthrough came in 1924 in Mauritz Stiller's film of Selma Lagerlöf's book The Atonement of Gösta Berling. The following year she moved to Hollywood, where she soon became the reigning star. Garbo appeared in 24 films, including Anna Karenina (1935) and Camille (1936). She never married and lived a solitary life until her death in 1990. Her ashes were interred at the Skogskyrkogården Cemetery in 1999.

Garbo in As You Desire Me (1932)

The silhouette of Globen arena dominating the surrounding area

THREE GUIDED WALKS

Stockholm is a perfect city for walking. Not only is it flat, but it is also one of Europe's less crowded capital cities, making it ideal for stress-free strolling through the streets and thoroughfares. Many of Stockholm's pedestrian areas also have cycle paths running alongside them, so take care to observe the painted signs on the ground, indicating which side of the line you should walk. These guided walks have been devised to cover some of the city's most appealing districts: discover residential Södermalm (also known as "Söder") south of the centre, with great views of the city centre; take in some of Stockholm's best parkland on Djurgården – the perfect destination for a picnic; and finally, explore the commercial heart of the Swedish capital, following a route which takes you past leading department stores and boutiques, as well as more sedate churches and monuments.

A view of Stockholm from Södermalm

Key

···· Walk route

Stadsbiblioteket (the city library) in central Stockholm *(see p119)*

0 kilometres 1

0 miles 1

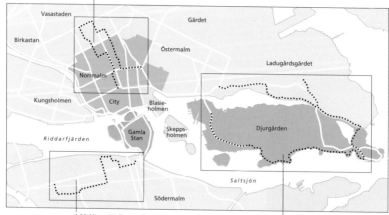

A 90-Minute Walk around the City Centre *(pp140–41)*

A 30-Minute Walk around Södermalm *(p137)*

A 90-Minute Walk on Djurgården *(pp138–9)*

A 30-Minute Walk around Södermalm

Winding through a charming mix of narrow residential streets and neighbourhood allotments with their red and white summer cottages, this walk also offers the best views of Stockholm from anywhere in the city. There is also the chance to browse in some of the more quirky stores or stop at a streetside café whilst exploring this largely undiscovered side of Stockholm.

Begin at Södermalms torg ①, the heart of one of Stockholm's main traffic interchanges, Slussen. Before leaving the

⑤ View of Riddarholmen from Blecktornsgränd

sought after addresses. Turn right into Bellmansgatan and head north towards Söder's northern shore, then take a left into pretty, cobbled Bastugatan ④, full of 18th-century houses. Turn right into Blecktornsgränd ⑤ to see some of the finest views in the city, with open vistas out over Riddarholmen, Gamla Stan and the city centre. Follow the narrow path of Monteliusvägen ⑥ west, enjoying the sweeping views

⑦ Boats serving as floating hotels lining Söder Mälarstrand

```
0 metres          500
0 yards           500
```

Key

••• Walk route

square, glance up at the roofs of the surrounding buildings and you'll see Sweden's first ever neon sign for the now defunct Stomatol toothpaste. From Södermalms torg, head west along Hornsgatan ②. Söder has a plethora of good restaurants and unusual shops, and on the initial stretch of this long road you will also find many small, interesting art galleries. On the left as you make your way along Hornsgatan you'll soon pass the 17th century Maria Magdalena Kyrka ③ designed by the same architects as the Royal Palace.

Now leave the main road to walk along some of Söder's residential streets which are among Stockholm's most

on your right; several of the house-boats below on Söder Mälarstrand ⑦ now serve as floating hotels.

At Timmermansgatan head south until you reach Wollmar Yxkullsgatan ⑧, considered by some to be the heart of Södermalm.

Now head right along Wollmar Yxkullsgatan until you reach Ringvägen. Cross this road and take the delightful Zinkens Väg ⑨ through an area of allotments and small summer cottages in the Zinkensdamm area ⑩. Owners often spend several days at a time here pottering in their gardens. After passing the Zinkensdamm youth hostel, head north up the

steps of Pipmakartrappan back to Hornsgatan and the end of the walk ⑪.

Tips for Walkers

Starting point: The easiest way to get to the start of the walk is to take the T-bana to Slussen; Södermalms torg is just outside the main exit.
Length: 2.5 km (1.6 miles)
Duration: Half an hour
Stopping-off points: There are plenty of cafés and shops along Hornsgatan for a break or rest.
Ending the walk: At the end of the walk you can take the Zinkensdamm T-bana located on Hornsgatan (two stops west of Slussen).

For map symbols see back flap

A 90-Minute Walk on Djurgården

This delightful walk offers a chance to explore the former royal hunting grounds of Djurgården, an island which forms the northern side of Stockholm harbour. Heavily wooded and dotted with grand old houses, the island offers peace, tranquillity and some of the city's most striking museums. There are also stunning views across Stockholm from the top of the Kaknäs TV tower.

Nordiska museet to Ryssviken
The walk starts at the palatial Nordiska museet ①, one of the city's best museums, which provides a good grounding in the history of everyday Swedish life. From the museum, follow Djurgårdsvägen south, looking out for the boat-shaped building behind the Nordiska museet. Here resides the former warship, *Vasa*. She sank in Stockholm harbour on her maiden voyage in 1628 *(see pp94–6)*.

Continuing on, you will soon come to the eclectic Liljevalchs Konsthall art gallery ② *(see p97)* which hosts frequently changing exhibitions of art and sculpture. Once at Almänna Gränd, you are entering the pleasure zone: there are often crowds of children here heading for the amusement park, Gröna Lund ③ *(see p97)*, which features several hair-raising rides including the "Free Fall", a

vertical drop of around 100 m (330 ft). From here Djurgårdsvägen swings east on its way around Djurgården. Follow the road to the small inlet, Ryssviken ④, where you could end the walk if you wish and take the Tram 7 back to the city.

The greenery of Djurgården as seen from the air

Tips for Walkers

Starting point: Tram number 7 or bus 44 will bring you closest to the Nordiska museet.
Length: 8.5 km (5.3 miles)
Duration: One and a half to 2 hours
Stopping-off points: A great spot for lunch or a cup of coffee is the Blå Porten, Djurgårdsvägen 64, near the Liljevachs Konsthall art gallery. The café at the top of the Kaknästornet TV tower has the best views of Stockholm.
End point: You could end this walk early at Blockhusudden, which is conveniently the terminus for the 69 bus which runs all the way back into the centre of the city via Strandvägen and Sergels torg. From the end of the walk at Strandvägen buses 69 and 79 run back to the centre.

Ryssviken to Blockhusudden
From Ryssviken, take the path south to the promontory known as Waldemarsudde ⑤ *(see p99)* with its good views across the harbour and excellent art gallery specialising in late 19th-century Nordic art. From here, it is a pleasant walk along the waterfront to another small promontory, Biskopsudden ⑥.

Heading east a short distance along Biskopsvägen, pick up another path along the shore

The Vasamuseet, home to the former warship, the *Vasa*

which begins just south of the junction with Djurgårdsvägen ⑦. This path leads to the eastern end of Djurgården, Blockhusudden ⑧, which gives views of the hi-tech business centre, Nacka Strand, on the southern side of the harbour and the residential area, Jarlaberg, high on the cliffs above. The arcing sculpture of a boy atop a crescent of steel that you can see across the water is *Gud på himmelsbågen*, by Stockholm sculptor Carl Milles *(see p152)*.

Carl Milles' sculpture, *Gud på himmelsbågen*

Blockhusudden to Berwaldhallen concert hall

On foot, continue northeast to Lilla Sjötullsbron bridge ⑩. The stretch of path before the bridge runs past a marshy pond, especially preserved for its birdlife. Once over the bridge, head west along the tranquil canal to meet up with Djurgårdsbrunnsvägen which leads towards the Kaknästornet TV tower ⑪ *(see p110).*

This is a long diversion from the main route, but worth it if you are feeling energetic. At 155 m (508 ft) high, the tower is one of the tallest buildings in Scandinavia and even boasts a café at around 120 m (390 ft) elevation.

From the tower, backtrack to the main walk and head west along the canal path past a clutch of museums on your right, including the Sjöhistoriska museet ⑫ *(see pp108–9)*, which reveals Sweden's maritime history. Further along the path, the imposing villas on the right are part of "Diplomatstaden" ("Diplomat's Town", *see p108*), home to several Embassies, including that of the United States of America ⑬. The spire rising from behind the waterfront houses belongs to Engelska Kyrkan ⑭, the English Church. To finish the walk, take the path around Nobel Parken and end at Strandvägen, with its elegant façades lining the waterfront ⑮.

Key

••• Walk route

0 metres 500
0 yards 500

Blockhusudden is also home to Thielska Galleriet ⑨ *(see p99)*, a superb art gallery with a fine collection of 19th-century Scandinavian art. If you wish to end the walk at this point, there is a bus from here back to the city.

⑮ Palatial waterfront houses along Strandvägen

A 90-Minute Walk around the City Centre

This walk will take you right through the heart of Stockholm, giving you a chance to browse in the city's best shops or to enjoy a coffee and pastry in one of the many cafés you'll pass. It also provides a chance to see some of the imposing buildings that Stockholm has to offer, such as the magnificent Konserthuset or the architecturally interesting Stadsbiblioteket. The route also includes a park or two where you can take a break and escape the bustling streets.

⑤ Plaque in memory of Olof Palme

⑦ Strindberg's study at Strindbergsmuseet Blå Tornet (The Blue Tower), Drottninggatan

Sergels Torg to Adolf Fredriks Kyrka

This walk begins at Sergels Torg (*see p69*) ①, a split-level square widely regarded as the very centre of the modern city. It is marked by a tall glass obelisk which is illuminated at night. From this point, take pedestrianised Sergelgatan north to reach the city's main market square, Hötorget (*see p70*) ②, full of vegetables and flowers for sale. It was in the PUB department store here in the square that film legend Greta Garbo sold hats in the millinery department; there is a small exhibition devoted to her by the ground floor entrance.

On the opposite side of Hötorget is the grand Konserthuset (*see p70*) ③, home to the Swedish Royal Philharmonic Orchestra. In front of Konserthuset stands Carl Mille's sculpture, *Orpheus*. Across Kungsgatan you will see the Kungshallen shopping mall ④, which also contains several cafés and restaurants. From Kungsgatan turn left into Sveavägen. At the junction with Olof Palmes Gata you will find a plaque in the pavement that marks the spot where the former Swedish Prime Minister, Olof Palme, was gunned down in 1986 as he left a nearby cinema with his wife ⑤.

③ The colourful Hötorget market, outside Konserthuset

For map symbols *see back flap*

A short distance to the north, still on Sveavägen, Palme's grave can be visited in the churchyard at Adolf Fredriks Kyrka (see p72) ⑥.

Blå Tornet to Odenplan

Just after the church, turn left into Kammakargatan to reach the former home of writer August Strindberg, now a museum, Blå Tornet (see p71) ⑦, at the corner of Drottninggatan. Head uphill on Drottninggatan, past small quirky shops and various popular cafés ⑧. Once past Kungstensgatan, Drottninggatan becomes Norrtullsgatan and continues north along the side of Observatorielunden ⑨, a leafy park which hides Stockholm's former observatory dating from 1753. At the end of the road you'll reach another of

⑮ The imposing Kungstornen (King's Towers) on Kungsgatan

Stockholm's main squares, Odenplan ⑩, a large open area of superb 19th-century architecture dominated by the Neo-Baroque Gustav Vasa Kyrka (see p119) ⑪. There is a T-bana station here if you want to cut the walk short.

Odenplan to Stureplan

From Odenplan, head east along Odengatan past some university buildings to reach the city library, Stadsbiblioteket (see p119) ⑫, designed by Gunnar Asplund and widely regarded as one of Stockholm's finest Functionalist buildings. Next, take a right into Sveavägen and head south towards the prestigious Stockholm School of Economics, Handelshögskolan ⑬, where competition for places is extremely fierce.

From here turn left into Rehnsgatan and walk a short distance east before turning right into Döbelnsgatan which, leading south, eventually becomes Malmskillnadsgatan. Johannes Kyrka ⑭, a 19th-century Neo-Gothic church set in a small park, can be seen on your left. The wooden steeple, which stands next to it was constructed much earlier in 1692.

Look out for a set of stone steps on the left which lead down onto Kungsgatan beside the Neo-Classical Kungstornen twin towers (see pp70–71) ⑮, which dominate this part of the city. Once on Kungsgatan, you will find a good selection of cafés and stylish shops, as well as several cinemas near the Kungstornen bridge. The walk ends with a short stroll downhill to Stureplan, (see pp72–3) ⑯ an open square that is the centre of Stockholm's vibrant nightlife and a popular meeting place.

⑪ The impressive doorway of the Neo-Baroque Gustav Vasa Kyrka

Tips for Walkers

Starting point: Sergels Torg is easily accessible from Stockholm's main T-bana station, T-Centralen. When leaving the platform simply follow the signs for Sergels torg.

Length: 3.5 km (2.2 miles)

Duration: One and a half hours

Stopping-off points: For cafés, try the Kungshallen shopping mall at Hötorget or Kungsgatan and Stureplan. The Saluhallen indoor market in Hötorget is the best place in Stockholm for ethnic treats and delicious Middle Eastern snacks.

HUMLEGÅRDEN

ENGELBREKTS-PLAN
AGARES GATA
HUMLEGÅRDSGATAN
BRUNNSGATAN
KUNGSGATAN ⑯
STURE-PLAN
LÄSTMAKARGATAN
JAKOBSBERGSGATAN
ÖSTER SAMUELSGATAN
REGERINGS-GATAN
HAMNGATAN
KUNGSTRÄD-GÅRDEN
NORRLANDSGATAN
BIBLIOTEKSGATAN
🇹 Östermalms-torg
RIDDARGATAN
SMÅLANDSGATAN
NYBROGATAN
GREV TURÉGATAN
NYBRO-PLAN
BERZELI PARK

RGS-EN | GATAN
IVERSONSG.
BACKE

Key
••• Walk route

0 metres   300
0 yards   300

EXCURSIONS FROM STOCKHOLM

Stockholm's strategic location between the Baltic Sea and Lake Mälaren provides the backdrop for a range of excursions that offer an insight into Swedish life and history. To the east lies the beautiful archipelago with its 24,000 islands and skerries. To the west are the more sheltered beaches and islands of Mälaren with a cultural heritage stretching back to the time of the Vikings and before.

The wide stretches of water to the east and west of Stockholm are markedly different, in terms of both their natural environment and history. The Vikings and their ancestors headed west from the capital towards the present-day Lake Mälaren for defensive reasons, before the gradual rising of the land transformed what was once a Baltic inlet into a freshwater lake.

Sweden's first town, Birka, was founded on the island of Björkö in the 8th century, but archaeological finds indicate that people have been using this area for trading with other countries since the 6th century. Evidence of these early residents can be found on Björkö to this day. Along with the royal palace of Drottningholm, on nearby Lovön, Birka is included on the list of UNESCO World Heritage Sites.

Around Lake Mälaren's shores are many other majestic palaces, elegant manor houses and small historic towns like Mariefred, which was established in the early 17th century and has retained its old-time character ever since. It is home to Sweden's National Portrait Gallery.

To the east of the city, the rising of the land since the Ice Age has provided a largely untouched archipelago with over 24,000 islands, rocks and skerries. The scene of many enemy attacks from the sea, the archipelago lacks the cultural treasures that characterize Mälaren, but it does boast plenty of splendid natural scenery. The boat trip from Nybrokajen or Slussen to the leafy Fjäderholmarna islands takes about half an hour, but a full day should be allowed for an excursion to the outer archipelago with its smooth rocks and wide bays.

Enjoying the sunny weather in the grounds of Drottningholm Palace

◀ The sun sets behind the bell tower of Stadshuset in Kungsholmen

Excursions from Stockholm

Stockholm is surrounded by a remarkable
natural landscape which provides an attractive setting for
excursions. Idyllic towns, majestic castles and prehistoric
settlements dot the shores of Mälaren to the west. On the
eastern side are the islands of the archipelago with their
traditional wooden houses, and cosy hotels and youth
hostels. Annual sailing regattas attract yachting enthusiasts
from all over the world. Everything is easily accessible by
scheduled boat services, making the journey itself a
memorable experience.

Key

== Motorway

— Major road

= Minor road

- Railway

— Minor railway

Drottningholms Slott on Lovön in Lake Mälaren

Getting There

*All the excursion destinations on this map
can be reached in summer by scheduled
boat services from Stockholm's city centre.
Those on Lake Mälaren are operated by
Strömma Kanalbolaget or Gripsholms-
Mariefreds Ångfartygs AB. Most of those in
the archipelago are operated by Waxholmsbolaget (see p204). Other destinations
on the mainland can be reached by car or
bus, and by train to Mariefred. See also the
checklist for individual sights.*

For map symbols *see back flap*

Sights at a Glance

❶ Drottningholm *pp146–9*
❷ Birka
❸ Mariefred
❹ Steninge Slott
❺ Millesgården
❻ Fjäderholmarna
❼ Vaxholm
❽ Grinda
❾ Finnhamn
❿ Sandhamn
⓫ Utö

Excursions by Steamboat

Traditional steamboats are a picturesque feature on the waters around Stockholm. Both in the archipelago and on Lake Mälaren visitors can still enjoy the quiet, calm atmosphere of a steamboat voyage. One of the real veterans, SS Blidösund (1911), is operated by voluntary organizations and serves mostly the northern archipelago. Some routes, for example Stockholm–Mariefred, are operated partly or completely by steamers. Most of the other passenger boats from the early 20th century have been fitted with oil-fired engines but still provide a nostalgic journey back in time.

SS Blidösund, one of the oldest in Stockholm's fleet of renovated steamboats still in regular service

Huvudskär in Stockholm's outer archipelago

❶ Drottningholm

With its palace, theatre, park and Chinese Pavilion, the whole of Drottningholm has been included in UNESCO's World Heritage list. The royal palace on the island of Lovön emerged in its present form towards the end of the 17th century, and was one of the most lavish buildings of its era. Contemporary Italian and French architecture inspired Tessin the Elder (1615–81) in his design, which was also intended to glorify royal power. The project was completed by Tessin the Younger, while 18th-century architects like Carl Hårleman and Jean Eric Rehn put the finishing touches to the interiors. The Royal Family uses part of the palace as its private residence.

Baroque Garden
The bronze statue of Hercules (1620s) by the Dutch Renaissance sculptor Adrian de Vries adorns the parterre in the palace's Baroque Gardens.

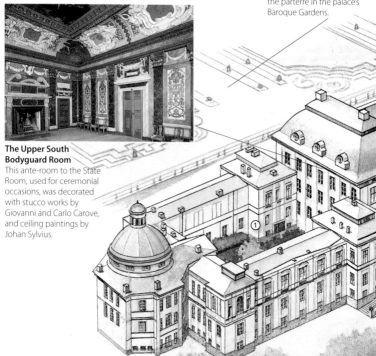

The Upper South Bodyguard Room
This ante-room to the State Room, used for ceremonial occasions, was decorated with stucco works by Giovanni and Carlo Carove, and ceiling paintings by Johan Sylvius.

KEY

① **Apartments of the Royal Family**

② **Writing Table by Georg Haupt** in the Queen's Room is a masterpiece (1770) commissioned by King Adolf Fredrik as a gift to Queen Lovisa Ulrika. Textiles for the walls and furnishings date from the 1970s.

③ **The Palace Church** in the northern cupola was completed by Hårleman in the 1720s.

★ Queen Lovisa Ulrika's Library
The Queen commissioned Jean Eric Rehn (1717–93) to decorate this splendid library, which emphasizes her influence on art and science in Sweden in the 18th-century.

VISITORS' CHECKLIST

Practical Information
10 km (6 miles) W of Stockholm.
Palace: **Tel** 08-402 62 70.
W royalcourt.se
Open Jan–Mar: noon–3:30pm Sat & Sun; Apr: 11am–3:30pm daily; May–Sep: 10am–4:30pm daily; Oct: 11am–3:30pm Fri–Sun; Nov–Dec: noon–3:30pm Sat & Sun.
Closed public hols. 🎫 🚫 📷
🏯 Chinese Pavilion: **Open** May–Aug: 11am–4:30pm daily; Sep: noon–3:30pm daily. 🎫 🚫 📷
Theatre Museum: **Tel** 08-759 04 06. **Open** May–Sep. 🎫 🚫

Transport
🚇 Brommaplan, then bus 176, 177, 301, 323. 🚢 May–Sep fr Stadshusbron.

Entrance

★ Queen Hedvig Eleonora's State Bedroom
Morning receptions ("levées") were held in this lavish Baroque room designed by Tessin the Elder. It took about 15 years for Sweden's foremost artists and craftsmen to decorate the room, which was completed in 1683.

★ The Staircase
Trompe l'oeil paintings by Johan Sylvius adorn the walls, giving the impression that the already spacious interior stretches further into the palace.

Exploring Drottningholm

The Palace of Drottningholm is complemented by the Court Theatre (Slottsteatern), the world's oldest theatre still in active use, the Theatre Museum (Teatermuseum) and the elegant Chinese Pavilion (Kina Slott). The complex is situated on the shores of Lake Mälaren, surrounded by Baroque and Rococo gardens, and lush English-style parkland. In summer the theatre stages opera and ballet; and the church is used for High Mass and concerts.

Karl XI's gallery at Drottningholm, featuring the victory at Lund, 1667

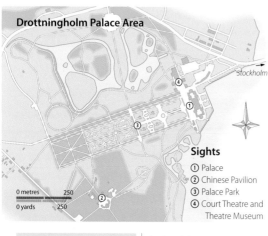

Drottningholm Palace Area

0 metres 250
0 yards 250

Sights

① Palace
② Chinese Pavilion
③ Palace Park
④ Court Theatre and Theatre Museum

The Palace Apartments

On entering the apartments, the first thing that meets the eye is a Baroque corridor with a view that frames part of the gardens, in all their splendour. The central part of the palace is dominated by the staircase, crowned by a lantern with ceiling paintings by Ehrenstrahl. There are examples of Baroque stucco work by Giovanni and Carlo Carove. Marble statues of the nine muses and their protector, Apollo, are placed at the corners of the balustrades.

The Green Salon is reached from the lower vestibule via the Lower Northern Bodyguard Room. This is the beginning of the main ceremonial suite, which continues with Karl X's Gallery where paintings illustrate his major military exploit, the crossing of the ice in the Store Bælt (Great Belt) by the Swedish army in 1658. Queen Hedvig Eleonora (1636–1715) held audiences in the Ehrenstrahl Salon, named after the artist whose paintings dominate the walls. More prominent guests were received in the State Bedroom. In Queen Lovisa Ulrika's time this room was used for sleeping. Her Meissen porcelain can be seen in the Blue Cabinet; the Library has her collection of more than 2,000 books. Behind the Upper Northern Guards Room with a ceiling by Johan Sylvius is a Gustavian drawing room, with a bureau by Johan Niklas Eckstein. In 1777, following Gustav III's assumption of power, the Blue Salon was decorated in the Neo-Classical style.

The Chinese Salon was used as a private bedroom by King Adolf Fredrik. It is directly above the Queen's State Bedroom and there is a hidden

Medallion showing life and death

staircase linking the two floors. The "bureau" opposite the tiled stove is also a sofa bed. The Oscar Room was refurbished by Oscar I (1799–1859) and is adorned by a tapestry dating from the 1630s. After the General's Room, Karl XI's Gallery – which commemorates the victory at Lund (1667) – and the Golden Salon, comes the Queen's Salon. Just as the adjoining State Room had portraits of all the European monarchs, the portraits in the Queen's Salon were of European queens. This floor finishes with the Upper South Bodyguard Room, an anteroom to the State Room and lavishly decorated by the Carove stucco artists and the ceiling painter Johan Sylvius.

The Chinese Pavilion

On her 33rd birthday in 1753 Queen Lovisa Ulrika was given a Chinese pavilion by her husband, King Adolf Fredrik. It had been manufactured in Stockholm and the previous night it was shipped to Drottningholm and assembled a few hundred metres from the palace. It had to be taken down after 10 years because rot had set in, and was replaced by the Chinese Pavilion

The Chinese Pavilion, an extravaganza in blue and gold

(Kina Slott) which is still one of the major attractions at Drottningholm. The polished-tile building was designed by C F Adelcrantz (1716–96).

At this time there was great European interest in all things Chinese. In 1733 the newly formed East India Company made its first journey to China. After Lovisa Ulrika's death in 1782 this interest waned, but it was rekindled in the 1840s. The Chinese Pavilion is a mixture of what was considered 250 years ago to be typical Chinese style along with artifacts from China and Japan. Efforts have been made to restore the interior to its original state with the help of a 1777 inventory.

Four smaller pavilions belong to the building. In the north-eastern pavilion the king had his lathe and a carpenter's bench. Alongside is the Confidencen pavilion, where meals were taken if he wished to be left undisturbed. The food was prepared in the basement, the floor opened and the dining table hauled up. The adjoining Turkish-style "watch tent" was built as a barracks for Gustav III's dragoons.

The Palace Park

The palace's three gardens are each of a completely different character but still combine to provide a unified whole. The symmetrical formal garden started to take shape in 1640. The garden was designed to stimulate all senses with sights, sounds and smells. It starts by the palace terrace with its "embroidery" parterre and continues as far as the Hercules statue. The water parterre is situated on slightly higher ground and is broken up with waterfalls and topiaries. The sculptures, mainly carved by the Flemish sculptor Adrian de Vries

(1560–1626) were war trophies from Prague in 1648 and from Fredriks-borg Castle in Denmark in 1659.

The avenues of chestnut trees were laid out when the Chinese Pavilion was completed, as well as the Rococo-inspired garden area – a cross between the formal main garden and the freer composition of the English park. The English park has natural paths and a stream with small islands, along with trees and bushes at "natural" irregular intervals. Gustav III is reputed to have been responsible for its design and also planned several buildings. Not all his plans were realized, but he added four statues which he had bought during his travels in Italy. The first 300 of a total of 846 lime

Tiled stove in a cabinet in the Chinese Pavilion

trees were planted in the avenues flanking the Baroque garden as early as 1684.

The Court Theatre and Theatre Museum

The designer of the Chinese Pavilion, Carl Fredrik Adelcrantz, was also responsible for the Drottningholm Court Theatre (Slottsteatern), which dates from 1766. The theatre was commissioned by Queen Lovisa

The magnificent 18th-century stage in the Drottningholm Court Theatre

Ulrika, but Adelcrantz did not have the same resources as the architects of the palace itself. This simple wooden building with a plaster façade is now the world's oldest theatre still preserved in its original condition. The interior and fittings are masterpieces of simple functionality. The pilasters, for example, are made from gypsum and the supports from papier maché. The scenery, with its wooden hand-driven machinery, is still in working order.

After Gustav III's death in 1792 the theatre fell into disuse until the 1920s, when the machinery ropes were replaced, electric lighting was installed, and the original wings were refurbished.

The scenery is adapted to 18th-century plays. It can be changed in just a few seconds with the help of up to 30 scene-shifters. The sound effects are simple but authentic: a wooden box filled with stones creates realistic thunder, a wooden cylinder covered in tent cloth produces a howling wind. Every summer there are about 30 performances, mainly opera and ballet from the 18th century. The theatre is open daily for visitors to the palace.

A Theatre Museum and shop are housed in Duke Carl's pavilion, built in the 1780s. The museum focuses on 18th-century theatre, with decoration sketches, paintings, scenery models and costumes. A *Commedia dell'arte* room contains paintings by Pehr Hilleström and sketches for Gustav III's dramatic productions by Louis Jean Desprez.

Court Theatre stage machinery: the world's oldest still in use

❷ Birka

30 km (19 miles) W of Stockholm.
🚢 May–Sep from Stadshusbron.
Birkamuseet: **Tel** 08-560 515 40.
Open hours vary, check website.
🎟 of exhibitions and excavations.
🏛 📷 ♿ 🌐 raa.se/birka

The first town in Scandinavia
was called Birka, on the island
of Björkö in Lake Mälaren. It
was founded in the 8th century
by the king of Svea who then
reigned over the central parts
of present-day Sweden. His
royal residence was on the
nearby island of Adelsö. About
100 years later a contemporary
writer gave the town this
description: "In Birka there are
many rich merchants and an
abundance of all types of goods,
money and valuable items."
It was not a large town. There
were only about 700 inhabitants, but they included
craftsmen, whose work
attracted merchants from
distant countries.
    The town was
planned on simple
lines. People lived
in modest houses,
which stood in rows
overlooking the jetties
where ships were
moored. These vessels
were used by the king's
warriors, the Vikings, for
their marauding expeditions.
In 830 a monk named Ansgar
came to Birka, bringing the
Christian faith to Sweden.
In the 10th century Birka was
abandoned in favour of

The 16th-century Gripsholms Slott just outside Mariefred

Sigtuna, 15 km (9 miles) to the
north, which is now Sweden's
oldest town.
    Today Björkö is a flourishing
island with gardens and
juniper-covered slopes.
But, most importantly, it
is a popular excursion destination with a fascinating
museum and continuing
archaeological digs.
    During the early 1990s
these excavations
provided a lot of
new information
about Birka and
the Vikings. Since
then, work has
continued around the
old fortifications,
revealing much about
the town's defences and
the life of its inhabitants. The
museum shows how Birka
looked in its heyday, along
with some of the archaeological finds. Visitors can also see
freshly dug artifacts while
excavations are in progress.

Birka crucifix

❸ Mariefred

65 km (40 miles) W of Stockholm.
Tel 0159–231 60. 🚢 summer from
Stadshusbron. 🚆 from Central-
stationen to Läggesta, then bus.
Gripsholms Slott: **Open** 15 May–Sep:
10am–4pm daily; Oct & Nov: noon–
3pm Sat & Sun.

Mariefred should ideally
be approached from the
water to get the best view of
the magnificent Gripsholms
Slott in all its splendour. The
first fortress on this site was
built in the 1380s by the Lord
High Chancellor, Bo Jonsson
Grip, who gave the castle its
name. Work on the present
building, initiated by King
Gustav Vasa, started in 1537
but parts have been rebuilt
or added – most notably
during the time of Gustav III
in the late 18th century. It was
during this period that the
National Portrait Gallery was
established. It now contains
more than 4,000 portraits
and covers some 500 years of
artistic endeavour, from the
time of Gustav Vasa to the
present day. It also has a
collection of notable foreign
portraits, which are shown
in a separate section.
    Gripsholms Slott's well-
preserved interiors feature a
wide collection of furniture,
art and handicrafts. There are
about 60 rooms. Highlights
include Gustav III's late
18th-century theatre and
the White Salon which is
also from the same era.
    The town of Mariefred, in the
shadow of the castle, derives its
name from a late 15th-century

Iron Age burial ground at Birka on the island of Björkö in Lake Mälaren

monastery, Monasterium Pacis Mariae. It received its charter as a town in 1605, and an inn has stood on the site of the monastery since the early 17th century. The elegantly restored and rebuilt restaurant is an attraction in itself.

Visitors to Mariefred can stroll through the town and admire the 17th-century

Duke Karl's bedchamber, Gripsholms Slott

church and the 18th-century Rådhus (law courts' building), which also houses the local Tourist Information Office. There are a number of specialist shops, galleries and an excellent antiques shop.

The vintage railway attracts visitors of all ages. Those interested in art should head for Grafikens Hus (House of Graphics) on a hill leading up to the former royal farm, where stables and haylofts have been converted into an exhibition area.

The excursion can be made into a varied round trip. From Stockholm to Mariefred one can travel on Sweden's oldest steamboat service, dating from 1832. The steamboat *Mariefred*, which has operated on the route since 1903, travels at 6–7 knots and the journey takes about three and a half hours. Beautiful scenery and a lunch of

classic "steamboat beef" is on offer along the way. For the return journey, a vintage steam railway runs from Mariefred to Läggesta (a 40-minute journey) from where it is possible to catch an express train back to Stockholm (30 minutes).

❹ Steninge Slott

40 km (25 miles) N of Stockholm. **Tel** 08-592 595 00. 🚢 summer from Stadshusbron to Rosersberg and connecting bus. Slottsgalleria: **Open** 11am–6pm Mon–Fri, 10am–5pm Sat & Sun. Palace: **Open** 11am–2pm Sat, 11am–3pm Sun; Jun–Aug: 11am–4pm daily. 📷 call for tour information. 🏠 💻 🌐 **steningeslott.com**

South-east of Sigtuna, Sweden's oldest town, and only 10 minutes from Arlanda Airport is Steninge Slott, one of the gems of Lake Mälaren. The palace ranks among the finest works of Tessin

the Younger *(see p39)* and was designed a decade before he started on Stockholm's Royal Palace. The roof is that of a traditional Swedish manor house of the time, but otherwise the design is influenced by Tessin's studies, mainly in Italy and France. The result is an Italianate palace in a rural Swedish setting, which Carl Gyllenstierna gave to his wife Anna Soop as a wedding gift in 1706. Since then Steninge has had several owners, the best known of whom was Count Axel von Fersen, reputed to have been the lover of the French Queen Marie Antoinette (1755–93). The park, planned by the landscape architect Johan Hårleman, has a monument of Count von Fersen.

In 1999 the estate was transformed into a cultural centre. The biggest attraction is the elegant Baroque palace. The staircase has similarities to its counterpart at the Royal Palace *(see p50)* and elsewhere there are details, which can also be seen in Tessinska Palatset *(see p54)*. The oval hall is a masterpiece of Swedish Baroque, decorated by the Italian stucco artist Giuseppe Marchi. It regained its original splendour as part of restoration work in the early 20th century, planned by the architect G Clason. At the same time Julius Kronberg contributed paintings on the door lintels and ceilings.

A 19th-century stone barn houses the Slottsgalleria with glassworks, pottery, candle-making, and a shop and restaurant.

Steninge Palace, one of the most perfect examples of late 17th-century manor house design

Millesgården, home of the sculptor Carl Milles in the early 20th century

❺ Millesgården

Herserudsvägen 30, Lidingö.
Ⓣ Subway to Ropsten, then bus to Torsviks Torg, then follow the signs to Millesgården. **Tel** 08-446 75 90.
Open May–Sep: 11am–5pm daily; Oct–Apr: noon–5pm Tue–Sun.
⬛ by appointment. ♿ 📷 💻 🏛
Ⓦ **millesgarden.se**

Carl Milles (1875–1955) was one of the 20th century's greatest Swedish sculptors and the best known internationally. From 1931 he lived for 20 years in the USA, where he became a prolific monumental sculptor with works such as the *Meeting of the Waters* fountain in St Louis and the *Resurrection* fountain in the National Memorial Park outside Washington DC. In Stockholm visitors can see 15 of his public works, including the *Orpheus* fountain in front of Konserthuset *(see p70)*.

In 1906 Milles bought land on the island of Lidingö, on which he built a house, completed in 1908. He lived here with his wife until 1931, and also after his return from the USA. In 1936 he and his wife donated the property to the Swedish people.

Millesgården covers 18,000 sq m (194,000 sq ft) in a series of terraces and includes Milles' studios with originals and replicas of his work. It has a magnificent garden – a real work of art in itself – and a fine view over the water.

❻ Fjäderholmarna

6 km (4 miles) E of Stockholm.
🚌 53. ⛴ May–Sep from Nybrokajen and Slussen.

With the inclusion of the Fjäderholmarna islands in the Royal National City Park *(see p123)* the city's "green lung" has acquired a small part of the archipelago. The main island, Stora Fjäderholmen, is only a 25-minute boat journey from Nybrokajen or Slussen.

The island already boasted an inn in the 17th century, conveniently sited for the archipelago islanders on their way to and from the city to sell their wares. The inn was closed during World War II, when the area was taken over by the military, and landing was forbidden.

Access to the public was restored in the mid-1980s, and the main island now offers an attractive harbour, three restaurants and an ice-cream parlour as well as a tour of the country's first whisky distillery, Mackmyra Distillery. There are also three museums, two of which are devoted to traditional and recreational boating and

The Fjäderholmarna islands – a popular summer excursion just 25 minutes by boat from the city

the third that explores the history of Vodka in Sweden and its growing popularity.

Various handicrafts are practised on the island, including metalwork, weaving, textile printing, wood-carving, pottery and glassmaking. There is also an art gallery and an outdoor theatre that, during the summer months, hosts popular theatre weeks for children.

The other three islands are especially rich with bird-life, and one of them, Libertas, has Sweden's last remaining gas-powered lighthouse.

Vaxholm Fortress, strategically sited on the approach to Vaxholm

❼ Vaxholm

25 km (16 miles) NE of Stockholm.
🚌 670. ⛴ from Strömkajen and Nybrokajen. Vaxholm Fortress and Vaxholm Fortress Museum:
Tel 08-541 718 90. **Open** Jun: 12:15pm–4pm daily; Jul–Aug: 12:15pm–5pm daily. 📷

The archipelago's main community, Vaxholm, has been a strategic point for shipping since the 19th century. It is easily reached by boat from Stockholm on a delightful one-hour journey through the inner archipelago.

Vaxholm has been inhabited since the 16th century. In 1548 Gustav Vasa ordered that the nearby island of Vaxholmen should be fortified. Some 300 years later a new fortress was built here, but it soon lost its military importance and was used as a civil prison. Today the imposing citadel houses an interesting military museum.

Two of Stockholm's best-known architects have left their mark on Vaxholm town. The 100-year-old law-courts' building was given its present appearance in 1925 by Cyrillus

Johansson. On the headland nearest to the harbour is a rather stately hotel designed in 1899 by Erik Lallerstedt, and traces of its Jugendstil ornamentation can still be seen.

The wooden buildings around the square and along Hamngatan with their souvenir shops provide a pleasant stroll, and the harbour is always busy.

❽ Grinda

30 km (19 miles) E of Stockholm. **Tel** 08-542 494 91. 670 from Stockholm Östra station to Vaxholm, then boat. from Strömkajen and Nybrokajen. (summer only).

Grinda is a leafy island, typical of the inner archipelago. It has some excellent beaches and rocks for swimming, as well as good fishing. Boats and bicycles can be hired, making it an ideal place to visit while exploring the archipelago. It takes about one and a half hours by boat from the city.

The architect Ernst Stenhammar (1859–1927), who designed the Grand Hôtel (see p81), built a large Jugendstil villa here, which is now a restaurant and pub and has guest rooms. There are chalets for rental, a campsite and a youth hostel in a former military barracks.

❾ Finnhamn

40 km (25 miles) NE of Stockholm. **Tel** 08-542 462 12. from Strömkajen and Nybrokajen.

Finnish ships used to moor at Finnhamn on their way to and from Stockholm. This attractive group of islands lies two and a half hours by boat from the city at the point where the softer scenery of the inner archipelago gives way to the harsher landscape of the outer islands. As on Grinda, the main island has a wooden villa designed by Ernst Stenhammar (1912). Today it is the largest youth hostel in the archipelago. There is a restaurant, chalets for rental and a campsite. Smaller islands nearby are accessible by rowing boat.

Sandhamn, a yachting centre in Stockholm's outer archipelago

❿ Sandhamn

50 km (31 miles) E of Stockholm. **Tel** 08-570 470 00. 433, 434 from Slussen to Stavsnäs, then boat. from Strömkajen and Nybrokajen.

Over the past 200 years Sandhamn, on Sandön, has been a meeting point for sailors, particularly yachting enthusiasts. The Royal Swedish Yacht Club has been based at Seglarrestaurangen (Sailors' Restaurant) for more than 100 years. Every year the world's yachting elite flock to Sandhamn to take part in the Round Gotland Race.

Once a pilot station, Sandhamn is a charming village with narrow alleys and houses adorned with decorative carvings. There are now about 100 permanent residents. The Customs House, built in 1752, is a listed

Smooth rock formations at Utö in the southern archipelago

heritage building. A customs inspector who worked here, Elias Sehlstedt (1808–74), made his name as a poet and artist.

Sandhamn has shops, handicraft centres, and a swimming pool. Guided tours can be arranged. Camping is not permitted, but hotel, bed-and-breakfast and chalet accommodation is available.

⓫ Utö

50 km (31 miles) SE of Stockholm. **Tel** 08-501 574 10. in summer, from Strömkajen. utoturistbyra.se

No other island in the archipelago has as rich a history as Utö, which was inhabited before the Viking era. In the 12th century the islanders started to mine iron ore, and this activity continued until 1879. Their story is told in the Mining Museum adjoining the hotel. Today's holiday homes along Lurgatan were built as miners' cottages in the 18th century. A windmill, built in 1791, provides an unrivalled view of the island.

Utö is one of the best seaside resorts in the Stockholm area, and is ideal for a weekend or full-day excursion. Its facilities include a variety of restaurants. The hotel's restaurant is sited in the old mine offices.

Hotel, youth hostel, camping, chalet and bed-and-breakfast accommodation are all available. Bicycles, rowing boats and canoes can be hired, and there are also regular fishing trips and archipelago safaris.

TRAVELLERS' NEEDS

WHERE TO STAY

Stockholm's hotel scene revolves around Blasieholmen, where the Grand Hôtel offers accommodation that is just as princely as the Royal Palace, on the opposite side of Norrström. Only a short distance away is *af Chapman*, a ship that is home to one of the world's most beautiful youth hostels.

Stockholm's hotels are not usually built in the same grandiose style as their counterparts in southern Europe, but they do offer high levels of comfort and service and often have magnificent views or locations. The listings on pages 158–61 cover a wide range of accommodation options.

Exterior of the imposing and elegant Diplomat hotel *(see p159)*

Choosing a Hotel

Although most of Stockholm's hotels are mid-range to expensive, the city also has perfectly acceptable budget accommodation. The cheapest alternative is offered by the dozen or so youth hostels, most of which have high standards. Other value-for-money options include the many bed-and-breakfast (B&B) establishments.

Stockholm has become one of the world's most popular cities for conferences, so occupancy at the city's hotels is high – around 80 per cent – between May and November, but much lower in July. Most of the locals head out to the countryside to soak in the summer sun during this period. Visitors are strongly advised to book hotel accommodation well in advance.

It is best to avoid the peak season for trade fairs and events such as the Stockholm Marathon in June. The **Stockholm Visitor Centre** website is useful for finding out when the busiest periods are.

How to Book

You can easily make a reservation at the **Stockholm Visitor Centre**. Staff can also offer tips and advice about lodging options for all tastes and budgets. Hotel reservations can also be made directly with the hotel, either over the telephone or, in most cases, online. Web addresses for the larger hotel chains' reservation centres are listed opposite.

Hotel Chains

Several international and national chains have hotels in Stockholm. **Scandic Hotels**, with over 230 establishments, is the leading Scandinavian chain, known for its environmentally friendly policies. It has eight hotels in the city and six outside, including two on the way to Arlanda Airport.

Radisson Blu has three large, luxurious hotels in central Stockholm and two at Arlanda Airport. **Choice Hotels Scandinavia** has two hotels in Stockholm under the "Comfort" banner, indicating

Smart seating area at the ultra-chic Scandic Malmen hotel *(see p161)*

a high-standard room-and-breakfast hotel. It also has a property near Arlanda and three conference hotels in the "Quality" category.

The environmentally conscious Scandinavian chain **First Hotels** has three categories: First Hotel, First Express and First Resort. There are three First Hotels in the city centre and three First Express properties outside the city.

Elite Hotels has six classic hotels located throughout Stockholm, each with its own unique style. Three of the hotels are within a 15-minute walk of the city centre.

The Collector's Hotels is a group of three small and exclusive hotels located in Gamla Stan – Victory, Lord Nelson and Lady Hamilton *(see p159)* – all of which have artistic and maritime decor.

Prices and Payment

Prices in the hotel listings are for a standard double room, including service charges and taxes. All hotels offer rooms at much reduced rates at weekends throughout the year and daily in the summer. For the cheaper hotels, this involves a price reduction of 100–300 kr per night; for medium-priced hotels about 500 kr; and for deluxe hotels up to 1,000 kr.

Nearly all hotels accept major credit cards; however, American Express is less commonly accepted in smaller establishments. Larger hotels usually help in changing foreign currency, but the cheapest way of changing money is to use a bureau de change *(see p194)*.

◀ Menu scribbled on a blackboard outside a café in Stockholm

Stately decor of the Bernadotte suite, Grand Hôtel *(see p160)*

Youth Hostels

There are more than 35 youth hostels in Stockholm, the four largest of which are affiliated to the **Swedish Touring Club** (STF/IYHF). Apart from the city's flagship floating hostel, *af Chapman (see p159)*, there are two more moored right in the city centre: MS *Rygerfjord* and *Den Röda Båten* at Södermälarstrand. These have about 100 beds each, as well as fully licensed restaurants and superb views.

The standard of Stockholm's youth hostels is generally high. Prices are around 300 kr per night in a double room, with a discount of about 50 kr for STF members, but they come down to about 150 kr – sometimes even less – in a larger room or dormitory. Prices usually exclude breakfast and bed-linen hire.

Visit Stockholm can help to book accommodation at most youth hostels at its offices. Be aware that some

hostels do not offer Internet booking, and some hostels are only open in the summer.

Bed & Breakfast

B&B accommodation is widely available in central Stockholm and the suburbs, as well as the archipelago. There is usually a choice between a single room, double room and a whole apartment. Breakfast is normally included in the price – apart from apartments, where self-catering is the rule; bed linen and hand towels are always included. B&B prices range from 400 kr to 600 kr per person per night. A double room costs 500–750 kr, while an apartment, which often has to be rented for at least four or five days, costs from around 700 kr per night.

Most B&Bs can be booked in advance through a number of agencies, such as **Stockholm Guesthouse** and **Bed & Breakfast Sweden**; you can find the full list on the Visit Stockholm website. Most B&Bs offer online booking services for guests.

Recommended Hotels

The lodging options featured in this guide have been selected across a wide price range for their excellent facilities and good location. All are listed by type, and then grouped by area, then by price. Choose from budget hotels and hostels, offering basic accommodation; places with striking design features; historic centuries-old buildings; luxury

Cozy cabin at the floating youth hostel, af Chapman *(see p159)*

hotels offering all kinds of opulence; and modern boutique hotels. The places highlighted as DK Choice have been chosen in recognition of an exceptional feature – a stunning location, notable history, inviting atmosphere or outstanding value. Most of these are extremely popular, so be sure to make reservations well in advance of your visit.

DIRECTORY

Central Booking

Stockholm Visitor Centre
Kulturhuset, Sergels Torg 3,
111 57 Stockholm.
Map 2 C4.
Tel 08-508 285 08.

Visit Stockholm
w visitstockholm.com

Hotel Chains

Choice Hotels Scandinavia
Tel 08-691 35 00.
w choicehotels.se

The Collector's Hotels
Tel 08-506 400 01.
w thecollectorshotels.se

Elite Hotels
Tel 0771-788 789.
w elite.se

First Hotels
Tel 08-442 84 00.
w firsthotels.com

Radisson Blu
Tel 020-238 238.
w radissonblu.com

Scandic Hotels
Tel 08-517 517 00.
w scandichotels.com

Youth Hostels

Swedish Touring Club (STF/IYHF)
Tel 08-463 21 00.
w svenskaturistforeningen.se

Bed & Breakfast

Bed & Breakfast Sweden
w bedandbreakfast.com/sweden

Stockholm Guesthouse
w stockholmguesthouse.com

Where to Stay

Budget

Gamla Stan

Archipelago Hostel Gamla Stan Ⓦ
Stora Nygatan 38, 111 27
Tel *08-22 92 40* **Map** 4 B3
Ⓦ archipelagohostel.se
Located in the heart of Old Town, with private rooms, fully equipped kitchens and shared bathrooms.

Castanea Hostel Ⓦ
Kindstugatan 1, 111 31
Tel *08-22 35 51* **Map** 4 C3
Ⓦ castaneahostel.com
A well-located modern hostel with spacious rooms. Free Wi-Fi.

Hotel Gamla Stan Ⓦ
Skeppsbron 22, 111 30
Tel *08-411 95 45* **Map** 4 C3
Ⓦ hotelgamlastan.se
Decent waterfront hostel with dorms and private rooms, as well as two fully equipped kitchens.

Old Town Hostel Ⓦ
Stora Nygatan 22, 111 10
Tel *08-20 77 17* **Map** 4 B3
Ⓦ oldtownhostel-stockholm.com
Four- and six-bed dormitories. Fabulous decor, as well as a big kitchen and dining area.

Old Town Lodge Ⓦ
Baggensgatan 25, 111 31
Tel *08-20 44 55* **Map** 4 C3
Ⓦ oldtownlodge.se
Rooms are clean but tiny; not all have windows. Bathrooms are shared but immaculately kept.

City

Crystal Plaza ⓌⓌ
Birger Jarlsgatan 35, 111 45
Tel *08-406 88 00* **Map** 2 C2
Ⓦ crystalplazahotel.se
Simple rooms, each individually decorated, in a historic building. Breakfast included.

Queen's ⓌⓌ
Drottninggatan 71a, 113 60
Tel *08-24 94 60* **Map** 4 A1
Ⓦ queenshotel.se
Rooms are spacious with modern conveniences. Relaxed atmosphere, central location.

Östermalm and Gärdet

Stureparken Ⓦ
Sturegatan 58, 114 36
Tel *08-662 72 30* **Map** 3 E3
Ⓦ stureparkens.nu
Small hotel with elegantly furnished rooms and apartments. Excellent breakfast.

Wellingtons Gästvåning ⓌⓌ
Skeppargatan 27, 114 52
Tel *08-663 50 70* **Map** 3 F2
Ⓦ wellington.se
A charming hotel in an old school building. Rooms are spacious. Free Wi-Fi.

Kungsholmen and Vasastan

2Kronor Hostel Vasastan Ⓦ
Surbrunnsgatan 44, 113 48
Tel *08-22 92 30* **Map** 2 C2
Ⓦ 2kronor.se
Clean rooms and dorms, but no private showers. Big shared kitchen and common room.

City Backpackers Ⓦ
Upplandsgatan 2, 111 23
Tel *08-20 69 20* **Map** 2 A1
Ⓦ citybackpackers.org
Hostel with dorms, private rooms and family rooms, sauna and guest kitchen. Tours offered.

Hansson Ⓦ
Surbrunnsgatan 38, 113 48
Tel *08-15 04 20* **Map** 2 C2
Ⓦ hotelhansson.se
This hotel boasts rooms with original wooden floors and period furniture. Great on-site restaurant.

Hotel Micro Ⓦ
Tegnérlunden 8, 113 59
Tel *08-545 455 69* **Map** 2 B3
Ⓦ hotelmicro.se
Small, newly decorated rooms in marine colours. Shared bathrooms are located on the same floor.

Wasa Park Ⓦ
Sankt Eriksplan 1, 113 20
Tel *08-545 453 00* **Map** 1 C1
Ⓦ wasaparkhotel.se
Bargain accommodation. Rooms are large and comfortable, some with private bathrooms.

Logo of the Tre Små Rum hotel in Södermalm

Price Guide
Prices are for a standard double room per night in high season, inclusive of all taxes. Breakfast is not included unless specified.

Ⓦ	under 1,000 Kr
ⓌⓌ	1,000–2,500 Kr
ⓌⓌⓌ	over 2,500 Kr

Södermalm

DK Choice

Mosebacke Hostel Ⓦ
Högbergsgatan 26, 116 20
Tel *08-641 64 60* **Map** 8 C3
Ⓦ mosebackehostel.se
This modern hostel offers clean single, double and triple rooms with shared facilities; choose the "VIP room" for extra space, private toilet and shower. Terrific value for money.

Tre Små Rum Ⓦ
Högbergsgatan 81, 118 54
Tel *08-641 23 71* **Map** 8 C3
Ⓦ tresmarum.se
Comfortable hotel with a homely atmosphere. Excellent breakfast included.

Further Afield

Attaché Ⓦ
Cedergrensvägen 16, 126 36 Hägersten
Tel *08-18 08 85*
Ⓦ hotelattache.se
A no-frills hotel with bright, airy and well-decorated rooms. Warm and friendly staff.

Design

Gamla Stan

Mälardrottningen Yacht Hotel ⓌⓌ
Riddarholmskajen, 111 28
Tel *08-120 902 00* **Map** 4 A2
Ⓦ malardrottningen.se
Boat-based hotel with spacious cabins and a great breakfast.

City

Micro Ⓦ
Tegnerlunden 8, 113 59
Tel *08-545 455 69* **Map** 2 B3
Ⓦ hotelmicro.se
Compact but stylish cabin-like rooms. No windows.

Stockholm Inn Ⓦ
Drottninggatan 67, 111 36
Tel *08-411 03 03* **Map** 4 A1
Ⓦ stockholminn.se
Central hostel with modern rooms, all with en-suite showers.

Freys ⊛⊛
Bryggargatan 12, 101 31
Tel *08-506 213 00*   **Map** 2 C4
🆆 freyshotels.com
Stylish boutique hotel with
Swedish design throughout.
Central location.

Berns Hotel ⊛⊛⊛
Näckströmsgatan 8, 111 47
Tel *08-566 322 00*   **Map** 3 D4
🆆 berns.se
Contemporary rooms in this
hotel popular with celebrities.
Restaurant and club on site.

Blasieholmen and Skeppsholmen

DK Choice

**af Chapman and
Skeppsholmen** ⊛
Flaggmansvägen 8, 111 49
Tel *08-463 22 66*   **Map** 5 D3
🆆 stfchapman.com
One of the most beautiful
youth hostels anywhere in the
world, offering beds on board a
tall ship permanently moored
across from the Royal Palace. It
fills up quickly, so reserve well
in advance. Breakfast included.

Djurgården

DK Choice

Scandic Hasselbacken ⊛⊛
Hazeliusbacken 20, 100 55
Tel *08-517 343 00*   **Map** 6 A3
🆆 scandichotels.com
Currently the only hotel on
Djurgården, this beautifully
restored mansion is surrounded
by lush woodland. It features
contemporary Swedish design
with elegant historic and
classical touches. Superb
in-house dining served
on the terrace in summer.

Östermalm and Gärdet

STF Gärdet Hotel and Hostel ⊛
Sandhamnsgatan 59, 115 28
Tel *08-463 22 99*
🆆 svenskaturistforeningen.se
Good-value singles, doubles and
twins with fresh decor, located
within the city national park.

Clarion Wellington ⊛⊛⊛
Storgatan 6, 114 51
Tel *08-667 09 10*   **Map** 3 F3
🆆 wellington.se
Vibrant rooms with huge
windows and terrific views.
Good service.

Diplomat ⊛⊛⊛
Strandvägen 7C, 114 56
Tel *08-459 68 00*   **Map** 3 E4
🆆 diplomathotel.com
Lovely waterfront period property
with bright, luxurious rooms.
Enjoy drinks on the terrace.

Mornington ⊛⊛⊛
Nybrogatan 53, 114 40
Tel *08-507 330 00*   **Map** 3 E2
🆆 mornington.se
Individually designed rooms
with wooden flooring, big beds
and comfortable sofas.

Kungsholmen and Vasastan

M/S Monika ⊛⊛
Kungsholms strand 133, 112 33
Tel *08-120 921 00*   **Map** 1 B1
🆆 msmonika.se
Boat-based hotel with charming
rooms that preserve many of the
ship's original features.

Södermalm

Columbus Loft ⊛
Tjärhovsgatan 11, 116 21
Tel *08-503 112 00*   **Map** 9 E3
🆆 columbusloft.se
The loft at the Columbus hotel
offers small but stylishly
furnished rooms.

Den Röda Båten ⊛
Söder Mälarstrand, Kajplats 10
Tel *08-644 43 85*   **Map** 4 A4
🆆 theredboat.com
A hotel and hostel spread over
two colourful ships. Only the
private rooms have their own
en-suite bathrooms.

Långholmen Hotel ⊛
Långholmsmuren 20, 117 33
Tel *08-720 85 00*   **Map** 1 B5
🆆 langholmen.com
Unique island accommodation.
Sleep in a former cell at this
converted prison.

Rygerfjord Hotel and Hostel ⊛
*Söder Mälarstrand,
Kajplats 12–14, 118 25*
Tel *08-84 08 30*   **Map** 4 A4
🆆 rygerfjord.se
Beautifully restored ship with
good hotel and hostel
accommodation. Shared
bathrooms for hostel guests.

Hellstens Malmgård ⊛⊛
Brännkyrkagatan 110, 117 26
Tel *08-465 058 00*   **Map** 4 A5
🆆 hellstensmalmgard.se
In an elegant mansion, this hotel
has a wide range of rooms, some
of which have original porcelain
heating stoves from 1770.

The majestic hostel af Chapman, on a boat
moored across from the Royal Palace

Further Afield

Elite Hotel Marina Tower ⊛⊛
Saltsjöqvarns kaj 25, 131 71 Nacka
Tel *08-555 702 00*
🆆 elite.se
A red-brick gem right on the
water with a wide range of
spacious rooms. Home to one
of Stockholm's best spas.

Historic
Gamla Stan

First Hotel Reisen ⊛⊛
Skeppsbron 12, 111 30
Tel *08-22 32 60*   **Map** 4 C3
🆆 firsthotels.com
Charming waterfront hotel in an
18th-century building. Excellent
service and renowned on-site
restaurant. Free Wi-Fi.

Lady Hamilton ⊛⊛
Storkyrkobrinken 5, 111 28
Tel *08-506 401 00*   **Map** 4 B3
🆆 thecollectorshotels.se
Classy hotel with gorgeous
rooms and excellent service.
A unique Ghost Walk is available
for guests.

Lord Nelson ⊛⊛
Västerlånggatan 22, 111 29
Tel *08-506 401 20*   **Map** 4 B3
🆆 thecollectorshotels.se
The small rooms in this 17th-
century building are excellent
value for money.

Scandic Gamla Stan ⊛⊛
Lilla Nygatan 25, 111 28
Tel *08-723 72 50*   **Map** 4 B3
🆆 scandichotels.se
Stylishly furnished hotel in a 17th-
century building. Cosy rooms,
graceful interiors and all modern
amenities. Relax on the roof
terrace in the summer.

For more information on types of hotels *see p157*

DK Choice

Sven Vintappare ⓦⓦ
Sven Vintappares Gränd 3, 111 27
Tel *08-22 41 40* **Map** 4 B3
Ⓦ hotelsvenvintappare.se
The centuries-old façade of
this historic Gamla Stan house
masks a bright, modern interior.
The wooden floors are a nod
to the past, while a number
of original features such as
fireplaces and ceramic heaters
have been incorporated into
the modern suites.

City

Scandic Kungsgatan ⓦⓦ
Kungsgatan 47, 111 56
Tel *08-723 72 20* **Map** 2 B4
Ⓦ scandichotels.com
Basic rooms and luxury suites
complete with terrific views in
this landmark building.

Blasieholmen and Skeppsholmen

Grand Hôtel Stockholm ⓦⓦⓦ
Södra Blasieholmshamnen 8, 111 48
Tel *08-679 35 00* **Map** 4 C2
Ⓦ grandhotel.se
Home to high-fliers since 1874,
this luxurious hotel features an
amazing underground spa.

Östermalm and Gärdet

Esplanade ⓦⓦ
Strandvägen 7a, 114 56
Tel *08-663 07 40* **Map** 3 E4
Ⓦ hotelesplanade.se
Cosy interiors behind a majestic
Art Nouveau façade. The
Esplanade offers old-fashioned
attention to detail in every aspect.

Kungsholmen and Vasastan

Elite Palace Hotel ⓦⓦ
Sankt Eriksgatan 115, 113 43
Tel *08-566 217 00* **Map** 1 C1
Ⓦ elite.se
Large and comfortable hotel
with three- and four-bed rooms;
great for families. Excellent gym
and spa facilities, too.

Södermalm

Hornsgatan ⓦ
Hornsgatan 66B, 118 21
Tel *08-658 29 01* **Map** 4 A5
Ⓦ hotelhornsgatan.se
Big, bright rooms at this lovely
hotel in a converted residential
building dating from 1905. Great
buffet breakfast. Friendly service.

DK Choice

Anno 1647 ⓦⓦ
Mariagränd 3, 116 46
Tel *08-442 16 80* **Map** 4 B5
Ⓦ anno1647.se
An ultra-modern hotel located
in a building dating from 1647.
The rooms are comfortable and
well appointed. Bathrooms, in
particular, are immaculate.
Excellent Swedish restaurant
and a stylish bar.

Columbus ⓦⓦ
Tjärhovsgatan 11, 116 21
Tel *08-503 112 00* **Map** 9 E3
Ⓦ columbus.se
Beautiful 1780s building with
rooms that feature high ceilings
and wooden beams.

Further Afield

Näsby Slott ⓦⓦ
Djursholmsvägen 30, 183 52 Täby
Tel *08-544 981 00*
Ⓦ nasbyslott.se
A lakeside manor house with a
delightful mix of classical and
modern decor throughout.

Åkeshofs Slott ⓦⓦⓦ
Åkeshovs Gårdsvägen, 168 39 Brooma
Tel *08-445 80 77*
Ⓦ akeshofsslott.se
Luxury accommodation in a
17th-century castle with stylish
rooms and excellent service.

Luxury

City

Nobis ⓦⓦⓦ
Norrmalmstorg 2–4, 111 86
Tel *08-614 10 00* **Map** 3 D4
Ⓦ nobishotel.se
Elegant decor, marble bathrooms
and some four-poster beds.

Colourful room with wooden flooring at
the Hornsgatan hotel

Sheraton Stockholm ⓦⓦⓦ
Tegelbacken 6, 101 23
Tel *08-412 34 00* **Map** 4 A2
Ⓦ sheratonstockholm.com
Oustanding hotel with elegantly
decorated rooms and sweeping
views. Excellent on-site dining.

Blasieholmen and Skeppsholmen

Lydmar ⓦⓦⓦ
Södra Blasieholmshamnen 2, 103 24
Tel *08-22 31 60* **Map** 4 C2
Ⓦ lydmar.com
An elegant hotel offering under-
stated luxury and cutting-edge
design. Gorgeous bathrooms.

Radisson Blu Strand ⓦⓦⓦ
Nybrokajen 9, 103 27
Tel *08-506 640 00* **Map** 5 D1
Ⓦ radissonblu.com
Expect the very best at this hotel.
Top-floor sauna with superb views
over the rooftops of Stockholm.

Östermalm and Gärdet

DK Choice

Villa Källhagan ⓦⓦ
Djurgårdsbrunnsvägen 10, 115 27
Tel *08-665 03 00* **Map** 6 B2
Ⓦ kallhagen.se
This modern yet elegant hotel
has rooms that are enormous
and luxuriously furnished. All of
the stunning bathrooms have a
skylight. Some rooms even offer
direct access to the lush gardens.
The on-site restaurant is great.

Södermalm

Hilton Stockholm Slussen ⓦⓦⓦ
Guldgränd 8, 104 65
Tel *08-517 353 11* **Map** 4 B5
Ⓦ www3.hilton.com
Seafront hotel offering typically
luxurious Hilton accommodation.
Good spa services available.

Further Afield

DK Choice

Villa Pauli ⓦⓦ
*Strandvägen 19, 182 60
Djursholm*
Tel *08-446 57 80* **Map** 3 E4
Ⓦ villapauli.com
Deluxe waterfront property in
a secluded setting right on the
Baltic Sea. Rooms are classically
furnished with modern touches.
Set in large grounds are a host
of sports facilities for the guests.

Sleek and classy room decor at the Hilton Stockholm Slussen, Södermalm

Modern

City

Clarion Hotel Sign ⊚⊚
Östra Järnvägsgatan 35, 111 20
Tel *08-676 98 00* **Map** 2 B4
🅆 clarionsign.com
A superbly furnished hotel in the heart of the city. Big rooms with huge bathrooms. Good spa.

Comfort Hotel Stockholm ⊚⊚
Kungsbron 1, 111 22
Tel *08-56 62 22 00* **Map** 2 B4
🅆 nordicchoicehotels.se
A business hotel close to the train station. Friendly service.

Radisson Blu Royal Viking ⊚⊚
Vasagatan 1, 101 24
Tel *08-506 540 00* **Map** 2 B4
🅆 radissonblu.com
Luxurious Swedish design hotel aimed at business travellers. Colourful decor and huge rooms.

DK Choice

Riddargatan ⊚⊚
Riddargatan 14, 114 35
Tel *08-55 57 30 00* **Map** 3 E4
🅆 profilhotels.se
One of Stockholm's finest business hotels, Riddargatan has spacious, striking rooms with contemporary design. It is the ideal base for clubbers and theatre-goers, and its location is hard to beat. Great service.

Scandic Anglais ⊚⊚
Humlegårdsgatan 23, 102 44
Tel *08-51 73 40 00* **Map** 3 D3
🅆 scandichotels.com
A vibrant hotel with spacious rooms and lovely wooden floors.

Scandic Sergel Plaza ⊚⊚
Brunkebergstorg 9, 103 27
Tel *08-51 72 63 00* **Map** 4 A1
🅆 scandichotels.com
Small, colourful rooms with large desks. Most have views over the city. There is also a gym and restaurant.

Tegnérlunden ⊚⊚
Tegnérlunden 8, 113 59
Tel *08-54 54 55 50* **Map** 2 B3
🅆 hoteltegnerlunden.se
Enjoy minimalist yet extremely elegant rooms, which come with extras such as free Wi-Fi and a great breakfast.

Radisson Blu Waterfront ⊚⊚⊚
Nils Ericsons Plan 4, 111 64
Tel *08-50 50 60 00* **Map** 2 C5
🅆 radissonblu.com
Plush, extremely spacious rooms and exceptional service. Excellent restaurant and bar.

Blasieholmen and Skeppsholmen

Skeppsholmen ⊚⊚⊚
Gröna gången 1, 111 86
Tel *08-407 23 00* **Map** 5 E3
🅆 hotelskeppsholmen.com
An island restreat; stylish rooms with original wooden floors and large windows. Friendly service and free Wi-Fi.

Östermalm and Gärdet

Best Western Karlaplan ⊚⊚
Skeppargatan 82, 114 59
Tel *08-31 32 20* **Map** 3 F2
🅆 hotelkarlaplan.se
Classic red-brick building with well-furnished rooms. Some budget single rooms do not have windows.

Clarion Tapto ⊚⊚
Jungfrugatan 57, 115 31
Tel *08-664 50 00* **Map** 3 E3
🅆 clarionhotel.com
Striking hotel featuring big, bright rooms with wooden floors. Some have balconies overlooking the courtyard.

Scandic Ariadne ⊚⊚
Södra Kajen 37, 115 74
Tel *08-51 73 86 00*
🅆 scandichotels.com
Bright, airy rooms and a fantastic Sky Bar on the 17th floor of this hotel. Exceptional service.

Scandic Park ⊚⊚
Karlavägen 43, 102 46
Tel *08-51 73 48 00* **Map** 2 C2
🅆 scandichotels.com
Enjoy stunning views from most of the spacious, gracefully decorated rooms here. Excellent value for money.

Kungsholmen and Vasastan

DK Choice

Courtyard by Marriott ⊚⊚
Rålambshovsleden 50, 112 19
Tel *08-441 31 00* **Map** 1 B3
🅆 marriott.co.uk
The best place to enjoy five-star comfort at half the price of similar hotels in the city centre. The stylish rooms and bathrooms are spacious. Great breakfast and free Wi-Fi.

First Hotel Norrtull ⊚⊚
Sankt Eriksgatan 119, 113 43
Tel *08-30 03 50* **Map** 1 C1
🅆 hotelnorrtull.se
A converted listed building with elegant rooms, some of which boast exposed original brickwork.

Södermalm

Scandic Malmen ⊚⊚
Götgatan 51, 102 66
Tel *08-51 73 47 00* **Map** 4 B5
🅆 scandichotels.com
Innovatively designed hotel with neat and cosy rooms.

Further Afield

Park Inn by Radisson Solna ⊚⊚
Hotellgatan 11, 171 25 Solna
Tel *08-470 91 00*
🅆 parkinn.com
Great option for business people, with clean rooms and a sauna. Complimentary breakfast buffet.

Quality Hotel Globe ⊚⊚
Arenaslingan 7, 121 26 Johanneshov
Tel *08-686 63 00*
🅆 nordicchoicehotels.se
Spacious, bright and comfortable rooms near the trade fair centre. The breakfast buffet is excellent.

Scandic Bromma ⊚⊚
Brommaplan, 168 76 Bromma
Tel *08-51 73 41 00*
🅆 scandichotels.com
A quiet retreat offering basic rooms. Nice courtyard and patio. Gym and kids' playroom on site.

For more information on types of hotels *see p157*

WHERE TO EAT AND DRINK

Stockholm is one of Europe's liveliest and most varied cities for eating out. Several of the country's restaurants have been awarded Michelin stars, and Swedish cuisine is well regarded internationally. Many of the best restaurants have been opened by a number of top Swedish chefs and they are relatively small and informal. International influences are often combined with Swedish food to create innovative and delicious cuisine. Lunchtime is the best time to sample traditional Swedish dishes, and they tend to represent excellent value for money. If you want to eat inexpensively in the evening, there are plenty of fast-food outlets, pubs, Chinese restaurants, pizzerias, hotdog stands and kebab houses all over the city.

Where to Eat

There is a great variety of restaurants all over the capital, not just in the city centre. Cafés can also be found in large department stores and shopping malls, as well as at most museums. Hot meals can be had on many of the archipelago ferries, and several of the boats offering sightseeing tours also include dinner (*see p204*).

Sandwiches with a variety of fillings can be bought at cafés and cake shops, which often serve inexpensive hot dishes at lunchtime.

Outdoor cafés spring up in the summer on many streets and squares, and also in green areas such as Djurgården and Hagaparken (*see pp124–5*).

Types of Restaurants

Fashionable restaurants usually attract a young crowd, and the trendiest places sometimes have a rather sparse decor and extremely high noise levels. If you are looking for somewhere quieter, it is best to choose an established restaurant. There are many restaurants serving cuisine from abroad, or "crossover" or fusion cooking, which is Swedish food with foreign influences, resulting in modern Swedish cuisine.

If you are looking for somewhere cheap to eat, choose a pizzeria, kebab house or café.

Those with a sweet tooth will be well catered for in Stockholm's many modern cafés or traditional cake shops, which serve delicious Danish pastries, cinnamon buns, cakes and gateaux.

Stockholm has few bars (*see pp178–9*) as such, and the

Inn sign, Gamla Stan

best can be found at the most popular restaurants (*see pp166–71*). Smoking is banned in all public bars and restaurants.

Opening Times

Most restaurants open for lunch at 11:30am and close at around 10pm. Dinner is served from 6pm or even earlier. A large number of restaurants are closed on Sundays or Mondays, as well as during the winter. Smaller restaurants may close for their annual holiday during July.

Prices for lunch are often extremely reasonable, even at the more elegant places, which makes lunchtime a good time to have your main meal. *Dagens lunch* (lunch of the day) is generally not served after 2pm, even if the restaurant is open in the afternoon.

For those who prefer to eat late, a number of restaurants and pubs serve food until midnight or even later, particularly those that have entertainment, music or a disco. For those who are still hungry, there are 24-hour hot-dog kiosks.

Vegetarian Food

Interest in vegetarian food is increasing in Sweden, and this is reflected by the fact that good-quality vegetarian cuisine is now served at most Stockholm restaurants. There are also several completely vegetarian restaurants.

The elegant and spacious dining area of the popular Grodan, on Grev Turegatan (*p166*)

The ever-busy Nytorget Urban Deli *(p171)*

Booking a Table

Reservations should be made for evening meals, but many restaurants do not accept bookings for lunch. If you want to be sure of a table at midday, it is best to arrive at the restaurant before 11:30am; or go after 1pm, by which time most of the lunchtime clientele will have left.

Children

Without exception, children are welcome in all restaurants in Stockholm. They will be offered a special children's menu or half-portions from the normal menu. Highchairs are generally available.

Prices

Meal prices at Stockholm restaurants are very similar. At most places hot dishes cost from about 125 kr, or 250 kr at the more expensive restaurants. Lunch prices are 75–100 kr, and that often includes bread, salad, a soft drink and coffee. The price of beer, wine and other alcoholic drinks can vary considerably. As in most places, the more expensive the restaurant, the higher the price of the wine. The house wine is usually the cheapest, with a bottle normally costing from 250 kr. Beer is cheaper in pubs than in restaurants. Tap water is free of charge, and Stockholm's drinking water is of excellent quality.

Tips are always included in the bill but, if you want to reward exceptionally good service, you can round it up. If the restaurant has a staffed cloakroom, the price is 10–20 kr per person. Credit cards are accepted in virtually every restaurant.

Reading the Menu

Dinner in Stockholm usually includes a starter, hot main course and a dessert. Most restaurants offer one or more fixed-price meals with a choice of two or three dishes at a lower price than the à la carte menu. Many restaurants have menus in English; if they don't, the staff are usually familiar with English and will be happy to explain the menu. A number of menus have a section labelled *Husmanskost*, which features traditional dishes of Swedish home-cooking.

Some restaurants serve a typical Swedish *smörgåsbord*, usually on Sundays. During December a *Julbord* is also usually available. This is similar to the *smörgåsbord*, but with a lavish buffet selection of traditional seasonal dishes. You can eat as much as you like at a fixed price, but drinks are not included.

What to Drink

Wine and beer are the normal accompaniments to a meal, as well as tap or mineral water. The wine list often features a good selection of wine from countries outside Europe, along with a house wine. Vintage wines are usually not available at the more medium-price restaurants.

Many pubs and restaurants offer a wide selection of beers, often with one or more on draught. Many smaller Swedish breweries make excellent craft beers that rival those around the world.

Spirits and wines are more expensive in Swedish restaurants because of the high duty on alcohol and the state retail alcohol monopoly.

Recommended Restaurants

The restaurants featured in this guide have been selected for their good value, great food, atmosphere or a combination of these things. A wide range of establishments from Stockholm's dining scene has been included, from bistros and trattorias to Swedish restaurants and the more elegant fine-dining restaurants, some with Michelin stars. Also featured are eateries serving ethnic cuisine from across the world. A number of select diners outside the main city are included for their outstanding food.

For the very best restaurants in Stockholm, look out for entries marked DK Choice. These places have been highlighted in recognition of an exceptional feature – a celebrity chef, exquisite food, an inviting ambience or simply for great value. Most are very popular among locals and visitors, so be sure to contact them regarding reservations well in advance to guarantee a table.

Stately entrance to the plush Mäster Anders restaurant in Kungsholmen *(p169)*

The Flavours of Stockholm

Thanks to strict regulations, Sweden is one of most unpolluted countries in Europe and produces some of the purest food. Salmon can be caught in the heart of Stockholm, zander and herring are fished from the nearby coastal waters and the lakes and rivers are full of crayfish and other delicacies. Fish is a staple, but other gastronomic treats are also on offer. Wild game, such as grouse, reindeer and moose, is abundant in autumn and winter. The forests are full of berries and mushrooms, and the rich pastures produce superlative dairy produce, including several fine cheeses.

Fresh dill

Fresh anchovies on offer at Östermalmshallen food market

The Smörgåsbord

The *smörgåsbord* made its first appearance on Swedish tables sometime in the 18th century, when it consisted of a spread of hot and cold hors d'oeuvres that would be served as a prelude to a grand lunch or dinner. All this was washed down with ice-cold snaps (vodka). Gradually, however, it has grown into a full-scale meal. A traditional *smörgåsbord* will start with a selection of different herring appetizers, followed by a variety of cold dishes such as hard-boiled eggs, meat pies and salads. Then a number of hot dishes are served, including such offerings as meatballs, fried potatoes and Jansson's Temptation (a gratin of potatoes, onions, anchovies and cream). Finally an array of desserts will be placed on the table. Diners help themselves, changing their plates between courses.

Some Swedes will prepare a *smörgåsbord* as a good way of using leftovers. Inventive cooks often improvise a very simple version when unexpected guests arrive,

Beetroot & orange salad
Cucumber salad
Rye crispbread
Pickled herring
Egg with lumpfish roe
Cheese
Pork liver pâté
Lingonberry tartlets
Smoked ham

Selection of items typically found on a cold *smörgåsbord*

Local Dishes and Specialities

A typical Swedish breakfast often includes yoghurt or *filmjölk* (a type of soured milk yoghurt) with cereal. Many Swedes, however, prefer a more savoury start to the day, and cheese, ham and even liver paté may be on offer. Bread spread with *kaviar* (a cod's roe paste) is also eaten at breakfast. For lunch, most people reach for something quick and simple to prepare. Salad, perhaps served with a seafood, ham or vegetable quiche, is common, and pasta is popular too. As well as the main meals, a break for coffee and pastries, known as *fika*, is taken at any time of the day. This strong Swedish tradition is a sociable event as much as an occasion to eat. In the evening, families usually get together for the main meal of the day, dinner, a more elaborate, but still homely, affair.

Gravad Lax, a salmon fillet marinated for two days in sugar, salt and dill, is served with a creamy mustard sauce.

A colourful vegetable stall at Hötorget market

Sweden's Dining "Revolution"

The turn of the 21st century has witnessed a renaissance of gourmet cooking in Sweden, with people now visiting Stockholm for its food as well as its culture. Traditional dishes, made with the finest – usually organic – ingredients are being given an original, modern twist. Instead of simple meatballs with lingonberries, chefs are increasingly offering delights such as foie gras with a spiced mixed berry and apple chutney, and turning cheap staples, such as pig's offal, into magnificent, melt-in-the-mouth mousses.

WHAT TO DRINK

Beer Along with vodka, beer is the most popular drink to accompany a smörgåsbord. In the past, little was on offer other than insipid lagers, but a beer-making revival has made styles from dark porters to pale ales available, including some interesting fruit beers.

Vodka About 60 types of snaps, each flavoured with different herbs and spices, are made in Sweden.

Punsch This sweet arak spirit is often taken with coffee or served hot with pea soup.

Wine A huge variety of fine wines are imported, but they are usually very expensive.

using larder staples, such as eggs, slices of cheese and cooked meats, and tinned or pickled fish. During the Christmas season, many Stockholm restaurants serve a special smörgåsbord, known as a Julbord, which will include dishes using nearly every part of the pig, such as various ham, trotters and a special brawn called sylta, made from the head.

Rustic Fare

The Swedes are very good at using cheap cuts to prepare delicious dishes, and seasoning is usually kept simple with salt, pepper and fresh dill. Such homely fare, known as husmanskost, is central to the Swedish diet and regularly features on the menus of many Stockholm restaurants. One favourite is yellow pea soup, traditionally served on Thursdays, accompanied by sausages or lightly salted meat and mustard. This is generally followed by pancakes with jam, washed down with hot punsch. Other popular dishes include pytt i panna (a hash of meat, onions and potatoes) and meatballs, served with lingonberry jam.

A selection of fine fish from Sweden's pristine coastal waters

Jansson's Temptation is a dish of layered potatoes, anchovies and onions with cream, and is baked until golden.

Meatballs made from beef or pork are drenched in a rich meaty sauce and served with lingonberries.

Apple cake is a delicious buttery dessert traditionally served piping hot with cold vanilla sauce.

Where to Eat and Drink

Gamla Stan

Vapiano Gamla Stan ⓚ
Bistro/Trattoria   **Map** 4 B3
Munkbrogatan 8, 114 27
Tel 08-22 29 40
Upmarket fast-food joint, where
a range of dishes – from pasta
to pizza – is rustled up in front
of the patrons in no time.

Bistro & Grill Ruby ⓚⓚ
Bistro/Trattoria   **Map** 4 C3
Österlånggatan 14, 111 31
Tel 08-20 57 76   **Closed** Sun
Choose between grilled food
in US Southern down-home
style, or French home-cooking
accompanied by wine in a more
formal set-up.

DK Choice

Bistro Pastis ⓚⓚ
Bistro/Trattoria   **Map** 4 C3
Baggensgatan 12, 111 31
Tel 08-20 20 18
Sample excellent, good-value
French bistro food in an area
otherwise packed with tourist
traps. The informal setting and
reasonably priced set lunch
menus make this a popular
choice. The *crème brûlée* is
one of Stockholm's finest.

Den Gyldene Freden ⓚⓚ
Fine Dining   **Map** 4 C4
Österlånggatan 51, 103 17
Tel 08-24 97 60   **Closed** Sun
Good Swedish and French cuisine
at this restaurant favoured by
artists and intellectuals.

Magnus Ladulas ⓚⓚ
Swedish   **Map** 4 C3
Österlånggatan 26, 111 31
Tel 08-21 19 57   **Closed** Sun
Guests choose the setting – a
cellar, a classic dining room or,
in the right weather, the street
terrace. Delectable fare.

Pubologi ⓚⓚ
Fine Dining   **Map** 4 B3
Stora Nygatan 20, 111 27
Tel 08-50 64 00 86   **Closed** Sun & Jul
Modern cooking mixed with
classic Swedish and international
dishes. The restaurant also brews
a couple of unique beers.

Djuret ⓚⓚⓚ
Fine Dining   **Map** 4 B3
Lilla Nygatan 5, 111 28
Tel 08-50 64 00 84   **Closed** Sun & Jul
Meat, and lots of it. The menu is
based around the meat of one

particular animal and usually
changes every couple of weeks.

Frantzen ⓚⓚⓚ
Fine Dining   **Map** 4 B3
Lilla Nygatan 21, 111 28
Tel 08-20 85 80   **Closed** Sun
Everything about this restaurant,
with two Michelin stars, is
designed to maximize the
feast of the senses. Exquisite set
menus and impeccable service.

Mr French ⓚⓚⓚ
Seafood   **Map** 4 C3
Tullhus 2, Skeppsbron, 111 30
Tel 08-20 20 95
The menu, prepared by one of
Sweden's top chefs, is inspired
by classic French brasserie food.
Great views across the water.

Le Rouge ⓚⓚⓚ
Fine Dining   **Map** 4 C3
Brunnsgränd 24, 111 30
Tel 08-50 52 44 30   **Closed** Sun
High-class French cuisine, with
the occasional Italian twist, is
served in luxurious surroundings.

City

Belgobaren ⓚⓚ
Bistro/Trattoria   **Map** 2 C4
Bryggargatan 12, 101 31
Tel 08-24 66 40
A Belgian restaurant serving
huge portions of fresh mussels
and frites with oodles of mayo.
Great range of Belgian beers.

Cloud Nine ⓚⓚ
Fine Dining   **Map** 2 B4
Torsgatan 1, 111 23
Tel 08-653 69 90   **Closed** Sun
Sample different cuisine – from
dim sum to Swedish seafood

Entrance to the chic Bistro Pastis,
Gamla Stan

Price Guide
Prices are for a three-course meal for
one, half a bottle of house wine and
other charges such as service and cover.

ⓚ	under 450 Kr
ⓚⓚ	450–1,000 Kr
ⓚⓚⓚ	over 1,000 Kr

and French classics. Eat on the
terrace in the summer months.

Grill ⓚⓚ
Fine Dining   **Map** 2 C3
Drottninggatan 89, 113 60
Tel 08-31 45 30
This huge bar and grill
appeals to a young crowd
who flock here for the sizzling
steaks and delicious cocktails.
Do not miss the elaborate
Sunday buffet.

Grodan ⓚⓚ
Swedish   **Map** 3 E2
Grev Turegatan 16, 114 46
Tel 08-679 61 00
Classic Swedish food in a
pleasant setting. The *raggmunk*
(Swedish potato pancakes) are
hard to resist. Popular with the
local crowd.

Hattori Sushi Devil ⓚⓚ
Japanese   **Map** 2 B3
Drottninggatan 85, 111 60
Tel 08-22 44 00
A small and cozy restaurant
serving good-quality sushi
and sashimi. The fried shrimp
is a popular choice. Serves
five kinds of sake.

Jamie's Italian ⓚⓚ
Italian   **Map** 3 D3
Humlegårdsgatan 23, 114 46
Tel 08-517 340 20
The first Jamie Oliver restaurant
in Sweden, located in the
heart of the city's entertainment
district. The menu features
appetizing, rustic dishes.

Nalen ⓚⓚ
Swedish   **Map** 3 D3
Regeringsgatan 74, 111 39
Tel 08-50 52 92 01   **Closed** Sun
Traditional Swedish food put
together using the finest local
ingredients, such as reindeer,
bleak roe and cranberries.

Operakällarens Bakficka ⓚⓚ
Seafood   **Map** 3 D5
Karl XII:s Torg, 111 86
Tel 08-676 58 00   **Closed** Sun
Savour generous helpings
of Swedish food, especially
fish. The daily specials are
listed on a chalkboard.
No reservations.

PA and Co ⊗⊗
Bistro/Trattoria **Map** 3 E4
Riddargatan 8, 114 35
Tel *08-611 08 45*
Another small yet famous Stockholm restaurant, for which you will almost certainly need a reservation. French food that is definitely worth the money.

Rolfs Kök ⊗⊗
Modern Swedish **Map** 2 C3
Tegnérgatan 41, 111 61
Tel *08-10 16 96*
Taste some of the best seasonal Swedish food in the city. The wine list runs to more than 450 varieties.

Sturehof ⊗⊗
Swedish **Map** 3 D4
Stureplan 2, 114 46
Tel *08-440 57 30*
This place offers a really good selection of meat and seafood in a traditional setting. There is also a lively bar at the back.

Supper ⊗⊗
South American **Map** 2 B3
Tegnérgatan 37, 111 61
Tel *08-23 24 24* **Closed** *Sun*
Spacious and bright restaurant serving South American-inspired food. Try the slow-cooked beef with chocolate and chilli, or fishcakes with lime and ginger.

Tjabba Thai ⊗⊗
Thai **Map** 2 B3
Wallingatan 7, 111 60
Tel *08-21 99 88*
Spicy and tasty Thai food prepared with authentic ingredients. Closes at 10pm. Try the *som tam tai* salad and the *geng som gong*, a dish of scampi in a spicy curry.

Zink Grill ⊗⊗
Bistro/Trattoria **Map** 3 D4
Biblioteksgatan 5, 111 46
Tel *08-611 42 22*
An outstanding bar and grill in an unbeatable location. It's open for breakfast too, which is rare in Stockholm. For lunch, the mixed grill for two offers great value.

DK Choice

Ekstedt ⊗⊗⊗
Modern Swedish **Map** 3 D3
Humlegårdsgatan 17, 114 46
Tel *08-611 12 10* **Closed** *Sun*
Michelin-starred Ekstedt serves amazing grilled meat and fish cooked over open fires by a team of young top Swedish chefs. The experience is made more enjoyable by the superb waiting staff. Set menus are expensive but offer a genuine culinary journey through Sweden.

Glitzy bar area at the classy Grodan

Griffins Steakhouse ⊗⊗⊗
Steak **Map** 2 C4
Klarabergsviadukten 67, 111 64
Tel *08-51 94 22 70* **Closed** *Sun*
Upmarket steakhouse offering a choice of sizes: 250 g (8.8 oz) or 350 g (12 oz). The burger with cheddar and bacon is heavenly.

Operakällaren ⊗⊗⊗
Swedish **Map** 4 C1
Karl XII:s Torg, 111 86
Tel *08-676 58 00* **Closed** *Sun & Mon*
Enjoy a lavish dining experience in surroundings that are an attraction in themselves. Reserve well in advance for weekends.

Riche ⊗⊗⊗
Swedish **Map** 3 E4
Birger Jarlsgatan 4, 114 34
Tel *08-54 50 35 60*
Swedish food at its best. The meatballs with mash and gravy are terrific. Informal ambience.

Teatergrillen ⊗⊗⊗
Fine Dining **Map** 3 E2
Nybrogatan 3, 114 34
Tel *08-54 50 35 65* **Closed** *Sun*
Come to one of Stockholm's oldest restaurants to enjoy

Elegant interior of the Wedholms Fisk, popular for seafood

a blend of French fine dining and classic Swedish dishes. Excellent service.

Wedholms Fisk ⊗⊗⊗
Seafood **Map** 3 E4
Arsenalsgatan 1, 111 47
Tel *08-611 78 74* **Closed** *Sun*
Great food with views to match, and arguably the finest selection of seafood in the land. Don't miss the signature turbot.

Blasieholmen & Skeppsholmen

DK Choice

B.A.R. ⊗⊗
Seafood **Map** 4 C1
Blasieholmsgatan 4a, 111 48
Tel *08-611 53 35*
Choose fish from the large counter and watch it get custom-cooked to perfection. There is lobster and crab too, waiting to be fished out of the aquarium and boiled or grilled. One of the most popular eateries in the city.

Hjerta ⊗⊗
Swedish **Map** 5 D2
Slupskjulsvagen 28b, 111 49
Tel *08-611 41 00* **Closed** *Sun & winter*
With its terrific Skeppsholmen setting and classic Swedish cuisine, Hjerta is a great place for a quiet lunch or private dinner.

Långa Raden ⊗⊗
Fine Dining **Map** 5 F3
Gröna gången 1, 111 86
Tel *08-407 23 00*
Situated in Hotel Skeppsholmen, this place offers formal dining with classic Swedish and international dishes on the menu. Great service.

For more information on types of restaurants *see p163*

Refreshing beer from the tap at Ulla Windbladh, Djurgården

Mathias Dahlgren Matsalen and Matbaren ⓦⓦ
Fine Dining   **Map** 4 C1
Grand Hotel, Södra Blasieholmshamnen 6, 111 48
Tel 08-679 35 84
The tasting menu at this Michelin-starred restaurant is a veritable treat of flavours and innovative combinations. There is also a more elaborate six-course themed menu. Well-stocked wine cellar.

Djurgården

Hasselbacken ⓦⓦ
Swedish   **Map** 6 A3
Hazeliusbacken 20, 100 55
Tel 08-51 73 43 00
Traditional Swedish food served in a finely restored 1850s setting. Good selection of desserts. A children's menu is also available.

Solliden Skansen ⓦⓦ
Swedish   **Map** 6 A3
Skansen Museum, 100 55
Tel 08-56 63 70 00
Enjoy breathtaking views of Stockholm at this charming eatery and savour a classic Swedish *smörgåsbord* at lunch.

Spritmuseum Restaurant ⓦⓦ
Fine Dining   **Map** 6 B4
Djurgårdsvägen 38, 115 21
Tel 08-12 13 13 09
Head Chef Petter Nilsson, who previously owned two renowned restaurants in France, uses seasonal, locally sourced ingredients to create sumptuous dishes.

Ulla Windbladh ⓦⓦ
Swedish   **Map** 6 A3
Rosendalsvägen 8, 115 21
Tel 08-53 48 97 01
Beautifully located restaurant with an old-fashioned atmosphere serving traditional and modern Swedish food.

Villa Godthem ⓦⓦ
Fine Dining   **Map** 6 A3
Rosendalsvägen 9, 115 21
Tel 08-50 52 44 15
Great location and excellent food, mostly Swedish classics. The emphasis is on organic fare, and local ingredients are used whenever possible.

Östermalm and Gärdet

Dell'Attore ⓦ
Bistro/Trattoria   **Map** 3 F2
Skeppargatan 60, 114 59
Tel 08-442 61 18
Small, bustling eatery decorated from floor to ceiling with photos of famous actors. The pizzas are the best in town.

Brasserie Elverket ⓦⓦ
Bistro/Trattoria   **Map** 3 D3
Linnégatan 69, 114 60
Tel 08-661 25 62
Scandinavian/European food served in an informal setting.

Softly lit dining area at sleek gastropub Restaurang Volt

The Norwegian cod with mashed potatoes is especially popular.

Funkalistic ⓦⓦ
Swedish
Sehlstedtsgatan 1, 115 28
Tel 08-12 20 37 77
Close to the cruise ship and ferry terminals, this family-run establishment offers traditional Swedish food at great prices.

Spring ⓦⓦ
Ethnic   **Map** 2 C2
Karlavägen 110, 115 26
Tel 08-655 11 22
Spring relies on a delicious and complex mix of influences, such as Asian, North African and South American, in its dishes.

Bistro Nouveau ⓦⓦⓦ
Fine Dining   **Map** 3 E3
Kommendörsgatan 7, 114 48
Tel 08-661 42 42   **Closed** *Mon*
Try snails, the fantastic steak tartare and mussels with fries at this excellent French eatery. Desserts are great, too.

Brasserie Bobonne ⓦⓦⓦ
Fine Dining   **Map** 3 E4
Storgatan 12, 114 51
Tel 08-660 03 18
Sample classic dishes such as *moules marinières* and boeuf bourguignon, and enjoy a range of well-matured French cheeses.

Cassi ⓦⓦⓦ
Fine Dining   **Map** 3 F3
Narvavägen 30, 115 22
Tel 08-661 74 61
This place dishes out modern European cuisine with a hint of French. Good steak Béarnaise and a legendary wine list.

Esperanto ⓦⓦⓦ
Fine Dining   **Map** 3 B3
Kungstensgatan 2, 114 25
Tel 08-696 23 23
Housed in a former theatre, this Michelin-starred restaurant serves superbly inventive food. Unpretentious service. Try the 15-course tasting menu.

Proviant ⓦⓦⓦ
Swedish   **Map** 3 E3
Sturegatan 19, 114 36
Tel 08-22 60 50
Lively restaurant serving excellent and inventive Swedish cuisine with a French twist. Don't miss the five-course "surprise" menu.

Restaurang Volt ⓦⓦⓦ
Swedish   **Map** 3 E3
Kommendörsgatan 16, 114 48
Tel 08-662 34 00   **Closed** *Sun & Mon*
This gastropub with minimalist decor serves traditional Swedish

food. Specialities include must-have dishes such as reindeer with berries and baked marrow.

Speceriet ⑩⑩⑩
Bistro/Trattoria **Map** 3 F2
Artillerigatan 14, 114 51
Tel *08-662 30 60*
This tiny place offers modern Nordic food with a contemporary take on classic dishes. It is best to reserve ahead.

Kungsholmen

La Famiglia ⑩
Bistro/Trattoria **Map** 1 B2
Alströmergatan 45, 112 47
Tel *08-650 63 10*
Particularly popular with families, this charming restaurant serves delectable classic Italian cuisine in a quirky setting at budget prices.

Great India ⑩
Indian **Map** 1 B2
Fleminggatan 62, 112 45
Tel *08-651 99 01*
One of the very few quality Indian restaurants in Stockholm. Delectable curries, good staff and a lovely terrace in the summer.

El Diablo ⑩⑩
Latin American **Map** 2 A4
Norra Agnegatan 43, 112 29
Tel *08-650 50 69*
Tequila recommendations with every dish. Offers delectable food made with seasonal ingredients served in a modern environment.

DK Choice

Mälarpaviljongen ⑩⑩
Bistro/Trattoria **Map** 1 B3
Norr Mälarstrand 64, 112 35
Tel *08-650 87 01*
An absolutely lovely place to eat outdoors, by the waterside, from spring to autumn. Soak in the laid-back ambience, complete with chill-out music and lounge-bar feel. The menu features upmarket burgers, salads and grilled fish. Prices are reasonable, and the service is exceptional.

Roppongi ⑩⑩
Japanese **Map** 1 B3
Hantverkargatan 76c, 12 38
Tel *08-650 17 72*
A great place that offers really good sushi, attentive service and a pleasant atmosphere. Roppongi also has another branch in Stockholm.

Spisa Hos Helena ⑩⑩
Bistro/Trattoria **Map** 2 A4
Scheelegatan 18, 112 28
Tel *08-654 49 26*
This restaurant serves up large portions of classic international dishes at affordable prices.

Sthlm Tapas ⑩⑩
Spanish **Map** 1 C3
Pontonjärgatan 28, 112 37
Tel *08-654 90 30*
Good tapas are hard to find in Stockholm, but this place won't disappoint. Loads of Spanish hams and quesadillas as well.

Tabbouli ⑩⑩
Lebanese **Map** 2 A4
Norra Agnegatan 39, 112 29
Tel *08-654 25 00*
Probably the best Lebanese restaurant in Stockholm. It specializes in grilled meats and meze, all served in a lively setting.

Trattorian ⑩⑩
Bistro/Trattoria **Map** 1 B3
Norr Malarstrand, Kajplats 464, 112 20
Tel *08-50 52 44 50* **Closed** *Sun*
Lively, trendy waterside Italian restaurant worth visiting for the chaotic yet stylish decor. The food matches the surroundings, and prices are good.

AG ⑩⑩⑩
Steak **Map** 1 C2
Kronobergsgatan 37, 112 33
Tel *08-41 06 81 00*
A meat lover's paradise, and home of one of Sweden's best bison steaks. Good tapas menu and decent cocktails, too.

Lux ⑩⑩⑩
Fine Dining
Primusgatan 116, 112 67
Tel *08-619 01 90* **Closed** *Mon*
Michelin-starred Swedish food served in the former Electrolux canteen. The lunchtime set menu offers great value for money.

Mäster Anders ⑩⑩⑩
Swedish **Map** 2 A4
Pipersgatan 1, 112 24
Tel *08-654 20 01*
Contemporary Swedish restaurant that offers an excellent lunch menu. Delicious meatballs.

Restaurang Jonas ⑩⑩⑩
Fine Dining **Map** 1 B2
Fleminggatan 39, 112 26
Tel *08-650 22 20*
There is a wide range of gourmet international dishes at this restaurant, and a great five-course set menu. Good service.

Stadshuskällaren ⑩⑩⑩
Fine Dining **Map** 1 B3
Hantverkargatan 1, 112 21
Tel *08-58 62 18 30*
Set in the basement of the City Hall, this restaurant hosts the annual Nobel Prize banquet. Serves traditional Swedish food.

Vasastan

Bistrot Paname ⑩⑩
Bistro/Trattoria **Map** 2 B1
Hagagatan 5, 113 48
Tel *08-31 43 38*
French bistro that offers gorgeous ambience and inventive food at great prices. Impeccable service.

I Cinque Sensi ⑩⑩
Bistro/Trattoria **Map** 1 B1
Rörstrandsgatan 23, 113 40
Tel *08-33 31 00*
Excellent Italian eatery. The grilled red tuna is great, as are the desserts. Good selection of wines.

Clas på Hörnet ⑩⑩
Swedish **Map** 2 C2
Surbrunnsgatan 20, 113 48
Tel *08-16 51 36* **Closed** *Sun*
Old-fashioned Swedish restaurant. Highlights include duck sausage and sautéed sweetbreads with leeks and cured ox tongue.

The simple dining room at Mäster Anders

For more information on types of restaurants *see p163*

Linguini ⓚⓚ
Bistro/Trattoria **Map** 2 A2
Frejgatan 48, 113 26
Tel 08-31 49 15
A small and homely Italian restaurant that serves tasty pasta dishes. There is also a good selection of Italian wines on offer.

Restaurang Malaysia ⓚⓚ
Malaysian **Map** 3 D4
Luntmakargatan, 111 37
Tel 08-673 56 69
Great selection of vegetarian dishes at this Asian place. The fish curry is highly recommended.

Tennstopet ⓚⓚ
Swedish **Map** 2 A2
Dalagatan 50, 113 24
Tel 08-32 25 18
Unpretentious neighbourhood joint that rustles up scrumptious Swedish food. It has been around for almost half a century.

Tranan ⓚⓚ
Swedish **Map** 3 F2
Karlbergsvägen 14, 113 27
Tel 08-52 72 81 00
A little off the beaten track, this bistro-style eatery offers superb international cuisine and Swedish home food at good prices. There is a lively bar downstairs.

Nortull and North of Stockholm

Döden I Grytan ⓚⓚ
Bistro/Trattoria **Map** 2 B2
Norrtullsgatan 61, Normalm, 113 45
Tel 08-32 50 95
Come to this superb restaurant for classic Italian countryside food. It is almost always full, and reservations are essential. Great value for money.

The brightly lit entrance to Tranan, a classy bistro, Vasastan

DK Choice

Stallmästaregården ⓚⓚ
Fine Dining
Stallmästaregården, Norrtull, 113 47
Tel 08-610 13 01
This former coaching inn dating from the 17th century is charmingly located on Brunnsviken lakeside. Tastefully renovated in 2012, it offers a wide range of modern Swedish cuisine with strong traditional influences. The *smörgåsbord* served on weekend afternoons offers good value. Warm and friendly service.

Södermalm

Ellora ⓚ
Indian **Map** 8 A2
Hornsgatan 85, 117 26
Tel 08-658 65 01
Good, relatively cheap Indian restaurant with gorgeous decor

and an excellent selection of curries. Try the prawn cocktail.

Faros ⓚ
Greek **Map** 9 E3
Sofiagatan 1, 116 40
Tel 08-442 14 14
A fine selection of Greek dishes draws the crowds here. Don't miss the *dolmadakia* and Faros pepper steak. The restaurant also serves excellent seafood and a good selection of wines.

Feca ⓚ
Bistro/Trattoria **Map** 8 B2
Torkel Knutssonsgatan 35, 118 49
Tel 08-428 98 28
One of the best places in Stockholm to gorge on cheap Italian food. Feca offers healthy portions of pizza and pasta at half the price of similar eateries.

Hermans ⓚ
Vegetarian **Map** 9 E2
Fjällgatan 23B, 116 28
Tel 08-643 94 80
Enjoy great views from the waterside tables at this restaurant. There is live jazz or bossa nova two or three times a week, and a vegetarian buffet that changes theme daily.

DK Choice

Indian Garden ⓚ
Indian **Map** 1 C5
Heleneborgsgatan 15, 117 31
Tel 08-84 94 28
An excellent Indian restaurant that dishes out delectable curries made to order, as spicy as one may choose to try out. Go for the devilishly hot vindaloo or the mild chicken korma. There are plenty of options for vegetarians as well, and it is perfect for large groups of diners. Service is fantastic and very friendly.

Blå Dörren ⓚⓚ
Swedish **Map** 9 D2
Södermalmstorg 6, 116 45
Tel 08-743 07 43
Good-value Swedish food in a lovely dining room complete with high, arched ceilings. The lunchtime buffet is particularly good and well priced.

Delikatessen Bistro Bar ⓚⓚ
Bistro/Trattoria **Map** 8 B2
Krukmakargatan 22, 118 51
Tel 08-658 42 50
Housed inside an old fire station. The food is an exquisite blend of modern European and classic French cuisine, and the decor is trendy and chic.

Outside seating at the Tennstopet in Vasastan

Häktet
Swedish   Map 8 A2
Hornsgatan 82, 118 21
Tel *08-84 59 10*   **Closed** *Sun*
Classic Swedish food in a minimalist and contemporary setting, away from the tourist hordes. Superb wine selection and cocktails complement the food.

Hjordis
Swedish/Thai   Map 9 E3
Borgmästargatan 7, 116 29
Tel *08-640 99 50*   **Closed** *Sun*
Contemporary Swedish and Thai fusion cuisine brings in a hip crowd. The retro design of the place appeals to youngsters. friendly and warm service.

Nostrano
Bistro/Trattoria   Map 8 C2
Timmermansgatan 13, 118 25
Tel *08-644 10 35*   **Closed** *Sun*
A bustling eatery serving outstanding Italian fare. The pasta is made fresh on the spot, and the list of sinful desserts is fantastic. There are no fewer than nine types of grappa.

Nytorget Urban Deli
Bistro/Trattoria   Map 9 E3
Nytorget 4, 116 40
Tel *08-59 90 91 80*
High-quality food and a quirky atmosphere have made this the eatery of choice of some of Stockholm's trendiest people. The cheese platter is delicious. Try the elaborate weekend brunch.

DK Choice

Pelikan
Swedish   Map 8 C4
Blekingegatan 40, 116 62
Tel *08-55 60 90 90*
A traditional Swedish beer hall serving all the usual Swedish favourites, from herring platter to fish stew. The cheeses are delicious, and the meatballs are arguably Stockholm's very best. Pelikan attracts both locals and tourists, and serves one of the best selections of Swedish beer in the city. Noisy and boisterous, so not the ideal place for a quiet night out.

Sardin
Seafood   Map 9 E3
Skånegatan 79, 116 35
Tel *08-644 97 00*   **Closed** *Sun*
Something of a cross between a French bistro and a tapas bar, this small but lively place serves good-value food to locals and visitors in the know.

Warm interiors and cozy couches at Gondolen, Södermalm

Sjögras
Swedish/French   Map 8 C2
Timmermansgatan 24, 118 55
Tel *08-84 12 00*   **Closed** *Sun*
A simple and lively restaurant whose trademark is its open kitchen. On the menu is mainly French food with a Swedish twist.

Gondolen
Swedish   Map 9 E2
Stadsgården 6, 105 65
Tel *08-641 70 90*   **Closed** *Sun*
Perched 33 m (108 ft) above the water, this restaurant offers great views and contemporary food, not to mention delicious cocktails at the sleek bar. It is always full, so reservations must be made in advance.

Further Afield

Båthuset
Seafood
Hamnen, Sigtuna
Tel *08-59 25 67 80*   **Closed** *Sun & Mon*
A good-value floating restaurant that mainly prepares seafood, with cod and crayfish being the specialities. Great choice for a romantic dinner.

The bar area at the ever-popular Nytorget Urban Deli

Edsbacka
Swedish
*Sollentunavagen 220, 191 35
Solentuna*
Tel *08-580 016 60*
Fine yet informal dining at an inn dating from 1626. On the menu is Swedish food with a modern twist. Don't miss the pork schnitzel.

DK Choice

Fjärderholmarnas Rökeriet
Swedish
Stora Fjärderholmen, Fjärderholmarna
Tel *08-716 50 88*
On a small island at the entrance to the archipelago, the Rökeriet serves great seafood, available as both buffet and à la carte. Do not miss the elaborate and sumptuous Archipelago Buffet. The restaurant also serves an interesting crayfish dinner every day in August and organizes a special Christmas dinner.

Holmen Kök & Bar
Modern Swedish
*Torben Gruts väg 5, 133 39
Saltsjöbaden*
Tel *08-717 77 67*
Open only during the summer, Holmen Kök & Bar primarily serves the many locals who keep their boats moored in the small harbour here. Good, simple food, live music and an exclusive feel.

Landet
Swedish
*LM Ericssons vag 27, 126 37
Midsommarkransen*
Tel *08-41 01 93 20*   **Closed** *Sun*
A trendy Swedish eatery, Landet is popular with Stockholm foodies. Try the exquisite veal entrecôte or the steak tartare.

For more information on types of restaurants *see p163*

Cafés and Pubs

Swedes love their coffee. At work people take a coffee break at around 3pm, and, if they are out and about, they are likely to pop into a café. The cake shops (indicated by the sign "Konditori") have a long tradition. They serve typical Swedish pastries, with everything from sweet small buns to tempting gateaux. The best cake shops have their own bakeries and sell a variety of pastries and sandwiches. Cafés were once cheaper and more popular than the elegant cake shops, but the differences have been evened out, and there are now many Continental-style cafés serving espresso, cappuccino and caffe latte. Many cafés open for breakfast early in the morning, and they usually serve lunch as well. The old Swedish "beer cafés" have been replaced by the city's many pubs, which also serve simple dishes at reasonable prices.

Cafés and Cake Shops

Café culture is flourishing in Stockholm, and the style ranges from American or Italian to traditional Swedish and classic cake shops. The café is a good choice if you feel peckish between meals, need to rest your legs or simply want a meeting place. Apart from coffee, sandwiches and cakes, nearly all cafés serve simple lunches – quiches and salad, for example – soft drinks and ice cream. Typical cafés serve Swedish-style strong coffee, along with sandwiches, buns and cakes. Don't miss the delicious *prinsesstårta* cream cake, by far the most popular one. Cafés usually close at around 6pm.

Many cafés have tables outside in the summer. If you feel like sitting under a fruit tree, where you can enjoy the birdsong, **Rosendals Trädgårdskafé** on Djurgården is the place. The salad buffet, consisting of organically grown vegetables and home-baked bread, is a feast for the eye and the palate. It is open only during the summer and in December. **Lasse i Parken** is another rustic idyll in the city with home-baked bread and delicious cheesecakes.

Sturekatten is a classic cake shop decorated in the style of an early 20th-century upper-class home with many small rooms and unrivalled pastries. **Vete-Katten** is one of Stockholm's most authentic cake shops. Its pastries are

outstanding, and chocaholics won't be able to resist the home-made pralines. After a hectic day's shopping, head for the trendy **Hotel Diplomat T/Bar**, which serves English-style afternoon tea. Another oasis in the shopping district is **Gateau**, one floor up in Sturegallerian. The pastries are delicious, and the gentle piano music is particularly enjoyable and relaxing.

Rather more unusual is **Legumes**, which serves nutritious yet tasty Middle Eastern vegetarian delicacies with biodynamic bread. Another one is **Bakverket**. Renowned for its fresh baked bread, it is also said to provide Stockholm's best breakfast.

Mellgvist Caffé is a very popular place for hanging out close to Sankt Eriksplan. The moreish turkey and horseradish cream panini is particularly addictive.

Wayne's Coffee is Södermalm's most popular meeting place, with giant sandwiches and cakes, comfortable armchairs and an elegant clientele. **Espresso House** serves bagels, sandwiches, fresh baked goods and many different types of coffee. At **Café Tabac** you can mingle with the locals as you enjoy a café au lait and home-baked brownies. Absolutely the finest espresso is served at **Tintarella di Luna**, an authentic Italian café, which also has the city's best *panini*. Coffee connoisseurs should not miss

Bagatelle Café, located in a bright and airy setting right at the entrance to the Kungshallen. They also offer freshly squeezed juices and delicious smoothies.

Pubs

The old Swedish beer cafés have either closed down, transformed into a local restaurant (Tranan at Odenplan is a typical example – *see p170*) or are now pubs with an international flavour. Irish, Scottish or English pubs are all popular, but there are also influences from Belgium, the Czech Republic, Germany, Australia and the USA.

Stockholmers generally have a great interest in beer, so the pubs usually have a wide selection of brews, and the staff are knowledgeable. Try some of the beers from three small, acclaimed, quality breweries: Tärnö, Stockholm's own brewery; Slottskällan in Uppsala; and Pilgrimstad from northern Sweden.

One of the busiest and most traditional pubs is the **Tudor Arms**, opened in the 1960s. English is the normal language here, and many of the regular customers are British. Scots and Americans head for the **Bagpiper's Inn**, where bagpipes are provided on the upper floor, and Scottish beers are available. One floor down is the **Bald Eagle**, where drinkers can enjoy rock music, and there is usually a queue for the billiards table. For some of the best craft beer in Stockholm, visitors can also head to the pub at **Omnipollo**, an award-winning brewery that has been listed among the top 100 brewers in the world.

Anyone feeling homesick for Ireland only needs to go through the door of **Limerick** to enjoy some Guinness or Kilkenny. Irish music is performed there at weekends. **O'Leary's** has many expat regulars and also serves excellent food. **The Dubliner** is yet another Irish pub, with a large selection of malt whiskeys. Live music contributes to the atmosphere. On Södermalm,

Soldaten Svejk specializes in Czech draught beer and offers rustic country cooking. **BrewDog Bar** serves a wide range of international and Swedish beers, as well as food.

Beer connoisseurs or whisky drinkers should head for **Akkurat**, which has about 400 different types of whisky and beer from all over the world, but particularly from Belgium. Mussels are always on the menu, but there is also a good choice of other hot dishes and delicious snacks. Beer and whisky tastings take place frequently, the staff are knowledgeable, and service is quick. **Oliver Twist** is reckoned to be one of the city's best pubs for draught beer, imported from all over the world. The staff here are also dedicated and knowledgeable. Business people head for **Man in the Moon** after work, and the atmosphere is

rather more refined than at most other pubs. A pleasant rural feel pervades the **Pub Anchor**, which specializes in unusual beers and has live music 3–4 nights a week.

Lundgrens is one of Sweden's best lagers and can be enjoyed on Kungsholmen, where it is brewed by the Tärnö brewery. It is served on draught at both **Mackinlay's Inn** and **Kings Head**, two pleasant local pubs. **Tennstopet** was once a meeting place for journalists, and some have remained loyal customers. It is pleasant but noisy, and there is a darts board. Swedish "home cooking" is available. The clientele is typically in the upper middle-age bracket.

Swedish pubs serve not just drinks but also snacks and value-for-money hot food from lunchtime till late in the evening. Many Stockholmers now regard

going out to the pub as a pleasant and often less expensive alternative to their local restaurant.

Most pubs are open daily. Many open for lunch and usually close at 11pm, while a few remain open to midnight or 1am *(see also pp178–9)*.

Fast Food

If you are looking for a quick snack, there are plenty of street kiosks selling hot dogs, hamburgers or kebabs. Several of them are open 24 hours. The Kungshallen complex at Hötorget has a lot of restaurants and fast-food outlets – particularly useful for groups who are undecided on the type of food they want to eat. There are also plenty of pizzerias of varying standards, as well as Chinese restaurants, where you can eat well and inexpensively.

DIRECTORY

Cafés and Cake Shops

Bagatelle Café
Kungsgatan 44.
Map 2 C4.
Tel 08-791 88 80.

Bakverket
Bondegatan 59. **Map** 9 E3.
Tel 08-640 91 07.

Café Tabac
Stora Nygatan 46.
Map 4 B4.
Tel 08-10 15 34.

Espresso House
Sergels Torg 12. **Map** 2 C4.
Tel 08-21 72 00.

Gateau
Sturegallerian. **Map** 3 D4.
Tel 08-519 791 01.

Hotel Diplomat T/Bar
Strandvägen 7 C.
Map 3 E4.
Tel 08-459 68 02.

Lasse i Parken
Högalidsgatan 56.
Map 1 B5.
Tel 08-658 33 95.

Legumes
Hornsgatan 80.
Map 8 B2.
Tel 08-669 35 35.

Mellgvist Caffé
Rörstrandsgatan 4.
Map 1 B1.
Tel 08-30 23 80.

Rosendals Trädgårdskafé
Rosendalsterrassen 12.
Map 6 C3.
Tel 08-545 812 70.

Sturekatten
Riddargatan 4.
Map 3 D4.
Tel 08-611 16 12.

Tintarella di Luna
Drottninggatan 102.
Map 2 C3.
Tel 08-10 79 55.

Wayne's Coffee
Götgatan 31.
Map 9 D2.
Tel 08-644 45 90.

Kungsgatan 14.
Map 3 D4.
Tel 08-791 00 86.

Vete-Katten
Kungsgatan 55.
Map 2 C4.
Tel 08-20 84 05.

Pubs

Akkurat
Hornsgatan 18.
Map 8 C2.
Tel 08-644 00 15.

Bagpiper's Inn
Rörstrandsgatan 21.
Map 1 C1.
Tel 08-31 18 55.

BrewDog Bar
St Eriksgatan 56.
Map 3 D3.
Tel 08-650 21 10.

Copperfields
St Eriksgatan 36–38.
Map 2 A2.
Tel 08-654 80 00.

The Dubliner
Hollandärgatan 1.
Map 2 C3.
Tel 08-679 77 07.

Limerick
Tegnérgatan 10.
Map 2 C3.
Tel 08-673 43 98.

Mackinlay's Inn
Fleminggatan 85.
Map 1 C2.
Tel 08-650 83 20.

Man in the Moon
Tegnérgatan 2 C.
Map 2 C3.
Tel 08-458 95 00.

O'Leary's
Vasagatan.
Map 2 B4.
Tel 073-688 16 86.

Oliver Twist
Repslagargatan 6.
Map 9 D2.
Tel 08-640 05 66.

Omnipollo
Tjärhovsgatan 6.
Map 9 E3.
Tel 073-785 57 41.

Pub Anchor
Sveavägen 90.
Map 2 C2.
Tel 08-15 20 00.

Soldaten Svejk
Östgötagatan 35.
Map 9 D3.
Tel 08-641 33 66.

Tennstopet
Dalagatan 50.
Map 2 A2.
Tel 08-32 25 18.

Tudor Arms
Grevgatan 31.
Map 3 F4.
Tel 08-660 27 12.

ENTERTAINMENT IN STOCKHOLM

Stockholm is an important city for entertainment. The capital, which was once said to have a "cold beauty", is now a vibrant, trend-setting metropolis full of theatres, bars and music venues. International stars increasingly put Stockholm on their touring schedule, not least because of its two magnificent indoor arenas, Globen and Tele2Arena. Another factor is Swedish pop music's great position on the world stage, which has made it an important export item. A wide range of entertainment is on offer, and the short distance between venues is another benefit. The Royal Opera House, for instance, is only a few minutes' walk from the intimate clubs of Gamla Stan. Stockholm also has a rich cultural life with concerts, drama and exhibitions.

Kungliga Operan (Royal Opera House), Gustav II Adolfs Torg *(see p66)*

Entertainment Listings

Daily newspapers offer detailed information on forthcoming events; this is printed either in a special section or in weekend supplements; note, however, that this information is only in Swedish.

The Internet has several good sites with up-to-date details on special events. **Stockholm Visitor Centre** *(see p191)* has an official "tourist site" (www.visit stockholm.com), which is constantly updated with detailed information and includes some useful links. For a wealth of information about entertainment and events in Stockholm, including museums, restaurants and concerts, visit www.**alltom stockholm.se**. Another useful website is www. **eventful.com**, where you can browse upcoming entertainment options such as concerts, festivals, kids' events and nightlife.

A fourth extremely useful and user-friendly site on entertainment in the Swedish capital is www.**ticnet.se**. Information on all four websites is at least partly in English.

Booking Tickets

Tickets for events can usually be bought at the ticket office of the relevant venue. But to be sure of a seat, it is advisable to book in advance either with the help of your hotel or the Stockholm Visitors Board's Visitor Centre, located at Kulturhuset, Sergels Torg 5. You can also use one of the city's ticket agencies, for example **Ticnet**, which can make bookings by telephone for theatres, concerts, sporting events and excursions. A booking fee of 10–45 kr is charged depending on the price of the ticket.

Swedish Music

Sweden is one of the world's leading music exporters. No matter the musical genre, you will find Swedish artists who have achieved international success. Bands including ABBA and Roxette paved the way for artists such as Robyn and songwriters such as Mike Snow, who has delivered hits for the likes of Lady Gaga, Madonna and Britney Spears.

Outdoor Concerts and Festivals

Major outdoor events get under way in mid-May with the annual **Kungsträdgården** programme. This includes a wide variety of music with regular lunchtime and evening concerts. In the second week of June the **Slottsgalorna** event takes place at Ulriksdals Slott with international stars and the country's top musicians. **Skansen** stages a wide range of

Stampen, in Stora Nygatan, one of Stockholm's great jazz clubs *(see p179)*

A sea of people at the Royal Philharmonic Orchestra's annual outdoor concert in August

music, especially in July, with jazz on Monday evenings. The **Stockholm Jazz Festival** is held on Skeppsholmen in mid-July, and attracts the big names in jazz and blues.

For classical music lovers, the **Royal Philharmonic Orchestra**'s outdoor concert at Sjöhistoriska (National Maritime Museum) on the second Sunday in August is one of the summer's highlights. The concert is an annual tradition and attracts audiences of 25,000–30,000.

Other events worth attending include **A Taste of Stockholm** at Kungsträdgården (first weekend in June) and the **Czech Culture and Beer Festival** (mid-July).

Night-Time Transport

The Tunnelbana stops around 3:30am Sunday to Thursday nights, but on Friday and Saturday nights it runs until 4am.

It is replaced by night buses. Several night buses depart from Sergels Torg, and most bus stops have maps showing the night routes. Taxis are not usually difficult to find, even on a Saturday evening (see p201).

Stockholm for Children

Compared with many major cities, Stockholm is an extremely child-friendly place and ideal for family visits.

It is easy to take prams and pushchairs on to the new buses, and there is plenty of space for them inside (see also p191).

Most of the museums have children's corners with special activities. Museums and other important sights often have a cafeteria or restaurant with special menus or smaller portions for children. Toilets with a baby-changing table are frequently available.

Many of the favourite places for children are on Djurgården. **Junibacken** has an exciting journey through the fantastic world of the children's author Astrid Lindgren. The nearby **Vasamuseet** is also child-friendly. For decades the **Gröna Lund** funfair has been a mixture of traditional and exciting modern attractions, making it an ideal excursion for families with both teenagers and younger children.

Gröna Lund's roller coaster

The open-air museum **Skansen**, with all its animals and exciting activities, can keep a family happily occupied for a whole day.

Special children's weeks are organized on **Fjäderholmarna**, a group of islands that can be reached from the city centre in only 25 minutes.

Leksaksmuseet (the Toy Museum) on Söder is a safe bet for children. At **Medeltidsmuseum** children can experience what life was like in Stockholm in the Middle Ages. In the city centre **Kulturhuset** has a variety of children's activities with a cultural content.

Naturhistoriska Riksmuseet (Museum of Natural History) houses the Cosmonova planetarium and IMAX cinema, which is a big attraction for children.

Drama and Classical Music

Stockholm's year as Cultural Capital of Europe in 1998 was a well-deserved honour, as all the city's various areas of culture reflect a high degree of dedication and talent. This applies particularly to the world of music, which has seen many top-class international artists emerge from the capital's stages. As a result opera, ballet and classical music is well supported by Stockholmers, who have a wide home-grown repertoire to enjoy. This is also complemented by a number of guest artists from all over the world.

Ballet and Dance

Classical ballet of the highest quality is mainly staged at the over 100-year-old **Kungliga Operan** *(see pp66–7)*. Every season three of the best-known ballets, for example *The Nutcracker, Swan Lake* and *Romeo and Juliet*, are performed to packed houses. Thanks to the late choreographer Birgit Cullberg, Stockholm has also become a noted centre for modern dance. Many established dance companies make guest appearances at **Dansens Hus** *(see p71)*, which has taken over the previous home of Stadsteatern. **Moderna Dansteatern** in the old torpedo factory on Skeppsholmen is another important stage for modern dance.

Opera

Traditional productions in their original language are staged mainly at **Kungliga Operan**. Lunchtime operas or concerts are sometimes performed in the Gustav III opera café. During the summer, major operas are presented at **Drottningholms Slottsteater** *(see pp146–49)*. Dating from the 18th century, the theatre's stage settings and scene-shifting machinery are preserved in their original condition and are still in good working order. All the operas performed here are also from the 18th century, and over the years the theatre has revived several unknown works by Mozart, using instruments typical of that era. The theatre is open for guided tours.

Sweden's oldest Rococo theatre, **Confidencen**, is located near Ulriksdal *(see p127)*. Between June and September weekly opera and ballet performances are held here. Another genre of classical opera is staged at **Folkoperan**, which performs the classics in Swedish and without elaborate scenery.

SpaghettiOperan Regina is a rebuilt cinema where audiences can dine in comfort while enjoying the opera.

Theatres and Musicals

Stockholm has a flourishing theatrical life, but performances are usually in Swedish. **Kungliga Dramatiska Teatern**, often known simply as "Dramaten" *(see pp74–5)*, is Sweden's national theatre and has five stages. International and Swedish classics are regularly performed here, from Shakespeare to Strindberg, as well as modern foreign and Swedish productions. Ingmar Bergman was the theatre's director from 1963–6, and he has returned as an acclaimed guest director many times since then.

Södra Teatern *(see p130)* often presents modern productions despite having roots that go back to the 19th century. **Stockholms Stadsteater**, based in Kulturhuset *(see p69)*, has a widely varied programme. A summer speciality is the popular series of **Parkteatern** productions in several of the city's parks with drama, dance and children's theatre. **Judiska Teatern** has a repertoire of new Jewish drama, as well as dance, poetry and film shows. **Teater Galeasen** is Stockholm's avant-garde stage

for new Swedish and foreign drama. **Marionetteatern** has a puppet shows for both children and adults, along with a puppet museum on the same premises. **Pantomimteatern** is a theatre company which performs not only in Stockholm but tours rural areas, too.

Light-hearted plays are often staged at **China-Teatern**, and its programmes include some highly popular musicals and some much-loved plays for children. High-quality musicals are also performed at **Oscars-Teatern**, **Göta Lejon** and **Cirkus**.

Classical Music

World-standard classical music is regularly performed at **Berwaldhallen** *(see p108)*. The hall is dedicated to the great Swedish composer Franz Berwald (1796–1868) and is home to the Swedish Radio Symphony Orchestra, which has thrived under musical directors such as Sergiu Celibidache and Esa-Pekka Salonen. The Swedish Radio Chorus, which is regarded as one of the world's great *a cappella* ensembles, is based here, too. Concerts are also given in the hall by other symphony orchestras and smaller ensembles.

Konserthuset *(see p70)* is the home of the Royal Stockholm Philharmonic Orchestra, an internationally acclaimed 100-piece ensemble whose season runs from August to May. Its programme includes a couple of chamber music series and a jazz series, as well as performances for families on Saturdays. An annual composition festival is held every November.

Musikaliska *(see p85)* was formerly the home of the Musical Academy. Apart from July and August, its large hall is now used almost daily for concerts. In addition to classical music, you can hear performances of jazz, choral music and folk music.

Music at the Palace is an annual summer series at the Royal Palace *(see pp50–53)* with two concerts every week, usually classical music but sometimes other styles. The concerts are normally staged in the Hall of State or the Royal Chapel. The majestic staircase of **Nationalmuseum** *(see pp84–5)* is the setting for summer concerts, although it is closed for renovation till 2018. **Riddarhusmusik** at Riddarhuset *(see p60)* is a series by the Stockholm Sinfonietta.

Folk and Church Music

Rural folk music still flourishes in the capital, and this tradition is particularly fostered at **Skansen** *(see pp100–101)*, where fiddlers and folk dance teams play a major role in the various festivals held there *(see pp28–31)*. Folk music is also on the programme at **Musikaliska**.

Concerts are regularly given in the city's churches, for example visitors can relax and enjoy beautiful church music in the tranquil surroundings of **Jacobs Kyrka** in Kungsträd-gården *(see p66)* every Saturday at 3pm. Afternoon concerts usually take place in **Storkyrkan** *(see p55)* on Saturday and Sunday during spring and autumn.

Booking Tickets

Tickets for Stockholm's theatres and concert halls can be booked through **Ticnet**; directly at the relevant box office; or ordered by telephone *(see p175)*.

DIRECTORY

Ballet and Dance

Dansens Hus
Barnhusgatan 12–14.
Map 2 C3.
Tel 08-508 990 90.
W dansenshus.se
Tickets on sale: 2–6pm
Tue–Fri, three hours
before performances
Sat & Sun.

Moderna Dansteatern
Slupskjulsvägen 30,
Skeppsholmen.
Map 5 E2.
Tel 08-611 14 56.
W moderna
dansteatern.se
Tickets on sale: from
Dansteatern/home page.

Ballet, Dance and Opera

Kungliga Operan
Gustav Adolfs Torg.
Map 4 B1.
Tel 08-791 43 00;
08-791 44 00 (tickets).
W operan.se
Tickets on sale: noon–5pm
Mon–Sat (to 3pm Sat).

Opera

Confidencen
Ulriksdals Slottsteater.
Tel 08-85 70 16.
W confidencen.se

Drottningholms Slottsteater
Drottningholm Palace,
Lovön. **Tel** 08-556 931 00.
W dtm.se

Folkoperan
Hornsgatan 72. **Map** 8 B2.
Tel 08-616 07 00;
08-616 07 50 (tickets).

W folkoperan.se
Tickets on sale from
Kulturdireckt, Sergels
Torg and Stockholm
Tourist Centers.

SpaghettiOperan Regina
Drottninggatan 71 A.
Map 2 C3.
Tel 08-411 63 20.
W regina-stockholm.se
Tickets on sale: noon–
6pm Tue–Sat.

Theatre

China-Teatern
Berzelii Park 9.
Map 3 D4.
Tel 08-566 323 50.
W chinateatern.se
Tickets on sale:
11am–6pm Mon–Fri.

Cirkus
Djurgårdsslätten 43–45.
Map 6 A4.
Tel 08-660 10 20 (tickets).
W cirkus.se
W ticnet.se
Tickets on sale: 2–4pm
(phone). Box office only
open during events.
Closed 6 Jul–10 Aug.

Drottningholms Slottsteater
Drottningholm Palace,
Lovön.
Tel 08-556 931 00.
W dtm.se

Göta Lejon
Götgatan 55.
Map 9 D3.
Tel 08-505 290 00.
W gotalejon.se
Tickets on sale: 11am–
6pm Mon–Fri (to 4pm Sat).

Judiska Teatern
Djurgårdsbrunnsvägen 59.

Map 7 E2.
Tel 08-660 02 71.
W judiskateatern.se

Kungliga Dramatiska Teatern
Nybroplan. **Map** 3 E4.
Tel 08-667 06 80.
W dramaten.se
Tickets on sale: noon–7pm
Tue–Sun (to 4pm Sun).

Marionetteatern
Sergels Torg.
Map 2 C4.
Tel 08-506 202 00.
W kulturhusetstads
teatern.se/ Teater/
Marionetteatern

Oscars-Teatern
Kungsgatan 63.
Map 2 B4.
Tel 08-20 50 00.
W oscarsteatern.se

Pantomimteatern
S:t Eriksgatan 84.
Map 1 C1. **Tel** 08-31 54 64.
W pantomimteatern.
com

Parkteatern
Tel 08-506 201 00.

Stockholms Stadsteater
Sergels Torg.
Map 2 C4.
Tel 08-506 201 00.
W stadsteatern.
stockholm.se
Tickets on sale: noon–
7pm Tue–Fri, noon–6pm
Sat & Sun.

Södra Teatern
Mosebacke Torg 1–3.
Map 9 D2.
Tel 08-531 994 90.
W sodrateatern.com
Tickets on sale:
10am–5pm Mon–Fri.

Teater Galeasen
Slupskjulsvägen 32,
Skeppsholmen.
Map 5 E2.
Tel 08-611 00 30.
W galeasen.se

Classical Music

Berwaldhallen
Dag Hammarskjölds
Väg 3.
Map 6 A2.
Tel 08-784 18 00.
W berwaldhallen.se

Konserthuset
Hötorget 8.
Map 2 C4.
Tel 08-506 677 88.
W konserthuset.se

Music at the Palace
The Royal Palace,
Slottsbacken.
Map 4 C2.

Musikaliska
Nybrokajen 11.
Map 4 C1.
Tel 08-407 16 00.
W musikaliska.com

Nationalmuseum
Södra,
Blasieholmshamnen.
Map 5 D2.
Tel 08-519 543 00.
W nationalmuseum.se

Riddarhusmusik
Riddarhuset,
Riddarhustorget 10.
Map 4 A3.
Tel 08-723 39 90.
W riddarhuset.se

Central Ticket Agency

Ticnet
Tel 077 170 70 70.
W ticnet.se

Nightlife and Entertainment

In common with most capitals, Stockholm has a rich variety of nightlife and entertainment, with something for everyone. Pop music is one of the country's biggest exports, so there is no shortage of groups following in the footsteps of ABBA. Top-class musical entertainment is provided on a large scale in Globen or on a smaller, more intimate basis in the pubs, clubs and bars. The Swedish jazz scene thrives in several venues where live music is played nightly.

Rock and Pop

Stockholm's **Globen** is the city's biggest stage for rock and pop music. It attracts all the biggest international artists as well as leading Swedish groups. **Cirkus** and **Södra Teatern** *(see pp 130 & 176)* are other favourite venues for rock and pop, and they stage both musical and theatrical productions in beautiful settings. **Münchenbryggeriet**, a former brewery, also provides a great venue. Hard rock enthusiasts are well-catered for at **Pub Anchor** three or four times a week.

Debaser is Sweden's biggest club scene for pop and rock. Based in three locations across the city, the club has attracted the likes of Bob Dylan, The Strokes, Bright Eyes and Sweden's very own, The Ark.

Tele2 Arena is a state-of-the-art arena that opened in 2013 and has since hosted two of the top football clubs in Sweden. Artists such as The Rolling Stones, Aerosmith and Avicii have also performed here.

Jazz Music

A wide choice of jazz can be found in Stockholm. **Fasching Jazzklubb** has an international reputation for good music with performances virtually every day of the week. Another classic jazz spot is Gamla Stan's **Stampen**, which attracts a rather older clientele. **Nalen** holds frequent jazz events, and usually provides live music to dance to on Sundays. **Glenn Miller Café** has a cosy atmosphere, with jazz nightly from Monday to Saturday. During the summer the vintage steamboat **SS** *Blidösund (see p145)* operates special jazz cruises around the archipelago four times a week. The annual **Stockholm Jazz Festival** hosts up-and-coming artists as well as international stars. See www.stockholmjazz.com for more details.

Music Pubs

Life in Stockholm's pubs and bars has changed in recent years as a number of establishments have introduced live music. Irish bands often play at **The Dubliner** *(see p172)*, and live music is also performed at the **Engelen** and **Akkurat** pubs. Engelen has a variety of music, while the accent is on rock at Akkurat.

Apart from these musical watering holes, there are plenty of traditional British and Irish pubs in the capital, generally with a wide choice of beer and whisky and snack meals *(see pp172–3)*.

Bars

The best bars are usually found in hotels and restaurants, but those in the latter are often noisier. The most fashionable tend to have a long queue, supervised by a doorman. For a quieter atmosphere with comfortable armchairs, hotel bars are the best bet. The minimum age for buying alcohol is 18, and young customers must be prepared to show proof of age.

The **Cadier Bar** in the Grand Hôtel *(see pp81 & 160)* undoubtedly has the most elegant clientele, and this is where the rich and famous stay. From the verandah there is a fine view of the Royal Palace and the archipelago boats, and in the background gentle music is played on the white grand piano.

Operabaren is a sight in itself with well-preserved Jugendstil decor, marble tables and leather sofas. The regulars often include authors, artists and intellectuals. **Erik's Gondolen** at the top of Katarinahissen *(see p129)* offers arguably the most beautiful view of Stockholm and is a perfect place for a drink at sunset. It has comfortable leather armchairs, skilled bartenders and a relaxing atmosphere. **Sky Bar**, high up in the Royal Viking Hotel, has a panoramic view of the city, seen at its best after dark when the lights come on.

Absolut Icebar Stockholm, located in the Nordic Sea Hotel, is the world's first permanent ice bar. All of the interior fittings are made of pure ice. The bar can cater for up to 30 people at a time. **Sturehof Bar** is a sophisticated and modern nightspot, particularly popular with people from the advertising and media worlds and other local night owls.

Nightclubs and Casinos

Most of Stockholm's best nightclubs are located around Stureplan *(see pp72–3)*. The traditional disco evenings are Friday and Saturday, and on other days of the week they are often hired by various clubs providing particular styles of music. The nightlife scene is changing all the time as new clubs come and go. **Café Opera**, Stockholm's most historic international-class nightclub, is located to the rear of Kungliga Operan *(see pp66–7)*. It has a mixed clientele of both the young and trendy and a more soberly dressed older generation. **Sturecompagniet** is a large disco on several floors which also has a rock bar at street level. **Fasching Jazzklubb** has soul from the 1960s and 1970s on Saturdays. **Spy Bar** is the place to rub shoulders with Swedish celebrities and international artists on tour. However, it is often crowded and a membership card may be necessary. **Ambassadeur** is another "in" place with a fashion-conscious clientele. The younger generation enjoy dancing to a variety of music at **Debaser Medis**. In the city centre is **Casino Cosmopol**, Stockholm's first casino.

Cabarets

Good food and top-class entertainment are on the menu at **Hamburger Börs**, which features cabaret shows performed by leading Swedish artists. **Wallmans Salonger** offers musical entertainment provided by the waiters and waitresses along with the food.

Film

Films are not dubbed into Swedish, so non-Swedish speaking visitors can more often than not go to a cinema and enjoy a film that is in their own language. Films in languages other than English are usually screened at **Zita**, and **Sture** is also a good venue for cineasts. There are both classic cinemas such as **Rigoletto**, showing quality international drama, and multi-screen complexes including **Filmstaden Sergel**, which screens most of the current Hollywood repertoire.

DIRECTORY

Rock and Pop

Cirkus
Djurgårdsslätten 43.
Map 6 A4.
Tel 08-660 10 20.

Debaser
Medborgarplatsen 8.
Map 9 D3.

Karl Johans Torg 1.
Map 4 C4.

Hornstulls Strand 4.
Map 4 C3.
Tel 08-462 98 60.

Globen
Globentorget 2.
Tel 0771 31 00 00. 3km (2 miles) S of Stockholm.

Münchenbryggeriet
Torkel Knutssonsg 2.
Map 8 B1.
Tel 08-658 20 00;
for tickets: 0771 707070.

Pub Anchor
Sveavägen 90.
Map 2 C2.
Tel 08-15 20 00.
Open 3pm–3am daily.

Södra Teatern
Mosebacke Torg 1–3.
Map 9 D2.
Tel 08-531 994 90.

Tele2 Arena
Arenaslingan 14.
Tel 07-131 00 00. 3km (2 miles) S of Stockholm.

Jazz

Fasching Jazzklubb
Kungsgatan 63.
Map 2 B4.
Tel 08-20 00 06.
Open 6pm–midnight Mon–Thu & Sun, 6pm–4am Fri–Sat.

Glenn Miller Café
Brunnsgatan 21 A.
Map 3 D3.
Tel 08-10 03 22.
Open 5pm–1am Mon–Thu, 5pm–2am Fri & Sat, 6pm–1am Sun.
Music from 8pm.

Nalen
Regeringsgatan 74.
Map 3 D3.
Tel 08-505 292 01.

Stampen
Stora Nygatan 5.
Map 4 B3. **Tel** 08-20 57 93.
Open 5pm–1am Mon & Tue, 5pm–2am Wed–Fri, 2pm–2am Sat.

SS Blidösund
Skeppsbron 10.
Map 4 C2. **Tel** 08-24 30 90.
Open mid-May–Oct: boat departing at 6:30pm Mon–Thu.

Music Pubs

Akkurat
Hornsgatan 18. **Map** 8 C2.
Tel 08-644 00 15.
Open 11am–1am Tue–Fri, 11am–midnight Mon, 3pm–1am Sat, 6pm–1am Sun.

The Dubliner
Holländargatan 1.
Map 2 C3. **Tel** 08-679 77 07.
Open 4pm–1am Mon & Tue, 4pm–1am Wed & Thu, 2pm–3am Fri, noon–3am Sat, 1–10pm Sun.
Music from 10pm daily.

Engelen
Kornhamnstorg 59 B.
Map 4 B4.
Tel 08-20 10 92.
Open 5pm–midnight Mon & Tue, 5pm–3am Wed–Sat, 5pm–12:30am Sun.

Bars

Absolut Icebar Stockholm
Vasaplan 4. **Map** 2 B4.
Tel 08-505 635 20.

Cadier Bar
Grand Hôtel, Södra Blasieholmshamnen 8.
Map 4 C1.
Tel 08-679 35 00.

Erik's Gondolen
Stadsgården 6.
Map 4 C5.
Tel 08-641 70 90.

Operabaren
Kungsträdgården.
Map 4 B1.
Tel 08-676 58 00.

Sky Bar
Vasagatan 1.
Map 2 B4.
Tel 08-506 540 00.

Sturehof Bar
Stureplan 2.
Map 3 D4.
Tel 08-440 57 30.

Nightclubs and Casinos

Ambassaduer
Kungsgatan 18.
Map 3 D4.
Tel 08-545 076 00.
Open 10pm–4am Fri & Sat.

Café Opera
Operahuset, Kungsträdgården.
Map 4 C1.
Tel 08-676 58 07.
Open 10pm–3am Wed–Sun.

Casino Cosmopol
Kungsgatan 65.
Map 2 B4.
Tel 08-781 88 00.
Open 1pm–5am daily.

Debaser Medis
Medborgarplatsen 8.
Map 9 D3.
Tel 08-694 79 00.
Open 5pm–midnight Mon–Sat (from 4pm Fri).

Fasching Jazzklubb
Kungsgatan 63.
Map 2 B4.
Tel 08-20 00 06.
Open Soul club: midnight–4am Sat.

Spy Bar
Birger Jarlsgatan 20.
Map 3 D3.
Tel 08-545 076 00.
Open 10pm–5am Wed–Sat.

Sturecompagniet
Sturegatan 4. **Map** 3 D3.
Tel 08-545 076 10.
Open 11pm–5am Thu–Sat.

Cabarets

Hamburger Börs
Jakobsgatan 6.
Map 3 D5.
Tel 08-787 85 00.

Wallmans Salonger
Teatergatan 3.
Map 3 E5.
Tel 0771-13 43 00.

Film

Filmstaden Sergel
Hötorget. **Map** 2 C4.
Tel 08-562 600 00.

Rigoletto
Kungsgatan 16.
Map 2 B4.
Tel 08-562 600 00.

Sture
Birger Jarlsgatan 41.
Map 3 D3.
Tel 08-562 948 80.

Zita
Birger Jarlsgatan 37.
Map 3 D3.
Tel 08-23 20 20.

OUTDOOR ACTIVITIES

As a city built around water and with the countryside reaching into the centre, Stockholm is ideally positioned for all kinds of open-air pursuits. The great outdoors plays an important role in the Swedish lifestyle, and the capital offers a plethora of activities throughout the year – for the energetic and not so energetic – from walking, cycling and ice-skating to fishing, skiing and hot-air ballooning. In spring, summer and autumn around 80 golf courses are open to visitors, as well as well-planned jogging and cycle tracks. Outdoor swimming pools are popular on hot summer days, and in winter long-distance skating between the islands and cross-country and downhill skiing are the things to do.

In many cases, it is simple to make your own contacts, but the Stockholm Visitor Centre *(see p191)* will be able to advise you.

Hagaparken *(see pp124–5)*, an inviting area for exercise and recreation

Jogging, Walks and Cycling

It can be both practical and rewarding to take some exercise while exploring the capital. Everything in the city centre is within easy walking distance, including major sights, beautiful

Fishing at Blasieholmskajen in the centre of the city

parks and modern shopping malls. A walk in Stockholm always takes you close to the water or some unusual sight. The organized walks in the city are usually conducted in Swedish, but there are also tours of Gamla Stan with English-speaking guides. Contact Visit Stockholm for advice on a route.

Even if you want to head out of the city centre, there is no need to travel far. The No. 7 streetcar goes out to Djurgården, where you can have a walk or jog along the shores, through the avenues under the oak trees, or over green fields. Walking paths along the city's waterfronts *(see pp42–3)* provide both good routes and stunning views. There are many floodlit jogging tracks, and plenty of fun-run events to choose from *(see pp28–31)*.

Those who prefer to move at a gentler pace can head for

Skansen open-air museum *(see pp100–101)* or the **Gröna Lund** amusement park *(see p97)*, both suitable for the whole family, providing a day out in the open air.

Djurgården has plenty of cycle paths, and bicycles can be hired from **Cykel Moped-uthyrningen** or **Stockholm City Bikes** *(see p205)*, which has locations all over Stockholm. Roller-blades can also be hired near the bridge.

Cyclists planning to take a longer tour should visit Visit Stockholm and ask to be put in touch with the Cykelfrämjandet cycling organization.

Horse Riding

Several riding schools near the city centre, such as **Stockholms Ridhus**, offer lessons. For those who prefer to discover Stockholm's surrounding areas, tours on Icelandic ponies are operated from quite a few stables.

Rundemars Gård hires out horses to experienced riders to explore the Tyresö nature reserve, southeast of the city, after an initial briefing.

Water Sports

There are excellent opportunities for water sports. Canoes, rowing boats, pedalos and larger boats for longer tours, can be hired from **Tvillingarnas Båtuthyrning** near Djurgårdsbron. A good area for canoeing is the canal near Djurgården *(see pp86–101)*, where **Djurgårds-brons Sjöcafé** hires out canoes.

Swimming

During the summer there are plenty of outdoor swimming pools to choose from. They include **Eriksdalsbadet** in Södermalm, **Kampementsbadet** at Gärdet and **Smedsuddsbadet** at Rålambshov Park Beach. There are several good places for a swim along the Kungsholmen shores of Riddarfjärden. And on Långholmen there are both sandy beaches or rocks to swim from (see p134).

For a completely different bathing experience, try the Japanese **Yasuragi** at Hasseludden. For indoor pools, try Centralbadet (see p71) or Sturebadet (see p73).

Golf

Golfers will find about 80 golf courses within easy reach of the city centre. The closest, such as **Djursholms Golfklubb**, are in delightful settings.

The courses are popular, and advance bookings are recommended. Golf information is available on Stockholm tourist board's website (www.visitstockholm.com).

Other Activities

Brightly coloured hot-air balloons hovering over the city are a common sight in the evening. Several companies operate charter trips in balloons. You can book via Visit Stockholm or directly with a company such as **Far & Flyg**.

Game fishing for salmon and trout is possible right in the city

Outdoor swimming in Stockholm

centre near the Royal Palace. Suitable tackle can be hired at **Naturkompaniet**. **Sportfiskarna Stockholm** can provide information on fishing in and around Stockholm.

Outdoor tennis courts are available at several places, including **Kungliga Lawn Tennishallen**, where the Stockholm Open ATP indoor tournament is held every November.

You can also go scuba-diving around Stockholm. Contact Visit Stockholm for details of diving schools and equipment hire.

Ice-skaters are in their element once the open waters of the archipelago have frozen over. Meanwhile, the artificial rink at Kungsträdgården is open throughout the winter, and hires out skates.

The outdoor activities organization **Friluftsfrämjandet** provides information on skating and skiing in the area.

Visitors with disablities can find out more about the availability of outdoor pursuits by contacting **De Handikappades Riksförbund** (see p191).

One of Stockholm's many golf courses

SHOPPING IN STOCKHOLM

Stockholm is worth visiting for the shopping alone. All the best shops in the central area are within easy walking distance and they stock virtually everything anyone could want. There are plenty of small boutiques for fashion and interiors, as well as antiques shops, luxury international designer outlets and well-stocked department stores.

Shopping is good all over the city. Exclusive shops can be found in fashionable Östermalm.

Gamla Stan is a good place for handicrafts and unusual knick-knacks. Södermalm and Vasastan have antiques and second-hand shops. Cameras, mobile telephones, furs, children's clothing, toys and Swedish glass are cheaper in Sweden than in most other countries. No expedition is complete without a visit to one of the city's splendid market halls, which sell Swedish delicacies including reindeer and moose meat, caviar and cloudberries.

Opening Times

Most shops usually open at 10am and close at 6pm, although many in the city centre remain open until 7pm. Most shops are open until 2pm on Saturdays, and the major department stores stay open until 5pm. Large stores, shopping malls and a number of shops in central Stockholm are open on Sundays. Market halls are closed on Sundays and public holidays. Larger super-markets are open daily until 8pm.

Payment

All the main credit cards and travellers' cheques are accepted in most shops. If you pay by card, you may be asked for proof of identity; many shops require a PIN number. Goods can be exchanged, if you produce the receipt. Purchases can usually be made on a sale-or-return basis, providing that this is noted on the receipt.

Value Added Tax

Value added tax ("moms" in Swedish) is charged on all items except daily newspapers. The VAT rate is 25%, except on food, for which the rate is only 12%. VAT is always included in the total price.

Tax-Free Shopping

Residents of countries out side the European Union are entitled to a refund of the VAT they have paid on their purchases. Tax-free shopping with Global Refund gives visitors a cash refund of 15–18 per cent on their departure from the EU. Look for the "Tax-free shopping" sign. Global Refund is at all departure points, including Arlanda Airport.

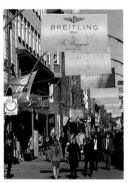

Biblioteksgatan, an attractive shopping street in Stockholm

Sales

Twice a year Stockholm's shops and department stores have sales with reduced prices on clothing, shoes and other fashion goods. Sales are indicated by the *rea* sign. The year's first sales start after Christmas and continue throughout January. The second sales period lasts from late June to the end of July.

Shopping Centres and Department Stores

Stockholm's best-known superstore is **IKEA**, which has become a popular tourist attraction in its own right. It sells not just furniture but also everything else for the home, and all at attractive prices. The textiles section is particularly good, as well as the kitchenware and porcelain departments. IKEA's store is located outside the city but is easy to reach by a free shuttle bus from

NK, Stockholm's most exclusive department store

Nordiska Kristall, a major outlet for Swedish glass in Stockholm

Regeringsgatan 13 to Kungens Kurva, hourly on weekdays from 10am to 5pm.

Another well-known store is the fashion house **H&M** (Hennes & Mauritz), which has branches in many European cities and several outlets in Stockholm. H&M stocks the latest fashions at low prices. It has its own designers and makes clothing for women, men, teenagers and children. The shops also sell accessories, jewellery, underwear, perfume and cosmetics.

Nordiska Kompaniet (NK) on Hamngatan is Stockholm's leading department store, where many well-known names in fashion and cosmetics have their own shops. NK also stocks Swedish-designed products, jewellery, handicrafts and souvenirs as well as cameras, films, books and CDs.

PUB on Hötorget is another established department store with a wide selection of goods. The **Cervera** boutique chain has a good choice of table coverings and decorations, both classic and modern.

Most shopping items can be purchased inexpensively at

Chandeliers and other treasures at one of Arsenalsgatan's fine antiques shops

Åhlens department store in City, Vasastaden, Kungsholmen and Östermalm, as well as some suburbs.

There are several indoor shopping malls. **Gallerian** on Hamngatan is the largest, and the prices are lower than in the elegant **Sturegallerian** near Stureplan with its many trendy boutiques. There are also shopping centres in most suburbs where nearly all the retail chains are represented.

Markets

A traditional Christmas market is held at Skansen *(see pp100–101)* every Sunday in December. Stortorget in Gamla Stan *(see p56)* also has a delightful market at Christmas.

Vegetables, fruit and flowers are sold from Monday to Friday at Hötorget *(see p70)*, Östermalmstorg *(see p73)* and Medborgarplatsen *(see p133)*. Street stalls along Drottninggatan and around Sergels Torg sell watches, clocks, toys and other knick-knacks.

Stockholm's flea market, **Skärholmens Loppmarknad**, offers a wide variety of clothes, practical objects and bric-a-brac for sale.

Wines and Spirits

The only shops selling alcohol in Sweden are run by Systembolaget, the State monopoly chain. They are open Monday to Friday 10am–6pm (some open on Saturdays 10am–3pm, but not on a public holiday weekend). The minimum age for buying alcohol at Systembolaget shops is 20 *(see also p191)*.

DIRECTORY

Shopping Centres and Department Stores

Cervera
Svavägen 24 .
Map 2 C4.
Tel 08-10 45 30.
W cervera.se

Fältöversten
Karlaplan 13.
Map 3 F3.
Tel 08-696 33 69.
W faltoverstencentrum.se

Gallerian
Hamngatan 37.
Map 3 D4.
Tel 073-531 94 96.
W gallerian.se

H&M
Hamngatan 22.
Map 3 D4.
Tel 08-524 635 30.

Sergels Torg 12.
Map 2 C4.
Tel 08-796 54 46.
W hm.com

IKEA
Kungens Kurva, Skärholmen.
Tel 08-744 83 60.

Järfälla, Folkungavägen 50.
Tel 08-795 40 00.
W ikea.se

NK
Hamngatan 18–20.
Map 3 D4.
Tel 08-762 80 00.
W nk.se

PUB
Hötorget. **Map** 3 C4.
Tel 08-789 19 30.
W pub.se

Sturegallerian
Grev Turegatan 9. **Map** 3 D4.
Tel 08-453 50 00.
W sturegallerian.se

Åhléns
Klarabergsgatan 50. **Map** 2 C4.
Tel 08-676 60 00.

Fridhemsplan. **Map** 1 B2.
Tel 08-617 97 00.

Odenplan. **Map** 2 B2.
Tel 08-728 53 00.
W ahlens.com

Markets

Skärholmens Loppmarknad
P-huset. Skärholmen.
Tel 08-710 00 60.
Open 11am–6pm Mon–Fri,
10am–4pm Sat, 11am–4pm Sun.

What to Buy in Stockholm

The Dala wooden horse must be the most typical Swedish souvenir. But it is facing strong competition from the moose, which has become a symbol for a country with vast tracts of unspoilt countryside. The Swedes love the great outdoors, so there are plenty of shops selling top-class sporting equipment. Swedish glass and crystal are renowned around the world. Orrefors and Kosta Boda are just two of several glassworks producing both classic and modern glassware. Educational toys in natural materials are a Swedish speciality, as are clogs, which can be found in many shoe shops.

Hand-painted clogs

Handicrafts and Design

Modern Swedish design is a familiar concept in many households worldwide, even for simple everyday items *(see pp40–41)*. Handicrafts have a long tradition in Sweden, and contemporary designers often use wrought-iron work, weaving, pottery and woodcarving.

Swedish Glass
Hand-blown sets of glassware are made in Sweden's glassworks, as well as artistic crystal creations and beautiful objects for everyday use.

Dala Horse and Cockerel
Originally the brightly painted Dala horses and cockerels were toys carved from left-over fragments of wood. Later the horse became a national symbol and is sold in many variants.

Nobel glass carafe from Orrefors by Gunnar Cyrén

Traditional snaps glasses

Tray with design by Josef Frank, Svenskt Tenn

Cheese slicer and knife by Michael Björnstierna

Designer Objects
The larger department stores often commission well-known designers for porcelain, glass, textiles and household items, which make highly desirable gifts.

Mama, a humorous clothes hanger

Crux rug by Pia Wallén

Children's Toys
Colourful wooden children's toys from Brio are worldwide favourites. Educational picture books, games and puzzles are all excellent gifts for children.

Outdoor Gear

Many Swedes enjoy outdoor pursuits such as fishing, hunting, sailing, golf, camping and all types of winter sports, so there are many well-equipped sports shops around. Unique items include Lapp handicrafts beautifully made from reindeer horn or skin.

Hand Knits

Caps and gloves with attractive designs, known as *lovikka*, are made from a special wool that gives good protection in cold or wet conditions.

Reindeer Skin Rucksack

Rucksacks are popular for both adults and children. This exclusive model is made in Lapland.

Drinking vessel in carved wood

Lapp Handicrafts

A hunting knife with a sheath of reindeer horn, or a *kåsa*, a drinking vessel carved in birch, are not only attractive but useful when out walking in the wild.

Spinning Reel and Lures

ABU-Garcia makes top-quality fishing tackle perfect for Sweden's long coastline, countless lakes and rivers with their rich and varied fishing.

Swedish Delicacies

Popular preserves are made from wild berries such as bitter lingonberries (for meatballs) or sweet cloudberries (served with whipped cream). Herring, crispbread and ginger biscuits can be bought in all groceries, and sweets are sold loose. Snaps miniatures come in gift packs.

Lingonberry preserve   Cloudberry jam

Pickled Herring

Pickled herring should be enjoyed with new potatoes cooked with dill, chopped chives and crème fraîche. Versions flavoured with mustard, dill or other herbs or spices are also available.

Swedish snaps gift-pack miniatures

"Raspberry boat" candy

Salt liquorice

Crispbread

Box of ginger biscuits

Where to Shop in Stockholm

Clothing from all the well-known international fashion houses can be found in Stockholm, and many have their own shops. If you want something rather different, it is worth seeking out the creations of younger Swedish fashion designers. Swedish interior design is famous for its clean lines, functionalism and the use of pale wood, and Stockholm is a paradise for anyone interested in design. Handicrafts are of a high quality. Leisurewear and sports goods offer excellent value for money.

Fashion

Stockholm's top places for fashion are in the "golden triangle" bounded by Stureplan, Nybroplan and Norrmalmstorg. Clothing at more moderate prices can be bought around Sergels Torg.

If you are looking for Swedish designers, **NK** has a selection of clothing created by younger designers as well as mainstream local products. Classic men's clothing of high quality is designed by Oscar Jacobsson, while Stenström shirts are sold in department stores and the more elegant menswear boutiques. **Björn Borg** has his own shops selling men's and women's clothing, underwear, perfume and accessories. **J Lindeberg** produces unusual fashions for the daring man, while fashion-conscious young people shop at **Sneakersnstuff**. The designer **Filippa K** produces smart clothing for trendy women. **Anna Holtblad** has a good selection of stylish women's garments, while **Thalia** in Östermalm has a good range of exclusive party outfits.

Design and Interior Decoration

The city centre, Östermalm and Hornsgatan in Södermalm have a number of interior decoration shops selling the products of young designers and artists. To see the latest on offer, visit **DesignTorget**, where young designers display their work. **R.O.O.M** on Kungsholmen, **Asplund** in Östermalm and **Norrgavel** in City are just a few of the most up-to-date shops, and they all have a good selection of products. **Svenskt Tenn** is the city's oldest shop for interior decoration, with both modern and classic designs. **Nordiska Galleriet** has exclusive modern furniture and decoration items, while **Georg Jensen** specializes in silver. **Kaolin, Nutida Svenskt Silver, Blås&Knåda** and **Galleri Metallum** stage exhibitions and sell Swedish-designed products. Hand-picked furnishings from floor to ceiling can be found at **Garbo Interior**. Orrefors **Kosta Boda** and **Nordiska Kristall** both have a wide choice of Swedish glassware, which can also be found at the various department stores.

Antiques

A large number of antiques shops can be found along Odengatan, Upplandsgatan and Roslagsgatan in Vasastan. Gamla Stan also has many shops offering collectables. Shops selling art, silver and porcelain of a more exclusive variety are on Arsenalsgatan on Blasieholmen, and also around Östermalmstorg. Södermalm has small shops selling bric-a-brac.

Music and Multimedia

Many Swedish pop bands now have an international reputation. Exciting new talents continue to find their way into the charts, and the latest products can often be bought in the record shops before they become available outside Sweden. Apart from pop and rock, Sweden has a long folk-music tradition, as well as many skilled jazz musicians and opera singers. **Pet Sounds** has a wide selection of CDs, as do the large department stores.

Sport and Leisure

The Swedes devote a lot of time to outdoor sports and activities. **Naturkompaniet** and **Peak Performance** have an exclusive selection of sportswear and equipment. **Stadium** and **Alewalds** have a varied choice of sports clothing and equipment at attractive prices. Equipment and exclusive clothing for hunting or fishing can be bought at **Walter Borg**.

Souvenirs and Handicrafts

Glasses for snaps, silver jewellery, hand-painted clogs, Lapp (*Same*) crafts, hand-knitted woollen gloves and caps, hand-made candles, traditional Christmas decorations and wrought-iron products can all be bought in the main department stores. Alternatively you can go to the Gamla Stan shops such as **Handkraft Swea**. **Svensk Hemslöjd** and the various museum gift shops are also good places to shop. Visitors to Skansen (*see pp100–101*) can buy handicrafts made in its shops. **Nordic Souvenirs** sells Swedish handicrafts and quality souvenirs.

Books

Photography books, cookery books, books on Swedish design and children's books make good souvenirs to take home. Apart from the **NK Bookshop** and at other department stores, **Hedengrens Bokhandel** has a large foreign-languages department. **The English Bookshop** has a good selection of books on Stockholm and Sweden in English, as well as a range of international newspapers.

Toys and Baby Equipment

It is worth buying high-quality baby prams and pushchairs produced by Emmaljunga and baby equipment by Babybjörn. **Babyland** and **Bonti** have a wide selection of these and other well-made products for children. Brio's wooden toys and other attractive toys are also favourite presents. **Bulleribock** and **BR Leksaker** offer a wide choice. Practical children's clothing can be found at **Polarn och Pyret** or at the larger department stores.

Swedish Delicacies

The capital has three superb market halls: **Östermalmshallen, Hötorgshallen** and **Söderhallarna**. Delicacies on sale include salmon, bleak roe, smoked eel and smoked reindeer meat, which all make

delicious culinary souvenirs. The food sections of the major department stores sell tinned herrings, lingonberry or cloudberry jam, crispbread, gingerbread and sweets, which also make good presents for the gastronomes back home.

DIRECTORY

Fashion

Anna Holtblad
Grev Turegatan 13.
Map 3 E4.
Tel 08-545 022 20.

Björn Borg
Sergelg 12.
Map 2 C4.
Tel 08-21 70 40.

Filippa K
Grev Turegatan 18.
Map 3 E4.
Tel 08-545 882 56.

J Lindeberg
Biblioteksgatan 6.
Map 3 D4.
Tel 08-400 500 41.

NK
Hamngatan 18–20.
Map 3 D4.
Tel 08-762 80 00.

Sneakersnstuff
Åsögatan 124.
Tel 08-743 03 22.

Thalia
Karlavägen 62. **Map** 3 E3.
Tel 08-660 54 30.

Design and Decoration

Asplund
Sibylleg 31. **Map** 3 E3.
Tel 08-662 52 84.

Blås&Knåda
Hornsgatan 26.
Map 4 B5.
Tel 08-642 77 67.

DesignTorget
Kulturhuset,
Sergels Torg 3.
Map 2 C4.
Tel 08-21 91 50.
Götgatan 31.
Map 9 D2.
Tel 08-644 16 78.

Galleri Metallum
Hornsgatan 30.
Map 4 B5.
Tel 08-640 13 23.

Garbo Interior
Brahegatan 21. **Map** 3 E2.
Tel 08-661 60 08.

Georg Jensen
Birger Jarlsgatan 13.
Map 3 D4.
Tel 08-545 040 80.

Kaolin
Hornsgatan 50.
Map 8 C2.
Tel 08-644 46 00.

Konsthantverkarna
Södermalmstorg 4.
Map 9 D2, 4 B5.
Tel 08-611 03 70.

Nordiska Galleriet
Nybrogatan 11.
Map 3 E4.
Tel 08-442 83 60.

Nordiska Kristall
Kungsgatan 9.
Map 3 D4.
Tel 08-10 43 72.

Norrgavel
Birger Jarlsgatan 27.
Map 3 D3.
Tel 08-545 220 50.

Nutida Svenskt Silver
Arsenalsgatan 3.
Map 3 D4.
Tel 08-611 67 18.

Orrefors Kosta Boda
Birger Jarlsgatan 15.
Map 2 C2.
Tel 08-611 91 15.

R.O.O.M
PUB, Plan 03, Högtorget.
Map 3 C4.
Tel 08-692 50 00.

Svenskt Tenn
Strandvägen 5.
Map 3 E4.
Tel 08-670 16 00.

Music and Multimedia

Pet Sounds
Skånegatan 53. **Map** 9 E3.
Tel 08-702 97 98.

Sport and Leisure

Alewalds
Kungsgatan 32.
Map 6 D3.
Tel 08-21 90 00.

Naturkompaniet
Sveavägen 62.
Map 2 C3.
Tel 08-24 30 02.
Kungsgatan 26.
Map 3 D4.
Tel 08-24 19 96.

Peak Performance
Biblioteksgatan 18.
Map 3 D4.
Tel 08-611 34 00.

Stadium
Sergelgatan 8. **Map** 2 C4.
Tel 08-14 09 90.

Walter Borg
Kungsgatan 57.
Map 2 C4.
Tel 08-14 38 65.

Souvenirs and Handicrafts

Handkraft Swea
Västerlånggatan 24.
Map 9 D1, 4 B3.
Tel 08-20 06 36.

Nordic Souvenirs
Hamngatan 27.
Map 3 D4.
Tel 08-24 24 70.

Svensk Hemslöjd
Norrlandsgatan 20.
Map 3 D4.
Tel 08-23 21 15.

Books

The English Bookshop
Lilla Nygatan 11.
Map 4 B3.
Tel 08-790 55 10.

Hedengrens Bokhandel
Stureplan 4. **Map** 3 D4.
Tel 08-611 51 28.

NK Bookshop
Hamngatan 18–20.
Map 3 D4.
Tel 08-762 80 00.

Toys and Baby Equipment

Babyland
Karlbergsvägen 40.
Map 2 A2.
Tel 08-555 912 10.

Bonti
Norrtullsgatan 33.
Map 2 B2.
Tel 08-30 69 16.

BR Leksaker
Gallerian, Hamngatan 37.
Map 3 D4.
Tel 08-545 154 40.

Bulleribock
Sveavägen 104.
Map 2 C2.
Tel 08-673 61 21.

Polarn och Pyret
Gallerian,
Hamngatan 35.
Map 3 D4.
Tel 08-411 22 47.

Swedish Delicacies

Östermalmshallen
Östermalmstorg.
Map 3 E4.

Hötorgshallen
Hötorget. **Map** 2 C4.

Söderhallarna
Medborgarplatsen.
Map 9 D3.

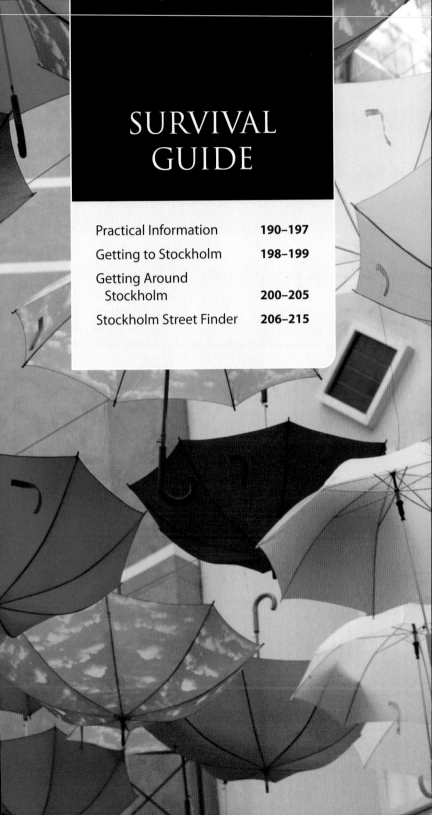

SURVIVAL
GUIDE

PRACTICAL INFORMATION

Over the years, Stockholm has become one of the most popular tourist destinations in Scandinavia. Its bustling cruise-ship terminals and its full event calendar bring thousands of tourists to the city each year, while many more come to experience the city's cultural and historical sites. It is easy to be a foreign visitor in the city, not least because most Swedes are happy to help tourists. The city's official tourism organization, the Stockholm Visitors Board, provides an excellent range of services. Stockholm is a small capital and is generally safe, but it still has its share of pickpockets. It is therefore wise to take care in the busy shopping areas and when travelling around the city at night.

Visas and Passports

Citizens of virtually all countries can enter Sweden without a visa. Since 2001, passports are not needed by visitors from European countries that have signed the Schengen agreement, as long as they are entering directly from a Schengen member country. However, to enter or depart from a Schengen country, visitors must carry a government-issued national ID card. Visitors arriving from outside the Schengen region must carry a valid passport.

Visitors are advised to check their visa and passport requirements with their local Swedish consulate or embassy prior to travelling.

Inside the Stockholm Visitor Centre at Sergels Torg 5

Tourist Information

Stockholm's official tourist information organization is the **Stockholm Visitors Board (SVB)**. The organization's website can answer most commonly asked questions and allows visitors to check the calendar of special events and purchase tickets. It also provides web addresses for the most important sights. Visitors to Stockholm and Sweden can also find a lot of useful information in different languages at the **Arrival Guides** website.

Hotel staff are usually well informed and can answer most questions related to sightseeing in the city. Visit What's On Stockholm's website or their Facebook page for information about events, culture and recreation. The site also contains links to other useful travel information.

Another good source of information is the **Museums in Stockholm** website, which provides an excellent overview of the city's museums and links to their respective websites.

Opening Hours and Admission Charges

Most museums and other sights are open between 10 or 11am and 5 or 6pm all year round, with extended opening hours in the summer. Some museums are closed on Mondays.

Entrance fees are generally between 50 and 100 kr, with discounts available for students, children and senior citizens.

Shops are generally open from 10am to 6pm during the week and from 10 or 11am to 4 or 5pm at weekends.

Tickets for theatres, concerts and sporting events can be bought at the venue box offices, at the SVB or through ticket agencies such as Ticnet (*see p174*).

Language and Etiquette

Visitors will find that English is widely spoken. This is especially true among hotel and restaurant staff, as well as most shop employees. The Swedes are usually friendly and glad to help foreign tourists. The use of first names is the norm, and "Hej!" (pronounced "Hay!") is a familiar greeting.

Casual clothing is acceptable almost everywhere, including restaurants and most theatres. Tips are always included in restaurant prices, but it is usual to round up the bill by up to 10 per cent for good service.

◀ Umbrellas, Sturegallerian shopping mall

Alcohol and Smoking

Swedish policy towards alcohol is restrictive. Wines, beers (above 3.5 per cent) and spirits can be bought only in the shops run by the state monopoly *Systembolaget*. They are open Monday to Friday from 10am to 6pm, and most are open on Saturdays from 10am to 3pm. The minimum age for buying liquor in these shops is 20, and you maybe required to show proof of age.

Most restaurants and pubs stop selling alcohol at 1am, but some city-centre bars stay open until 5am. The minimum age for buying liquor in restaurants is 18, with some establishments setting higher age minimums.

The maximum permitted blood alcohol level is only 0.2 mg per mil, so drinking is effectively banned for drivers.

Bans on smoking are widespread in Sweden. Smoking is not permitted in all public places, including all forms of public transport, bars and restaurants. Customers wishing to purchase tobacco must be over 18, and establishments will often ask for ID as proof of age.

Travellers with Special Needs

Under Swedish law, public areas have to be accessible to physically or visually disabled people, and Stockholm is well ahead of many other cities in this respect. The Tunnelbana network is adapted for disabled passengers, and most buses "kneel" at bus stops to make it easier to board or disembark. Those travelling with pets on public transport even have allocated areas to separate them from allergy sufferers. Car drivers with a disability permit from their home country can park in designated areas. Disabled visitors can obtain information in English before they travel from **De Handikappades Riksförbund**.

Travelling with Children

Families with children will find it easy to travel around Stockholm. The under 20s travel at a reduced rate on all forms of public transport, while children under 7 do not need a ticket when travelling with a paying passenger. Children between the ages of 7–11 travel free with a paying passenger from Fridays at noon through to midnight on Sunday. In addition, at all times, one adult may accompany a baby or toddler in a pram on city buses free of charge.

Children are warmly welcome in Stockholm's many cafés and restaurants, and most museums and cinemas offer reduced tickets for children (*see p175*).

Responsible Tourism

Stockholm is known for its efforts to reduce pollution and improve the level of environmental awareness among its inhabitants. The city has established over 700 km (435 miles) of cycle lanes, while all inner city buses and trains run on renewable fuels. Greenhouse emissions have been lowered by 25 per cent since 1990, and Stockholm was presented with the European Commission's first European Green Capital Award in 2009.

Hötorget market sells fruit, vegetables and flowers

DIRECTORY

Tourist Information

Arlanda Visitor Centre
Arrival Hall Terminal 5,
Arlanda Airport, 190 45
Stockholm-Arlanda.
Tel 010-109 10 00.

Arrival Guides
🌐 arrivalguides.com

Museums in Stockholm
🌐 stockholmmuseum.com

Stockholm Visitor Centre
Kulturhuset, Sergels Torg 5.
Map 2 C4.
Tel 08-508 285 08.
🌐 visitstockholm.com

Travellers with Special Needs

De Handikappades Riksförbund
Tel 08-685 80 00.
🌐 dhr.se

Embassies and Consulates

United Kingdom
Skarpögatan 6–8. **Map** 6 B2.
Tel 08-671 30 00.
🌐 gov.uk/government/world/sweden

United States
Dag Hammarskjölds väg 31.
Map 6 B2.
Tel 08-783 53 00.
🌐 sweden.usembassy.gov

Recycling containers for cans and plastics are found in public areas throughout the city and travel by public transport is highly encouraged.

More than 30 Stockholm hotels are deemed eco-friendly, and numerous restaurants offer purely organic menus. The Stockholm Visitors Board lists many such establishments. For those wishing to sample local produce, a farmers' market can be found at Hötorget seven days a week, while other markets are open at Katarina Bangata on Södermalm and at Tessinparken in Gärdet from 10am to 3pm on Saturdays during the summer, as well as during the Christmas holidays.

Personal Security and Health

Stockholm is outstandingly safe compared with virtually any other major city. To a great extent the city has been spared violence and terrorism, and natural disasters including earthquakes and severe storms do not occur. However, as with any major city, caution is recommended in the centre of town, particularly at night. Sweden has a well-developed network of emergency services as well as highly efficient hospital emergency clinics and rescue services.

Policeman   Security guard

Police

In Stockholm, the police are usually extremely helpful and competent in English and visitors can feel free to address them with any questions or concerns.

Police patrolling on foot or in cars are a routine sight in the city centre, and mounted police are common at special events. There are police stations in every part of the city, and police are also available at the Central Station/T-Centralen. To report an incident that does not require immediate police help call the **non-emergency** number (114 14).

In addition to the police, security guards are a familiar feature in many public places, such as shopping centres.

Safety

Although Stockholm is basically safe, as with any major city, tourists can still run into trouble. The many popular events attract bag-snatchers and pickpockets, especially during the summer months. Always keep an eye on your bag and valuables in crowded public areas.

When going out, it is a good idea to lock passports and travel documents in your room safe or in the hotel strongbox. It is equally important not to leave any valuables in your car; ideally, choose a hotel with its own parking facilities. There is no need to carry large amounts of cash when exploring the city. ATM machines are widely available, and all of the main credit and debit cards are accepted in virtually all shops and restaurants. Note that many places now require you to enter your PIN number when using a debit or credit card.

Stockholm is easy to explore on foot or by Tunnelbana (underground railway). The Tunnelbana is safe at most times, but avoid empty carriages. Care should also be taken when walking around the city at night. In addition, visitors should avoid using unauthorized taxis, particularly when arriving at Arlanda Airport.

It is illegal to buy sexual services in Sweden, so it is the buyer, not the prostitute, who is prosecuted. As a result of this law, street prostitutes are a rare sight in the inner city.

In an Emergency

The emergency telephone number for police, fire or ambulance is **112**. It can be dialled free of charge from all public and mobile telephones, but should be used only in emergencies. For minor illnesses or concerns, ring the **Healthcare Information Service** *(Sjukvårdsupplysningen)*.

Lost and Stolen Property

Lost or stolen property should be reported to the nearest police station. The **Police Lost Property Office** *(Polisens Hittegodsexpedition)* is open Monday to Friday from 10am to 3pm (until 6pm on Thursdays). Telephone enquiries are accepted Monday and Tuesday from 1pm to 3pm and Friday from 10am to noon. The **Swedish State Railways** *(Statens Järnvägar)* has its own lost property office for items lost on SJ trains. For property lost on *Storstockholms Lokaltrafik* (SL) buses, Tunnelbana trains or local trains, check with the **SL Lost Property Office** *(Hittegodsavdelning)*, which is open from 11am to 7pm Monday, 11am to 6pm Tuesday to Friday and 10am to 4pm Saturday.

Ambulance

Police car

Fire engine

Entrance to Karolinska Sjukhus, a hospital in Stockholm

Hospitals and Pharmacies

Several city hospitals have accident and emergency clinics, including **Karolinska Sjukhus**, **Astrid Lindgrens Barnsjukhus** (children), **Danderyds Sjukhus**, **S:t Görans Sjukhus** (privately owned) and **Södersjukhus**.

Patients should not report to individual emergency clinics without contacting the **Healthcare Information Service** beforehand. This service can provide advice in English, and its staff are responsible for assigning patients to a suitable hospital or duty doctor. It is always advisable to make use of this service; those who do not and go directly to a hospital emergency clinic with minor ailments are likely to experience long waiting times.

For severe toothache or eye emergencies, patients can report to **S:t Eriks Sjukhus** between 7:45am and 8:30pm.

Pharmacies can dispense medicines for most minor ailments without a prescription, and staff can usually give good advice on suitable medication. Pharmacies across the city are normally open Monday to Friday from 8:30am to 4 or 6pm. Some are also open on Saturday. The **C W Scheele** pharmacy near Central Station is open 24 hours. There is also a **Pharmaceutical Information** line that gives advice on prescription and non-prescription medication.

Visitors to Sweden do not need special vaccinations.

Pharmacy sign

Minor Hazards

Mosquitoes can be a nuisance between June and late September, especially at dusk. This is particularly the case in parks, along waterways and, above all, in the archipelago. Pharmacies can supply mosquito repellent.

In the wooded areas around Stockholm and in the archipelago, ticks are a serious problem. As ticks in this region often carry borrelia or TBE, they should be removed from the skin with tweezers as quickly as possible. If redness develops around the bite, a doctor should be consulted.

The cobbled streets of Gamla Stan, the city's old quarter, can prove treacherous for tourists. Sturdy shoes are recommended when visiting this area, particularly in the winter.

Travel and Health Insurance

Foreign visitors are advised to take out medical insurance before departure to cover medical care or hospital in-patient treatment. EU citizens are entitled to free medical care in Sweden on production of a European Health Insurance Card (EHIC) and a valid passport or other form of identification. As not all treatment is covered by the card, separate medical insurance is advisable.

DIRECTORY

Banking and Local Currency

As Sweden remains outside the European Monetary Union (EMU), goods are priced only in Swedish kronor and not in euros. Visitors can change currency in banks, which provide an efficient service, but better rates can often be obtained at bureaux de change, which have longer opening hours and are strategically located in the city centre. Automatic cash machines can be found outside most banks and in shopping centres. Credit and debit cards are accepted nearly everywhere, and some of the larger stores accept the major foreign currencies. Traveller's cheques are no longer accepted in shops and can only be exchanged in banks and bureaux de change.

Bankomat ATM

Banks and Bureaux de Change

There are plenty of banks in the city centre, all of which offer currency exchange services, and can help visitors who need to report lost or stolen bank or credit cards. The major banks – **Handelsbanken**, **Nordea** and **SEB** – have numerous branches throughout Stockholm. Their opening times vary, but the normal hours are from 9:30am to 3pm. Some banks stay open until 6pm at least once a week.

All banks are closed on weekends and on public holidays, as well as the day before a public holiday.

Various bureaux de change chains are represented in Stockholm, including **Forex** and **X-Change**. They generally provide a better exchange rate than the banks and they are easily accessible. In the city centre, there is always an office close at hand.

Currency and traveller's cheques can be changed at one of Forex's or X-Change's Arlanda Airport locations from 5:30am, and from 7am at the Forex or X-change offices at Stockholm Central Station. All of these outlets are open for more than 12 hours daily. At Central Station, Forex and X-Change are both located in the main entrance hall and on the underground train level. Other exchange offices can be found in the Nordiska Kompaniet and PUB department stores, and in the Gallerian shopping centre on Hamngatan (see p183).

Changing money in your hotel can be an expensive option, so remember to check the exchange rates and commission charges before going ahead.

ATMs

Automatic cash machines (ATMs) are widely available, operate efficiently and are generally safe to use. Foreign visitors can use all the city's cash machines to make withdrawals,

DIRECTORY

Banks

Handelsbanken
Kungsträdgårdsgatan 2.
Map 4 C1.
Tel 08-701 10 00.

Nordea
Hamngatan 12.
Map 3 D4.
Tel 077-122 44 88.

Seb
Sergels Torg 2.
Map 2 C4.
Tel 077-136 53 65.

Bureaux de Change

Forex
Central Station.
Map 2 C5.
Tel 08-411 67 34.

Arlanda Airport, Terminal 2.
Tel 08-593 622 71.

Arlanda Airport, Terminal 5.
Tel 08-593 622 20.

Klarabergsgatan 60.
Map 2 C5.
Tel 010-211 16 10.
W forex.se

X-Change
Arlanda Airport, Terminal 5.
Tel 010-211 16 93.

Central Station.
Map 2 B4.
Tel 08-545 230 30.
W x-change.se

Credit and Debit Cards

American Express
Tel 08-429 56 00

Diners Club
Tel 08-14 68 78.

MasterCard
Tel 020-791 324 (emergency assistance for international visitors).

Visa
Tel 020-795675.

The head office of Handelsbanken at Kungsträdgårdsgatan

provided that they have an internationally accepted credit or debit card with a PIN code. The majority of ATMs accept **Visa** and **MasterCard**. Please note that credit card companies often charge a high fee for such cash advances.

Machines usually have instructions in several languages, including English. The charge for withdrawing cash varies according to the type of card, and additional fees may be charged by the cardholder's bank. As criminals are known to watch ATMs to gather PIN code information, make sure that you shield the keypad with your hand or body when entering your PIN.

Credit and Debit Cards

All the well-known credit and debit cards, including Visa, MasterCard, **American Express** and **Diners Club**, are accepted not just by the larger hotels and restaurants but by nearly all shops and services. Customers paying by credit or debit card may be asked to produce proof of identity, and many stores require use of the PIN code associated with the card.

If your credit or debit card is lost or stolen, contact your card company immediately.

In order to ensure your card works overseas, it is worth contacting your bank or credit card provider in advance of travelling.

Currency

Sweden's currency is the Swedish krona (plural kronor). The krona (abbreviated as SEK or kr) is divided into 100 öre. The smallest coin is 1 kr and the largest note is 1,000 kronor, which is not commonly used. If possible, it is advisable not to carry notes of more than 500 kr.

Many of Stockholm's larger shops and department stores will accept euros as payment for goods, but, to avoid disappointment, it is best to check with a shop employee that this is indeed the case before trying to purchase your goods.

50 kronor

500 kronor

20 kronor

100 kronor

1,000 kronor

Notes

Swedish currency notes are issued in denominations of 20, 50, 100, 500 and 1,000 kronor. They depict historic Swedish artists, authors, scientists and monarchs.

Coins

Coins are issued in values of 1, 5 and 10 kronor. The 1 kr coin depicts Sweden's monarch on the obverse side, while the 5 kr has his monogram on the reverse side.

1 krona

5 kronor

10 kronor

Communications and Media

Sweden has a top-ranking telecommunications industry, one of the most successful and innovative in the world. High living standards have placed the Swedes among the world's biggest users of mobile telephones, and there is a very high level of Internet usage. Telephone cards – and usually credit or debit cards – can be used to make a call from a public telephone, while a mobile phone can be purchased at a relatively low price. With Internet access readily available, there is no risk of being cut off from the world here.

Logo of Telenor network provider

The major network providers in Sweden include **Telia**, **Telenor**, Tele2/Comviq and 3 Sweden. Inexpensive GSM mobile phones can be purchased at a number of stores, including **The Phone House**, Telia or Telenor, together with a pre-paid SIM card for local phone calls.

Within the Stockholm area, mobile users need to dial the area code 08 before a local number – the country code is not needed.

The interior of the Stadsbiblioteket (City Library)

International and Local Telephone Calls

The prefix for international calls from Sweden is 00 followed by the country code, the area code (omitting any initial 0) and the local number.

Public telephones are usually operated by phone cards, which are sold at newspaper kiosks and shops. Normal credit cards and most international telephone cards can also be used, although the charge per minute is generally higher. It is possible to make reverse-charge (collect) calls and calls to the emergency number 112 (free of charge) from all phones. Coin-operated phones are becoming increasingly rare.

Local numbers can be obtained by ringing directory enquiries on 118 118, or on the Internet at Eniro (www.eniro.se) or at Hitta (www.hitta.se). Computer-to-computer phone calls allow visitors to call free of charge using the Internet. Popular service providers include Skype and Google Talk.

Mobile Phones

The number of telephone kiosks in Sweden has shown a marked decline in recent years because virtually every Swede has a mobile phone. Sweden's mobile network is based on GSM, and most foreign visitors can use their GSM phones. However, visitors from North America should check with their service providers to ensure their phones are GSM-compatible.

A typical Swedish telephone kiosk

Internet Facilities

Most hotels offer guests email and fax services. Furthermore, nearly all hotels and hostels in the Stockholm area offer Internet access, although they may charge a daily fee. Public computers are generally available at local libraries, such as the Stockholm City Library at Odengatan 63. Users may be asked to present some form of identification.

Sidewalk Express offers pay-per-minute Internet access from computer terminals at Arlanda Airport, Central Station, and a number of Pressbyrån and 7-Eleven stores throughout the city. The cost varies by location but usually ranges from 25–35 kr per hour.

Wireless Internet (Wi-Fi) access is widely available for visitors with their own computers. Most hotels, many cafés and all **Max Hamburgers** restaurants offer free Wi-Fi.

Postal Services

The Swedish postal system – easily recognized by its blue-and-gold symbol – is based on a series of small postal kiosks located in local grocery stores, such as **Hemköp** which is one of the most central. These kiosks offer the most common services and are open during normal

Pressbyrån kiosks, newsagent selling stamps

shop hours. Some official post offices remain to handle more specialized services; one is located on Klarabergsvia-dukten 84 near Central Station and is open on weekdays from 8:30am to 6pm.

Stamps can be bought at post offices and postal kiosks, as well as at Pressbyrån kiosks and tourist information offices. It costs 7 kr to send a postcard or letter under 20g (0.04 lb) within Sweden and 14 kr to the rest of the world. Post boxes are painted in different colours: the yellow boxes are for national and international mail and the blue boxes for letters destined for the Stockholm area (post codes starting with "1"). In some areas, there are only yellow boxes, which can then be used for local mail as well. Collection times vary and are always shown on the post box.

Post Office logo

Most international courier services, including **DHL**, **UPS** and **FedEx**, are represented in

Stockholm. DHL and UPS services are available at **Mailboxes Etc.**, which is located in the city centre and open on week days from 8am to 7pm. In addition, special courier services are also offered through the Swedish post office.

Television and Radio

Virtually all hotel rooms have a TV with a range of national and foreign channels. The most common channels are the Swedish SVT1, SVT2, TV3, TV4 and Channel 5, as well as the international CNN, Sky News, MTV and Eurosport. SVT1 and 2 are State-run public-service channels. SVT2 and TV4 broadcast local programmes in the morning and evening, which include weather forecasts.

There are a number of local radio stations that broadcast a selection of international and Swedish music. P6, Stockholm International, broadcasts English- and German-language programmes on 89.6 MHz.

Newspapers and Magazines

Many foreign newspapers and magazines can be bought in Stockholm. For the broadest range, visit Press Stop, Press Center or Press Specialisten. Alternatively, the Pressbyrån kiosks and tourist information offices around the city stock a limited number of foreign publications. A wide variety

Yellow postbox for national and international, blue for local mail

DIRECTORY

Mobile Phones

The Phone House
Brunkebergstorg 10.
Map 3 D4.
Tel 08-796 47 50.

Telenor Store
Ringvägen 132.
Map 8 B2.
Tel 020-015 90 80.

Telia Store
Kungsgatan 36.
Map 2 C4.
Tel 08-696 96 80.

Internet Facilities

Café String
Nytorgsgatan 38.
Map 9 E3.
Tel 08-714 85 14.

Max Hamburgers
Kungsträdgårdsgatan 20.
Map 3 D4.
Tel 08-611 38 10.

Sidewalk Express
Located in Stockholm Central Station, Arlanda Airport, and 7-Eleven and Pressbyrån stores.

Postal Services

DHL
Tel 077-134 53 45.

Federal Express (FedEx)
Arlanda Airport.
Tel 0200 252 252.

Hemköp
Mäster Samuelsgatan 57.
Map 2 C4.
Tel 020-23 22 21.

Mailboxes Etc.
Mäster Samuelsgatan 20.
Map 3 D4.
Tel 08-411 70 10.

Swedish Post
Klarabergsviadukten 84.
Map 2 B5.
Tel 08-781 20 42.

UPS
Tel 077-662 20 77.

of foreign titles can be found at the Plattan Library at Kulturhuset, which is open Monday to Friday from 9am to 7pm, and Saturday to Sunday from 11am to 5pm.

GETTING TO STOCKHOLM

Stockholm's location at the centre of the Baltic region has made it an important transport hub. Direct, daily flights link the capital to most major European and North American cities. Arlanda Airport, served by about 60 international and domestic airlines, is one of the most efficient in the world. In addition, Sweden's infrastructure is constantly being improved, with new motorways under construction and the railway system being upgraded for high-speed trains. Car ferries operate between Stockholm and Finland and other points in the Baltic, and from Sweden's west and south coasts, the capital can be reached by high-speed trains and motorways in 6 hours. Sweden also has a direct link to the Continent via the Öresund bridge to Denmark in the south.

Duty free at Stockholm's Arlanda Airport

Arriving by Air

Most major European cities have direct flights to Stockholm. Many of the world's leading airlines, such as **British Airways**, serve Arlanda Airport, located about 40 km (25 miles) north of the city centre. Some Swedish domestic airlines also use Arlanda Airport, including **SAS** (Scandinavian Airlines).

Stockholm is also served by two other airports. Bromma, close to the city centre, is used by several of the smaller domestic airlines as well as Finnair and Brussels Airlines. Skavsta, about 100 km (62 miles) south of Stockholm, is used by **Ryanair** for flights to and from London Stansted Airport. A bus takes travellers into Stockholm.

Direct flights between Stockholm and North America are run by SAS, Delta and United.

Air Fares and Tickets

Fare options are varied, particularly if you can be flexible about departure and arrival dates, or can book well in advance. SAS, for example, has low-cost fares, which must be booked at least seven days before departure and require a Saturday night stay at the destination. Bookings on this type of ticket cannot usually be changed.

Scheduled airlines generally maintain their basic fare structure throughout the year. However, special offers and last-minute online deals are frequently available.

Customs

Travellers arriving from within the EU are able to bring an unlimited amount of alcohol into the country for their own consumption, provided they are at least 20 years old, and an unlimited amount of tobacco for their own consumption, as long as they are at least 18 years of age. Travellers from outside the EU may only bring 1 litre of spirits or 2 litres of fortified wine, 4 litres of wine and 16 litres of beer, and 200 cigarettes or 50 cigars, all of which must be for personal use only.

Visitors from within the EU can bring any amount of food into Sweden, with the exception of fish, which is subject to an import restriction of 15 kg (33 lb). Those wishing to import fresh food from other areas must be in possession of a health certificate and understand that such food will be inspected at the border. Visitors from non-EU countries travelling by commercial airlines or ferries can take in goods, including beer and food, with a value of up to 4,300 kr.

Tax-free sales in Sweden are permitted only for travellers with a final destination outside the EU.

SAS

SAS logo

Getting to the City from Arlanda Airport

There are several ways of getting to the city from Arlanda Airport. The "Flygbussarna" bus service, which operates every 10 minutes at peak times, takes 45 minutes to the City Terminal at Central Station and costs about 120 kr one way or 215 kr for a return ticket. Tickets can be cheaper if bought online in advance. An onward journey by taxi can be booked on the bus. A taxi from the airport is quicker but more expensive. Most taxi firms have a fixed charge of about 500 kr to the city centre. Use only authorized taxis waiting in the official taxi queues at Arlanda and agree

Ferry from Finland on the way to its terminal at Stadsgården

on the fare with the driver before departure. The Arlanda Express train takes 20 minutes to Central Station and costs about 280 kr each way.

The Arlanda Express, linking Arlanda Airport with the city

Arriving by Train or Coach

Rail and coach travel from the Continent to Stockholm is quick, inexpensive and comfortable. The opening, in 2000, of the Öresund bridge, which carries both rail and road traffic between Denmark and southern Sweden, significantly shortened travel times.

Within Sweden, the state-owned railway company **Statens Järnvägar (SJ)** operates most of the long-distance trains. Some routes are run by private companies, notably **Tågkompaniet** (Stockholm–northern Sweden). Air travel between Stockholm and Malmö or Gothenburg faces strong competition from SJ's X 2000 high-speed train. The lowest fares can usually be purchased 90 days in advance. The journey by train from Malmö to Stockholm is about 5 hours; from Gothenburg it is 3 hours.

The same routes are served by express coaches, most of which are run by **Swebus**. Journey times are longer (about 9 hours from Malmö and about 7 hours from Gothenburg), but fares are generally much lower and advance booking is not required.

Arriving by Ferry

Large passenger/car ferries sail to Stockholm from Finland. Both **Viking Line** and **Tallink Silja Line** operate daily services and have their own terminals at Stadsgården near the city centre and Värtahamnen respectively. The journey from Helsinki takes about 15 hours, while it takes 11 hours from Turku. Both shipping lines offer excellent passenger facilities, including good food, entertainment and shopping. Tallink Silja Line operates daily from Tallinn in Estonia to the Värtahamnen terminal.

Arriving by Car

Visitors driving from Denmark can use the Öresund toll bridge between Copenhagen and Malmö. The toll costs around 425 kr for a normal passenger vehicle. On the Swedish side, the bridge connects with the E4, a 550-km (340-mile) motorway to Stockholm. Another option is the 20-minute car ferry from Helsingør in Denmark to Helsingborg in Sweden.

Car ferries to Gothenburg operate from Denmark (Frederikshavn) and Germany (Kiel), with an onward journey

Warning, moose on the road

on the E3 of about 450 km (280 miles) to Stockholm. The fastest route from Germany to Sweden is the catamaran ferry from Rostock to Trelleborg in southern Sweden, then the E6 to Malmö and the E4 to Stockholm.

Speed limits are usually clearly signed. On Swedish motorways, the limit is typically 110 km/h (68 mph) or 120 km/h (75 mph). On other main roads, the limit is 90 km/h (56 mph), while it is 50 km/h (31 mph) in built-up areas. Take care when driving in the countryside, as moose and deer can suddenly appear on the road. Accidents involving these animals must be reported to the police.

DIRECTORY

Arriving by Air

British Airways
Tel 0770 110 020.
Tel 0844 381 63 05 (UK).
W britishairways.com

Ryanair
Tel 0900 100 0550.
Tel 0843 658 08 99 (UK).
W ryanair.com

SAS
Tel 0770 727 727.
Tel 0871 226 77 60 (UK).
W flysas.com

Arriving by Train or Coach

Statens Järnvägar (SJ)
Tel 0771 757 575.
W sj.se

Swebus
Tel 0771 218 218.
W swebusexpress.se

Tågkompaniet
Tel 0771 444 111.
W tagkompaniet.se

Arriving by Ferry

Tallink Silja Line
Tel 08-22 21 40.
W tallinksilja.com

Viking Line
Tel 08-452 40 00.
W vikingline.se

GETTING AROUND STOCKHOLM

Stockholm is a perfect city for pedestrians. Distances between sights are usually short, and around every corner there is something interesting to explore. The capital extends across a large number of islands, offering eye-catching vistas and waterfront scenes. Public transport on buses, underground trains, trams and local trains is efficient and covers the entire city and surrounding region. Apart from the area of Gamla Stan, and during rush hours, driving in Stockholm is relatively easy, and indoor parking facilities are adequate. However, the best way of exploring the city centre is on foot.

Green Travel

In recent years, Stockholm has focussed on encouraging travellers and inhabitants alike to move about the city in the most environmentally friendly way possible. For tourists, day tickets on public transport are significantly cheaper than paid parking, and visitors arriving or travelling across the city by bus, Tunnelbana or train are not subject to the city's congestion tolls. Every major site in the city is easily accessible by public transport, and switching from one form of transport to another is very straightforward.

A good alternative to public transport during the summer months is the Stockholm City Bikes system *(see p205)*, through which visitors can borrow a bike and tour the city on their own. The cheapest method of getting around, however, is walking and doing so is easy because of Stockholm's compact city centre. Many roads are pedestrian friendly and, in most cases, it is easy to walk from one attraction to the next.

Stockholm on Foot

While walking is the best way to see the sights in central Stockholm, there are regulations to be aware of. Pedestrians are not allowed to cross a road at a red light, and motorists must stop and give way to pedestrians at zebra crossings without traffic lights (always look carefully). Don't forget to press the pedestrian crossing button at intersections

Pedestrianized square in Gamla Stan, the city's Old Town

Pedestrian crossing sign

– otherwise you may wait a long time before the light changes to green.

The city's clear street signs make it simple to find your way around. There are sidewalks everywhere, as well as plenty of pedestrian streets and park areas.

Gamla Stan is a popular area for exploring on foot, and there is always something to see around Kungsträdgården. A stroll along the quayside opposite the Grand Hôtel and the Nationalmuseum can be followed by a walk around Skeppsholmen. Another delightful area is Djurgården, with a host of attractions set in a park environment a short distance from the city centre.

Those who like to walk along the waterfront can follow the quaysides from Stadshuset along Norr Mälarstrand or the Riddarfjärden bay. Fjällgatan *(see p131)* is also recommended, not least for its magnificent views of the city.

Guided walks are organized regularly, often with a special theme, such as architecture, history or parks. Sometimes they are available in different languages, especially during the summer months. Most walks take place in Gamla Stan, but there are a number of other routes. Ask at the **Stockholm Visitor Centre** for details.

Driving in Stockholm

Driving around Stockholm is straightforward, except during rush hours (7:30–9:30am, noon–1pm and 3:30–6pm). It is also best to avoid driving in Gamla Stan, due to narrow one-way streets. However, cars are not necessary in the city centre given the short distances between sights and the excellent public transport system.

Fines for speeding are high, and you can lose your driving licence even if the limit is only slightly exceeded. Vehicle headlights must always be on, and drivers and passengers are required to wear seatbelts. Sweden's drink-drive laws are zero-tolerance: the maximum permitted blood alcohol level is 0.2 mg per ml. Motorists must give way to pedestrians at crossings without traffic lights.

Reading Street Signs

Street name

Roslagsgatan

kv. Ingemar **46-34**

Block

Street number range in block

Restored vintage tram, a popular way of getting to Djurgården

Buses

Stockholm's network of red city buses run on the main inner-city routes, and the blue "feeder" buses operate on the routes out to the suburbs. Many streets have special bus lanes, which make travel quick and easy. The buses are all modern and comfortable, with easy access for prams and wheelchairs, and they use environmentally friendly fuels such as ethanol and natural gas.

The best routes for sightseeing are 2, 3, 44, 65 and 69, which cover most of the central area and stop near many sights. Route 69, which can be boarded at Norrmalmstorg, is particularly useful for reaching sights not served by the Tunnelbana. Route 69 goes to southern Gärdet with its four important museums and Kaknästornet before continuing to Blockhusudden at the easternmost tip of Djurgården.

Buses run every few minutes throughout the day and about 20 to 30 minutes in the late evening. There are also three night buses that operate hourly.

Trams

In 2010, Stockholm opened the first stage of the new tramline, Spårväg City. This line takes travellers from Kungsträdgården to Waldemarsudde on a regular SL ticket. The trams run every 15 minutes from 5:30am to 1:30am Monday to Friday, from 6am to 1:30am on Saturday, and from 6:30am to 1:30am on Sunday.

A charming way of travelling to Djurgården, particularly in the summer, is to take one of the lovingly restored vintage trams. In fact, since there is no subway service on the island, trams provide a good alternative to driving.

Djurgårdslinjen, a voluntary organization of tram enthusiasts, run services on the former line 7 (now Line 7N) between Norrmalmstorg and Djurgården, where 14 trams are stabled. The trams run approximately every 15 minutes between 10am and 7pm daily from early July until late August. The rest of the year, they run on weekends and holidays only. Refreshments are served on some services.

Every year more than 300,000 passengers enjoy a trip using this popular method of travel. SL tickets cannot be used on

Trams

Djurgårdslinjen
W sparvagssallskapet.se

the vintage trams, but holders of an SL Access card may ride for free.

Local trains

Stockholm's inner-city public transportation system is complemented by an extensive network of local trains (pendeltåg), many of which accept the same SL tickets used on the Tunnelbana system. Travellers can therefore easily visit a number of towns and villages around Stockholm, including Täby, Södertalje, Åkersberga, Nynäshamn and Kungsängen. While most regional trains leave from Central Station, the regional trains on the Roslagsbanean line leave from Östra Station, which is adjacent to the Tekniska Högskolan stop on the red Tunnelbana line.

Tickets

A single ticket for travel on public transportation costs 36 kr and is generally valid for 60 minutes. Travel cards valid for 1 day (115 kr), 3 days (230 kr) or 7 days (300 kr) are also available. They are issued through the SL Access system and are valid for all zones. To use an SL Access card, hold it against the blue entry pad when entering a bus or a Tunnelbana station. Reduced-price tickets are available for children (see p191), students and pensioners with a valid ID. Tickets and Access cards can be bought at Pressbyrån kiosks, the SL Central Ticket Office or at most stations.

Red city bus and blue "feeder" bus

Around by Ferry and Boat

olm's location between Lake Mälaren and the Baltic
ipelago means that its waterways play an important
ole in city life. A large number of scheduled boat services,
ferries and sightseeing tours offer visitors endless
opportunities to enjoy Stockholm from the water. Note
that from mid-August transport schedules are adjusted
for winter, so always check the times.

Djurgården ferry in front of Nordiska museet

Ferries

One of the best ways to visit
Djurgården is to take a ferry
from the city centre. Operated
by **Waxholmsbolaget**, the ferry
service links with bus and
Tunnelbana routes, and is free
for holders of SL's 1–3- or 7- day
cards. Single tickets cost 45 kr.

The ferry runs year-round from
Slussen via Skeppsholmen to
Allmänna Gränd near Gröna Lund,
and operates from 6:30am
until midnight. From May to
August there is a route from
Nybroplan to Vasamuseet,
Skeppsholmen and Gröna
Lund from 10am to 6pm.

Sightseeing by Boat

A pleasant way of enjoying
Stockholm is to take one of the
many sightseeing boat tours
(see maps below). **Strömma**
offers several tours including a
hop-on, hop-off tour that costs

around 85 kr. Their
"Historical Canal" tour
departs hourly from the
quayside near the City
Hall and costs 185 kr. The
"Under the Bridges of
Stockholm" tour and
"Royal Canal" tour depart
from Strömkajen near
the Grand Hôtel
(passengers can also board at
Nybroplan). The former tour
operates from April to October
between 10am and 8pm and
costs about 240 kr. The latter
operates from April to
December between 10:30am and
6pm for about 85 kr. On all tours,
guides speak English and Swedish.

Waxholmsbolaget operates a
number of scheduled public
transport boat services year-
round. An excellent way of
exploring the archipelago is to
take one of the regular services
from Strömkajen: these call at
countless picturesque jetties
along the way. The ferry company
and tourist information offices
can suggest suitable itineraries.

Organized excursions both in
the archipelago and on Lake
Mälaren are run by Strömma
and other operators. You can,
for instance, take a gastronomic evening cruise to
Vaxholm. A number of sights

that can be reached by fast
passenger boats or traditional
steamers are listed on pages
142–153.

Hiring Boats and Canoes

Enjoying the city from the
water is an exciting experience.
Rowboats, canoes, kayaks,
pedalos and small boats with
outboard motors can be hired
near the Djurgården bridge at
Djurgårdsbrons Sjöcafé.
The gentle waters of the
Djurgården Canal are ideal
for rowing, paddle-boating
or canoeing.

DIRECTORY

Ferries

Waxholmsbolaget
Strömkajen.
Map 3 D5. **Tel** 08-679 58 30.
W waxholmsbolaget.se

Sightseeing by Boat

Strömma
Södra Blasieholmshamnen 11.
Map 3 D5.

Nybrokajen 9.
Map 3 E4. **Tel** 08-12 00 40 00.
W stromma.se

Hiring Boats

Djurgårdsbrons Sjöcafé
Galärvarvsgatan 2.
Map 3 F5. **Tel** 08-660 57 57.
W sjocafet.se

Key To Ferry Routes

— Djurgårdsfärjan *(see inset map)*
⎯ Under the Bridges of Stockholm Tour
— Historical Canal Tour (Jun–Aug)
— Royal Canal Tour (Apr–Dec)
— Drottningholm Tour (Jun–Aug)

Key
····· Djurgården Ferry (May–Aug)

Nybroplan
City
Strömkajen
Vasa-
varvet
Stadshusbron
Skepps-
Holmen
Allm.
Gränd
Gamla
Stan
Slussen

Drottningholm
Kungsholmen
City
Djurgården
Södermalm

0 kilometres   3
0 miles   2

Getting Around by Bicycle

Stockholm and its surrounding area are tailor-made for cycling. The capital's network of bicycle tracks is increasing all the time, and you do not need to be a very experienced city cyclist if you want to explore the central area from the saddle. Furthermore, anyone wanting to go out into the countryside and enjoy the fresh air and beautiful surroundings will not have to travel far from the city centre.

Cycling in Stockholm

With over 700 km (435 miles) of bike lanes, and numerous bike paths in Djurgården and other parks, Stockholm is easily accessible to biking enthusiasts and casual bikers alike. In recent years, the city has significantly increased the number of bicycle lanes on major streets and run several campaigns to increase awareness of bicycles as an environmentally friendly alternative to cars.

A Stockholm City Bikes stand

Djurgården, with its gently graded cycle tracks and roads, that are mostly free of cars, is an excellent area for those wishing to explore by bike. Gärdet, Lilljanskogen and Hagaparken are other good areas for biking. It is also possible to cycle in parts of the Royal National City Park (Ekoparken; see p123), which are virtually traffic-free.

Bicycle routes are clearly posted throughout much of Stockholm, and there are marked routes that stretch further out from the city centre. Maps can be bought from **Kartbutiken** and in most bookstores and are also available from the tourist office.

Under Swedish law, all cyclists 15 years old and under are required to wear helmets, and all bicycles must have electric lights after dusk. Cyclists generally do not have right of way at intersections and should watch for turning cars. Bike racks can be found almost everywhere, and it is advisable to lock any bike left unattended to avoid the risk of theft.

There are numerous cycling tours available in the city. **Bikeguide Stockholm**, located outside Historiska museet, organize various tours that take in all the major sites as well as paths along the waterfront. To find out more about cycling, or cycling tours in Stockholm and throughout Sweden, contact **Cykelfrämjandet**.

DIRECTORY

Cycling Tours and Maps

Bikeguide Stockholm
Narvavägen 13.
Map 3 F4.
Tel 07-330 956 26.
w bikeguide-stockholm.se

Cykelfrämjandet
Tel 08-545 910 30.
w cykelframjandet.se

Kartbutiken
Mäster Samuelsgatan 54.
Map 2 C4.
Tel 08-20 23 03.
w kartbutiken.se

Bicycle Rental

Cykel & Mopeduthyrningen
Strandvägen, quay berth No. 24.
Map 3 F4. **Tel** 08-660 79 59.

Cykelstallet
Scheelegatan 15.
Map 2 B5. **Tel** 08-651 00 66.
w cykelstallet.se

Djurgårdsbrons Sjöcafé
Galärvarvsgatan 2.
Map 3 F5. **Tel** 08-660 57 57.
w sjocafet.se

Stockholm City Bikes
Tel 077-444 24 24.
w citybikes.se

Bicycle Rental

Stockholm City Bikes offers an excellent option for visitors wishing to explore the city by bike. Tourists can purchase a 3-day rental card for 165 kr at the Stockholm Visitors Board or at the main SL office at Central Station. After swiping the card at any one of the city's 80 bicycle stands, the renter can borrow a bike for up to 3 hours. Bikes can be returned to any stand, which creates a great deal of flexibility. Renters must use their own bicycle helmets to use this service.

Two rental firms, **Djurgårdsbrons Sjöcafé** and **Cykel & Mopeduthyrningen**, are located on Strandvägen near the Djurgården bridge. These companies offer bicycle rental by the day and also hire out rollerblades. **Cykelstallet** is the best place in town to go for mountain bike rental.

A bicycle rank on the waterfront

STOCKHOLM STREET FINDER

The map below shows the areas of Stockholm covered by the street map only. Gamla Stan (Old Town) is shown on a larger scale than the rest of the city. The map references listed in the guide for many sights, restaurants, hotels, shops and entertainment spots refer to the maps in this section. The first figure of the reference indicates the map page, while the letter and following figure shows its location on the map grid. All the more important sights are marked so that they are easier to find. The key below explains other symbols on the map, including post offices, tunnelbana stations and churches. An overview map of Stockholm is on pp14–15.

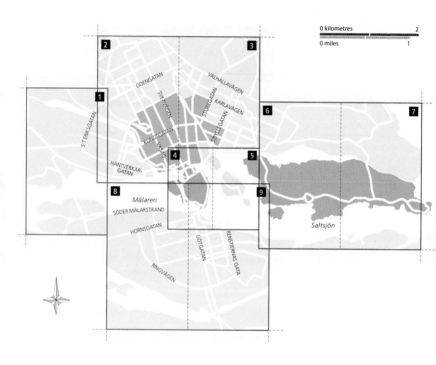

| 0 kilometres | | 2 |
| 0 miles | | 1 |

Key to Street Finder

- ▢ Major sight
- ▢ Place of interest
- ▢ Other building
- 🚉 Train station
- Ⓣ Tunnelbana station
- 🚌 Coach station
- ⛴ Car ferry
- ⛴ Passenger ferry
- 🚊 Tram stop

- 𝒊 Tourist information office
- ✚ Hospital with casualty unit
- 🏛 Police station
- ✝ Church
- ✡ Synagogue
- ☪ Mosque
- ❋ Viewpoint
- ═ Railway line
- Pedestrian street

Scale of Map Pages

1-3 and 6-9
| 0 metres | 200 |
| 0 yards | 200 |

4-5
| 0 metres | 200 |
| 0 yards | 200 |

Street name index on pp216–18

General Index

Acknowledgments

Dorling Kindersley would like to thank the following people whose contributions and assistance have made the preparation of this book possible.

Main Contributor
Kaj Sandell began his career as a journalist, writing for the Swedish publishers Åhlén & Åkerlund and *Dagens Nyheter*, Sweden's largest daily newspaper, and has contributed to other guidebooks. For some decades, Kaj Sandell was the Head of Information at Scania Trucks and Busses and he has in recent years written several monographs on leading Swedish companies.

Additional Contributors
Anna Mosesson, Tina Pedersen, James Proctor, Kristin Prouty

Special Assistance
The Publisher would like to thank Stockholm Visitors Board (SVB) and their representatives Roland Berndt, Kjell Holmstrand, Charlotta Lorentz and all other SIS employees for their efforts and support throughout the project. Particular thanks are also due to: Irina Chiriboga, Dorothée Greitz (food and drink consultant), Olof Hultin (architectural consultant) Christina Sollenberg-Britton (Swedish design consultant).

Senior Managing Editor
Louise Bostock Lang.

Editorial Director
Vivien Crump.

Managing Director
Douglas Amrine.

English Translation
Philip Ray.

Editors, English Edition
Jane Hutchings, Caroline Radula-Scott.

Proofreader
Michelle Clark, Clare Peel.

Factchecker
Sharon A. Bowker, Kathleen Sauret.

DTP, Design & Editorial Assistance
Asad Ali, Emma Anacootee, Jasneet Arora, Liz Atherton, Marta Bescos Sanchez, Sonal Bhatt, Hilary Bird, Kathleen Blankenship Sauret, Lucinda Cooke, Karen Fitzpatrick, Lydia Halliday, Kaberi Hazarika, Stuart James, Priya Kukadia, Maite Lantaron, Hayley Maher, Alison McGill, Sam Merrell, Deepak Mittal, Casper Morris, Viveka Mörk, Claire Naylor, Monica Nilsson, Vikki Nousiainen, Anna Ohlsson, Susie Peachey, Helen Peters, Marianne Petrou, Lee Redmond, Marisa Renzullo, Lucy Richards, Ellen Root, Simon Ryder, Sands Publishing Solutions, Azeem Siddiqui, Neil Simpson, Sadie Smith, Rebecca Taylor, Priyanka Thakur, Nikhil Verma, Sophie Wright.

Additional Illustrations
Jan Rojmar, Jane Bark.

Additional Photography
Neil Fletcher, Ian O'Leary, Ulf Svensson.

Artwork Reference
Svenska Aerobilder AB.

Photography Permission
Dorling Kindersley would like to thank all those who gave permission to photograph at various churches, museums, restaurants, hotels, shops and other sights that are too numerous to list individually. Particular thanks to the Guild of Museum Directors in Stockholm for permitting access to picture archives as well as making additional photographing of objects and exhibitions possible.

Picture Credits
a = above; b = below/bottom; c = centre; f = far; l = left; r = right; t = top.

The publisher would like to thank the following individuals, companies and picture libraries for permission to reproduce their photographs.

4Corners Images: SIME/Anna Serrano 205bl.

Alamy Images: Sten Andersson 79tc; Marie-Louise Avery 164cla; Frank Chmura 76; Chad Ehlers 194cl; Peter Forsberg 165c; imagebroker/Thomas Schneider 205ca; Andrea Innocenti 35crb; Jon Arnold Images Ltd/Russell Young 200ca; Nicholas Pitt 165tl; pixonnet.com/Ingemar Edfalk 141cr; Sweden And Swedish 192cr; Anna Yu 193tl.

Bergianska Trädgården: Åsa Stjerna 126b; Bistro pastis Restaurant 166bc; **Kosta Boda**: Ann Wåhlström 41bl.

Camera Press: Scanpix/Thure Wikberg 139tr; **Corbis**: Malcom Hanes 44-5; John Hicks 142; Leemage 6–7; Keith Levit 154-5; **Gunnar Cyrén**: © BUS 2000 184cl.

Dansmuseum: 37bc; **Dreamstime.com:** Alexander Avdeev 10t; Gelia 191bl; Sophysweden 11t; Tupungato 64tr; Vvoevale 35cr; **Drottningholm Slottsteate**r: Bengt Wanselius 149tr, 149bc.

Fjärils & Fågelhuset: 124cla; **Fotolia**: madeleineforsberg 1c; Fredrik Rollman 31cr.

Getty Images: Sven Nackstrand 201bl; Photo Filip Nystedt 102; David Rynde Photography, Sweden, david.rynde@ gmail.com 86; Korhan Sezer 2-3; Gondolen Restaurant 171tr. **Grand Hôtel**: 81br; 157tl; **Grodan Grev Ture Restaurant**: 167tr; **Grona Lund**: 175bl.

Hallwylska museet: 37tr; S. Uhrdin 75c; **Hilton Stockholm Slussen**: 161tr; **Hornsgatan Hotel**: 160bc.

IMS Bildbyrå: 27tl.

Kungliga Myntkabinettet: 49crb, 70br; Jan Eve Olsson 54c; **Kungliga Biblioteket**: 20br, 21cr, 72ca; **Kungliga Husgerådskammaren**: *Karl XI's Triumph*, Jacques Foucquet 21tl, 51tc, 51ca; Alexis Daflos 52tr, 52clb, 53tr, 125bl, 151tc, 146cl, 147tc 147bc, 148tr, 148clb; Håkan Lind 5cl, 50cb, 50cl, 50br, 52cla, 147cra; **Kungliga Operan**: Mats Bäcker 64bc, 67tl, 67cl.

Livrustkammaren: 21bl, 25br; Göran Schmidt 25cla, 36cla, 49tl; Nina Heins 54bl.

Märta Måås-Fjetterstrom: 40br; **Master Anders Restaurant:** 163br, 169br; **Medical Products Agency**: 193cl; **Moderna museet**: *Breakfast Outdoors*, Pablo Picasso 82bl; *Monogram*, Robert Rauschenberg © BUS 2000 82crb, *The Child's Brain*, Giorgio De Chirico ©BUS 2000 83bl; Per Anders Allsten 82br; Wassily Kandinsky 82tr; **Museum Tre Kronor**: 53br.

Nationalmuseum: 40clb, 41tr, 51cr, 84clb; *The Parhelion Painting*, Urban Målare 16; *The Entry of King Gustav Vasa of Sweden in Stockholm 1523*, Carl Larsson 18t; *Portrait of Erik XIV*, Steven van der Meulen 18c; *The Fire at the Royal Palace May 7th 1697*, Johan Fredrik Höckert 19tr, *Portrait of Queen Kristina*, David Beck 19cl; *The Death of Gustav II Adolf of Sweden at the Battle of Lützen*, Carl Wahlbom 20bl; *The Crossing of the Belt*, Johan Philip Lemke 20–21c; *Bringing Home the Body of King Karl XII of Sweden*, Gustaf Cederström 21br; *King Gustav III of Sweden*, Lorens Pasch the Younger. 22tl; *Portrait of the Bernadotte Family*, Fredrik Westin 22crb; *The Coronation of Gustav III of Sweden*, Carl Gustav Pilo 24cla; *The Battle at Svensksund*, J.T. Schoultz 24clb; *A Noisy Dinner*, Johan Tobias Sergel 24bc; *Conversation at Drottningholm*, Pehr Hilleström 24–25c; *The Murder of Gustav III*, A.W. Küssner 25tr; *Bacchanal on Andros*, Peter Paul Rubens 34clb *Flowers on the Windowsill*, Carl Larsson 40–41c; *The Conspiracy of the Batavians under Claudius Civilis*, Rembrandt 84cla; *David and Bathsheba* 84bl; *The Love Lesson*, Antoine Watteau 84tr; *The Lady with the Veil*, Alexander Roslin 85tl; Åsa Lundén 127br; Hans Thorwid 150tr; **Naturhistoriska Riksmuseet**: Staffan Waerndt 126tl, 126c; **Peter Nordahl**: 137cla, 139br, 140tr; **Nordiska museet**: 35bc 92tr, 93tr; Mats Landin 92cl, 93crb, 93tc; Peter Segemark 33tc; Sören Hallgren 92bc.

Östasiatiska museet: 74tl, 80bl.

Posten.se: 197bl; **Postmuseum**: 57crb; **Pressbyran**: 197tl; **Pressens bild**: 135br; Rolf Hamilton 27cr; Hans T. Dahlskog 27br; Jan Collsiöö 51br, 72bl, 73br; Jan Delden 69bl; Hans Dahlskog 90br; Hans Rossel: 140bl; Gunnar Seijbolds 111bc; Axel Malmström 119bl; Riksarkivet: Richard Ryan: 136cr.

Courtesy of SAS Group: 198cb; **Scandic Hotels**: 156b; **Sjöhistoriska museet**: 109 all; **Skansen**: 9tr, 100-101c; 101tc, 101cra, 101b; Marie Andersson 89bc; **Skogskyrkogården**: 135c; **Spiritmuseum**: 91bc; **Stadsbiblioteket**: 119tr; **Statens Historiska Museum**: 36br, 106 all, 107 all, 150c, 150bl; Christer Åhlin 35tr; Statens **Museum für Världskultur**: Etnografiska museet – Bo Gabrielsson 110bc, 110cra; Medelhavsmuseet – Ove Kaneberg 64cla; Ostasiatiska museet – Erik Cornelius 78cla; Karl Zetterstorm 80bl; **Steninge Slott**: 151b; **Stockholm Arlanda Airport**: 198cla; **Stockholm Public Library**: 196cl; **Stockholm Visitor Center**: 190cr; **Stockholms Auktionsverk**: 25bl; J. L. Sánchez, Hans

Hedberg © BUS 2000 40tr, Sigurd Persson © BUS 2000 41tl; **Stockholms Stadsbyggnadskontor**: Stockholms Stadshus: Jan Asplund 116br, 117tl; *The Mosaics in the Golden Hall*, Einar Forseth © BUS 2000 116tr; **Stockholms Stadsmuseum**: 26clb, 27clb; *The Three Crowns Castle*, Govert Camphuysen 20cla; Gustaf Carleman 23cb; *Newspaper Readers*, J. A. Cronstedt 23tl; *The Regicide Anckarström punished in front of the House of Nobility*, 25cr; **Stockholms Universitet**: Per Bergström 118b; **Storstockholms brandforsvar**: 192br; **STF Af Chapman**: 159tr; **Strindbergsmuseet**: 140cla; Per Bergström 71br; Stromma Media Bank: 8br; **Superstock**: image Source 62: Stock Connection 85bc; **Svenska Akademien**: Leif Jansson 24tr; Svenska Handelsbanken AB: Bengt Wanselius 194bl; **Svenska Filminstitutet**: Mark Standley 111crb.

Telenor Group: 196tr; **Courtesy of TeliaSonera**: 196bc; **Thielska Galleriet**: *Hornsgatan*, Eugène Jansson 99tr; **Tidningen Svensk Polis**: 192crb.

Urban Deli Restaurant: 171br, Urban Orzolek 163tl.

Vasamuseet: 88cla, 88cl, 95cra, 95tl, 95cr; Hans Hammarskiöld 4tr, 94tr, 94cla, 94clb, 94br, 95tc, 95crb, 95bl, 96br, 96cla, 96tr; **Ingrid Vang Nyman**: Claes Westlin 40cla; Restaurang Volt: 168bc.

Pia Wallén: © BUS 2000 184bl; **Wedholms Fisk Restaurant**: 167br; **Jeppe Wikström**: 5tr, 8cla, 9cl, 9br, 17bc, 28cr, 28bl, 29cr, 33cra, 38tr, 38cl, 40cl, 42tr, 42cl, 42clb, 42br, 57tr, 61tc, 64bl, 65bc, 65cra, 69t, 70tl, 74bc, 75tc, 75bl, 81ca, 89cra, 91t, 97tr, 98bl, 104bl, 118tr, 123bl, 124clb, 128tr, 128bl, 129c, 129bl, 130tc, 131crb, 133tr, 136cla, 137tr, 138tr, 138br, 141tc, 144cla, 145br, 152cr, 153tr, 153bc, 175tl, 180cla, 180bl, 188-9, 199tl.

Sheet Map front cover: Alamy Images: Michael Abid.

Front Endpapers – Alamy Images: Frank Chmura Ltr; **Getty Images**: David Rynde Photography, Sweden, david. rynde@gmail.com Rtc; **Superstock**: image Source Lbl.

Jacket
Front – Alamy Images: Michael Abid; **DK Images**: James Tye bl

All other images © Dorling Kindersley.
For further information see: www.dkimages.com

Special Editions of DK Travel Guides

DK Travel Guides can be purchased in bulk quantities at discounted prices for use in promotions or as premiums. We are also able to offer special editions and personalized jackets, corporate imprints, and excerpts from all of our books, tailored specifically to meet your own needs.

To find out more, please contact:
in the United States: **specialsales@dk.com**
in the UK: **travelguides@uk.dk.com**
in Canada: DK Special Sales at **specialmarkets@dk.com**
in Australia: **penguincorporatesales@penguinrandomhouse.com.au**

Phrase Book

When reading the imitated pronunciation, stress the part that is underlined. Pronounce each syllable as if it formed part of an English word, and you will be understood sufficiently well. Remember the points below, and your pronunciation will be even closer to the correct Swedish.

ai:	as in 'fair' or 'stair'
ea:	as in 'ear' or 'hear'
ew:	like the sound in 'dew'
EW:	try to say 'ee' with your lips rounded
oo:	as in 'book' or 'soot'
OO:	as in 'spoon' or 'groom'
r:	should be strongly pronounced

Swedish Alphabetical Order

In the list below we have not followed Swedish alphabetical order. The letters **å**, **ä** and **ö** have been interfiled within the Latin alphabet, not ordered after **z**.

You

There are two words for 'you': 'du' and 'ni'. 'Du' is the familiar form; 'ni' is the polite form. It is not impolite to address a complete stranger with the familiar form.

In an Emergency

Help!	**Hjälp!**	yelp
Stop!	**Stanna!**	stanna!
Call a doctor!	**Ring efter en doktor!**	ring efter ehn doktor
Call an ambulance!	**Ring efter en ambulans!**	ring efter ehn ambewlanss
Call the police!	**Ring polisen!**	ring poleesen
Call the fire brigade!	**Ring efter brandkåren!**	ring efter brandkawren
Where is the nearest telephone?	**Var finns närmaste telefon?**	vahr finnss nairmasteh telefawn
Where is the nearest hospital?	**Var finns närmaste sjukhus?**	vahr finnss- nairmasteh shewkhews

Communication Essentials

Yes	**Ja**	yah
No	**Nej**	nay
Please (offering)	**Varsågod**	vahrshawgOOd
Thank you	**Tack**	tack
Excuse me	**Ursäkta**	ewrshekta
Hello	**Hej**	hay
Goodbye	**Hej då/adjö**	haydaw/ahyur
Good night	**God natt**	goonytt
Morning	**Morgon**	morron
Afternoon	**Eftermiddag**	eftermiddahg
Evening	**Kväll**	kvell
Yesterday	**Igår**	ee gawr
Today	**Idag**	ee dahg
Tomorrow	**I morgon**	ee morron
Here	**Här**	hair
There	**Där**	dair
What?	**Vad?**	vah
When?	**När?**	nair
Why?	**Varför?**	vahrfurr
Where?	**Var?**	vahr

Useful Phrases

How are you?	**Hur mår du?**	hewr mawr dew
Very well, thank you.	**Mycket bra, tack.**	mewkeh brah, tack
Pleased to meet you.	**Trevligt att träffas.**	treavlit att traffas
See you soon.	**Vi ses snart.**	vee seas snahrt
That's fine.	**Det går bra.**	dea gawr brah
Where is/are …?	**Var finns …?**	vahr finnss…
How far is it to …?	**Hur långt är det till …?**	hewr lawngt ea dea till
Which way to …?	**Hur kommer jag till …?**	hewr kommer yah till …
Do you speak English?	**Talar du/ni engelska?**	tahlar dew/nee engelska
I don't understand	**Jag förstår inte.**	yah furshtawr inteh
Could you speak more slowly, please?	**Kan du/ni tala långsammare, tack?**	kan dew/nee tahla lawng-ssamareh tack
I'm sorry.	**Förlåt.**	furrlawt

Useful Words

big	**stor**	stOOr
small	**liten**	leeten
hot	**varm**	varrm
cold	**kall**	kall
good	**bra**	brah
bad	**dålig**	dawleeg
enough	**tillräcklig**	tillraikleeg
open	**öppen**	urpen
closed	**stängd**	staingd
left	**vänster**	vainster
right	**höger**	hurger
straight on	**rakt fram**	rahkt fram
near	**nära**	naira
far	**långt**	lawngt
up/over	**upp/över**	ewp/urver
down/under	**ner/under**	near/ewnder
early	**tidig**	teedee
late	**sen**	sehn
entrance	**ingång**	ingawng
exit	**utgång**	ewtgawng
toilet	**toalett**	too-alett
more	**mer**	mehr
less	**mindre**	meendre

Shopping

How much - is this?	**Hur mycket - kostar den här?**	hewr mewkeh - kostar dehn hair
I would like …	**Jag skulle vilja …**	yah skewleh vilya
Do you have?	**Har du/ni …?**	hahr dew/nee …
I'm just looking	**Jag ser mig bara omkring**	yah sear may bahra omkring
Do you take credit cards?	**Tar du/ni kreditkort?**	tahr dew/nee kredeetkoort
What time do you open?	**När öppnar ni?**	nair urpnar nee
What time do you close?	**När stänger ni?**	nair stainger nee
This one.	**den här**	dehn hair
That one.	**den där**	dehn dair
expensive	**dyr**	dewr
cheap	**billig**	billig
size (clothes)	**storlek**	stOOrlek
white	**vit**	veet
black	**svart**	svart
red	**röd**	rurd
yellow	**gul**	gewl
green	**grön**	grurn
blue	**blå**	blaw
antiques shop	**antikaffär**	anteek-affair
bakery	**bageri**	bahgeree
bank	**bank**	bank
book shop	**bokhandel**	bOOkhandel
butcher's	**slaktare**	slaktareh
cake shop	**konditori**	konditoree
chemist	**apotek**	apoteak
fishmonger	**fiskaffär**	fisk-affair
grocer	**speceriaffär**	spesseree-affair
hairdresser	**frisör**	frissurr
market	**marknad**	marrknad
newsagent	**tidningskiosk**	teednings-cheeosk
post office	**postkontor**	posstkontOOr
shoe shop	**skoaffär**	skOO-affair
supermarket	**snabbköp**	snabbchurp
tobacconist's	**tobakshandel**	tOObaks-handel
travel agency	**resebyrå**	reasseh-bewraw

Sightseeing

art gallery	**konstgalleri**	konnst-galleree
church	**kyrka**	chewrka
garden	**trädgård**	traidgawrd
house	**hus**	hews
library	**bibliotek**	beebleeotek
museum	**museum**	mewseum
square	**torg**	tohrj
street	**gata**	gahta
tourist information office	**turist-informations-kontor**	tureest-informashOOns kontOOr
town hall	**stadshus**	statshews
closed for holiday	**stängt för semester**	staingt furr semester
bus station	**busstation**	bewss-stashOOn
railway station	**järnvägsstation**	yairnvaigs-stashOOn

Staying in a Hotel

Do you have any vacancies?	Har ni några lediga rum?	hahr nee negra lediga rewm
double room wih double bed	dubbelrum med dubbelsäng	doobelrewm med doobel seng
twin room	dubbelrum med två sängar	doobelrewm med tvaw sengar
single room	enkelrum	enkelrewm
room with a bath	rum med bad	rewm med bahd
shower	dusch	dewsh
key	nyckel	newckel
I have a reservation	Jag har beställt rum	yah hahr bestellt rewm

Eating Out

Have you got a table for…	Har ni ett bord för…?	hahr nee ett bOOrd furr …
I would like to reserve a table.	Jag skulle vilja boka ett bord.	yah skewleh vilya bOOka ett bord.
The bill, please.	Notan, tack.	nOOtan, tack
I am a vegetarian	Jag är vegetarian	yah air vegetariahn
waitress	servitris	sairvitreess
waiter	servitör	sairviturr
menu	meny/ matsedel	menew/ mahtseadel
fixed-price menu	meny med fast pris	menew med fast prees
wine list	vinlista	veenlista
glass of water	ett glas vatten	ett glahss vatten
glass of wine	ett glas vin	ett glahss veen
bottle	flaska	flaska
knife	kniv	k-neev
fork	gaffel	gaffel
spoon	sked	shead
breakfast	frukost	frewkost
lunch	lunch	lewnch
dinner	middag	middahg
main course	huvudrätt	hewvewdrett
starter	förrätt	furrett
dish of the day	dagens rätt	dahgens rett
coffee	kaffe	kaffeh
rare	blodig	blOOdee
medium	medium	medium
well done	välstekt	vailstehkt

Menu Decoder

abborre	abborreh	perch
ägg	aigg	egg
älg	ail-y	moose
ansjovis	anshOOvees	anchovies
apelsin	appelseen	orange
äpple	aippleh	apple
bakelse	bahkelse	cake, pastry, tart
banan	banahn	banana
biff	biff	beef
bröd	brurd	bread
bullar	bewllar	buns
choklad	shooklahd	chocolate
citron	sitrOOn	lemon
dessert	dessair	dessert
fisk	fisk	fish
fläsk	flaisk	pork
forell	fooraill	trout
frukt	fruckt	fruit
glass	glass	ice cream
grönsaksgryta	grurnsahks-grewta	vegetable stew
gurka	gewrka	cucumber
hummer	hummer	lobster
kallskuret	kall-skuret	cold meat
korv	koorv	sausages
kött	churtt	meat
kyckling	chewkling	chicken
lamm	lamm	lamb
lök	lurk	onion
mineralvatten med/utan kolsyra	minerahl-vatten mehd/ewtan kawlsewra	mineral water still/sparkling
mjölk	m-yurlk	milk
nötkött	nurtchurtt	beef
nötter	nurtter	nuts
öl	url	beer
oliver	oleever	olives
olja	olya	oil
ost	oost	cheese
paj/kaka	pa-y/kahka	pie/cake
potatis	potahtis	potatoes
peppar	peppar	pepper
räkor	raikoor	prawns
ris	rees	rice
rökt skinka	rurkt sheenka	cured ham
rostat bröd	rostat brurd	toast
rött vin	rurtt veen	red wine
saft	safft	lemonade
salt	sallt	salt
sås	saws	sauce
sill	seell	herring
skaldjur	skahl-yewr	seafood
smör	smurr	butter
socker	socker	sugar
soppa	soppa	soup
stekt	stehkt	fried
strömming	strurmming	baltic herring
te	tea	tea
torr	torr	dry
ungsstekt	ewngs-stehkt	baked, roast
vinäger	vinager	vinegar
vispgrädde	veesp-graiddeh	whipped cream
vitlök	veet-lurk	garlic
vitt vin	veett veen	white wine

Numbers

0	noll	noll
1	ett	ett
2	två	tvaw
3	tre	trea
4	fyra	feara
5	fem	fem
6	sex	sex
7	sju	shew
8	åtta	otta
9	nio	nee-oo
10	tio	tee-oo
11	elva	elva
12	tolv	tolv
13	tretton	tretton
14	fjorton	f-yoorton
15	femton	femton
16	sexton	sexton
17	sjutton	shewton
18	arton	ahrton
19	nitton	nitton
20	tjugo	chewgoo
21	tjugoett	chewgoo-ett
22	tjugotvå	chewgoo-tvaw
30	trettio	tretti
31	trettioett	tretti-ett
40	fyrtio	furrti
50	femtio	femti
60	sextio	sexti
70	sjuttio	shewti
80	åttio	otti
90	nittio	nitti
100	(ett) hundra	(ett) hewndra
101	etthundraett	ett-hewndra-ett
102	etthundratvå	ett-hewndra-tvaw
200	tvåhundra	tvawhewndra
300	trehundra	treahewndra
400	fyrahundra	fewrahewndra
500	femhundra	femhewndra
600	sexhundra	sexhewndra
700	sjuhundra	shewhewndra
800	åttahundra	ottahewndra
900	niohundra	nee-oohewndra
1,000	(ett) tusen	(ett) tewssen
1,001	etttusenett	ett-tewssen-ett
100,000	(ett) hundra- tusen	(ett) hewndra tewssen
1,000,000	en miljon	ehn milyOOn

Time

one minute	en minut	ehn meenewt
one hour	en timme	ehn timmeh
half an hour	en halvtimme	ehn halvtimmeh
ten past one	tio över ett	teeoo urver ett
quarter past one	kvart över ett	kvahrt urver ett
half past one	halv två	halv tvaw
twenty to two	tjugo i två	chewgoo ee tvaw
quarter to two	kvart i två	kvahrt ee tvaw
two o'clock	klockan två	klockan tvaw
13:00	klockan tretton	klockan tretton
16:30	sexton och trettio	sexton ock tretti
noon	klockan tolv	klockan tolv
midnight	midnatt	meednatt
Monday	måndag	mawndahg
Tuesday	tisdag	teesdahg
Wednesday	onsdag	oonssdahg
Thursday	torsdag	toorsdahg
Friday	fredag	freadahg
Saturday	lördag	lurrdahg
Sunday	söndag	surndahg